TEXT BOOK OF

ENVIRONMENTAL ENGINEERING - I

FOR
SEMESTER - V
THIRD YEAR DEGREE COURSE IN CIVIL ENGINEERING
AS PER NEW REVISED SYLLABUS
NORTH MAHARASHTRA UNIVERSITY, JALGAON.

(JUNE 2014)

Dr. R. K. LAD
B.E. (Civil), M.E. Civil (Env. Engg.), Ph.D.
REC TOPPER
Dean. Engineering
JSPM Technical Institute Campus
Narhe, PUNE

Dr. M. R. GIDDE
M.E. (Env. Engg.)Ph.D.
Professor
Department of Civil Engineering
Bharati Vidyapeeth's College of Engineering
Dhankawadi, PUNE - 411037.

Dr. S. T. MALI
B.E. (Civil), M.E. (Civil) (Env. Engg.) Ph.D
Associate Professor
Department of Civil Engineering
Sinhagad College of Engineering
Vadgaon (BK), PUNE - 411041.

ENVIRONMENTAL ENGINEERING – I (TE CIVIL SEM – V, NMU) ISBN 978-93-5164-101-8
First Edition : **August 2014**
© : **Authors**

The text of this publication, or any part thereof, should not be reproduced or transmitted in any form or stored in any computer storage system, or device for distribution including photocopy, recording, taping or information retrieval system or reproduced on any disc, tape, perforated media or other information storage device etc., without the written permission of Authors with whom the rights are reserved. Breach of this condition is liable for legal action.

Every effort has been made to avoid errors or omissions in this publication. In spite of this, errors may have crept in. Any mistake, error or discrepancy so noted and shall be brought to our notice shall be taken care of in the next edition. It is notified that neither the publisher nor the authors or seller shall be responsible for any damage or loss of action to any one, of any kind, in any manner, therefrom.

Published By :
NIRALI PRAKASHAN
Abhyudaya Pragati, 1312, Shivaji Nagar,
Off J.M. Road, PUNE – 411005
Tel - (020) 25512336/37/39, Fax - (020) 25511379
Email : niralipune@pragationline.com

Printed at
Repro Knowledgecast Limited
India

DISTRIBUTION CENTRES
PUNE

Nirali Prakashan
119, Budhwar Peth, Jogeshwari Mandir Lane
Pune 411002, Maharashtra
Tel : (020) 2445 2044, 66022708, Fax : (020) 2445 1538
Email : bookorder@pragationline.com

Nirali Prakashan
S. No. 28/27, Dhyari,
Near Pari Company, Pune 411041
Tel : (020) 24690204 Fax : (020) 24690316
Email : dhyari@pragationline.com
bookorder@pragationline.com

MUMBAI
Nirali Prakashan
385, S.V.P. Road, Rasdhara Co-op. Hsg. Society Ltd.,
Girgaum, Mumbai 400004, Maharashtra
Tel : (022) 2385 6339 / 2386 9976, Fax : (022) 2386 9976
Email : niralimumbai@pragationline.com

DISTRIBUTION BRANCHES

NAGPUR
Pratibha Book Distributors
Above Maratha Mandir, Shop No. 3, First Floor,
Rani Jhanshi Square, Sitabuldi, Nagpur 440012,
Maharashtra, Tel : (0712) 254 7129

BENGALURU
Pragati Book House
House No. 1, Sanjeevappa Lane, Avenue Road Cross,
Opp. Rice Church, Bengaluru – 560002.
Tel : (080) 64513344, 64513355,
Mob : 9880582331, 9845021552
Email:bharatsavla@yahoo.com

JALGAON
Nirali Prakashan
34, V. V. Golani Market, Navi Peth, Jalgaon 425001,
Maharashtra, Tel : (0257) 222 0945
Mob : 94234 91860

KOLHAPUR
Nirali Prakashan
New Mahadvar Road,
Kedar Plaza, 1st Floor Opp. IDBI Bank
Kolhapur 416 012, Maharashtra. Mob : 9855046155

CHENNAI
Pragati Books
9/1, Montieth Road, Behind Taas Mahal, Egmore,
Chennai 600008 Tamil Nadu, Tel : (044) 6518 3535,
Mob : 94440 01782 / 98450 21552 / 98805 82331, Email : bharatsavla@yahoo.com

RETAIL OUTLETS
PUNE

Pragati Book Centre
157, Budhwar Peth, Opp. Ratan Talkies,
Pune 411002, Maharashtra
Tel : (020) 2445 8887 / 6602 2707, Fax : (020) 2445 8887
Pragati Book Centre
Amber Chamber, 28/A, Budhwar Peth,
Appa Balwant Chowk, Pune : 411002, Maharashtra,
Tel : (020) 20240335 / 66281669
Email : pbcpune@pragationline.com

Pragati Book Centre
676/B, Budhwar Peth, Opp. Jogeshwari Mandir,
Pune 411002, Maharashtra
Tel : (020) 6601 7784 / 6602 0855
PBC Book Sellers & Stationers
152, Budhwar Peth, Pune 411002, Maharashtra
Tel : (020) 2445 2254 / 6609 2463

MUMBAI
Pragati Book Corner
Indira Niwas, 111 - A, Bhavani Shankar Road, Dadar (W), Mumbai 400028, Maharashtra
Tel : (022) 2422 3526 / 6662 5254, Email : pbcmumbai@pragationline.com

PREFACE

This book tittled '**Environmental Engineering – I**' is written according to the New Revised Syllabus of Third Year Degree North Maharashtra University. Jalgaon.

This book is intended for the junior and senior students of the Civil Engineering course and also for the students of Environmental Science Course; who wish to take Environmental Engineering Course. Practicing Engineers, Students and professors would find this book useful both as a reference book or as a text book.

The aspects like Water supply scheme, Water Demand, Quality of Water, Filtration, Disinfection of water and Water Distribution System are essentially covered in this book. As a result, this book is an ideal one for the courses in Environmental Engineering. Both principles and design are explained in this book. The principles are enunciated in the simplest possible way.

This book is an outcome of the author's experiences both in the class while teaching and problems faced on the field.

The authors are thankful to all who have directly or indirectly helped us at all stages of bringing out book. Special thanks are to Shri. Dineshbhai Furia, Shri Jignesh Furia, Shri. M. P. Munde, and the team of Nirali Prakasha namely Mrs. Deepali Lachake, Miss. Mandakini Jadhavar who took great efforts to publish this book within a very short time at their disposal.

Suggestions and comments are always welcome for the improvement of this book.

29th July 2014
Pune   – Authors

SYLLABUS

UNIT-I
A: Introduction to water supply schemes: data collection for water supply scheme, components and layout, design period, factors affecting design period.
B: Water intake structures: General design considerations, intake structures, such as river intake, canal and reservoir intake, conveyance of raw water, hydraulic design
of pumping station.,
C: Water demand, rate of water consumption for various purposes, like domestic, industrial and institutional and commercial. Fire demand. Water system losses. Factors affecting the rate of demand. Population forecasting: arithmetical increase method geometrical increases method, incremental increase method logistic curve methods.

UNIT-II
A: Water quality: impurities in water, physical, chemical and biological characteristics, water quality standards as per IS 10500-1991, USEPA and WHO.
B: Water treatment processes: introduction to different water treatment processes, flow sheets, aeration- principle, concept, necessity, methods and design of aeration fountains (Stepped aerators), Flash mixer, function, design and power requirements.
C: Flocculation and sedimentation: coagulation, flocculation theory, zeta potential and its significance, mean velocity gradient G, power consumption, common coagulants, coagulant aids, principle of sedimentation, efficiency of ideal settling basin, types of settling and related theory. Design of settling tanks, clariflocculators, tube settlers.

UNIT-III
A: Filtration: theory of filtration, mechanism of filtration, filter materials, types of filters, rapid Sand Filter, Slow Sand Filter, multimedia and dual media filters, components- under drainage system, working and cleaning of filters. Operational troubles, design of filters-RSF and SSF. Design of under drainage system.
B: Disinfection- objectives, theory, types of disinfection, chlorination, free and combined chlorine, effect of pH, types of chlorination, pre and post chlorination, break point chlorination, de-chlorination bleaching powder estimation.

UNIT-IV
A: water softening- theory, methods, lime soda, zeolite, and ion exchange processes,
quantity estimation of lime soda process, re-carbonization. Demineralizationmethods
like reverse osmosis, electro-dialysis
B: Miscellaneous methods- adsorption: theory, Frendlich isotherms design. effect of
fluoride, fluoridation and de-fluoridation.
C: Water treatment of swimming pool.

UNIT-V
A: Water distribution system, types of distribution system, continuous and intermittent system, gravity, pumping and combined system. Wastage of waterdetection and prevention. Lay out of distribution system. Design of hydraulic network. Residual pressure, Hardy-Cross method, design of ESR capacity.
B: Service reservoir, ESR, GSR, balancing reservoir- necessity, location, capacity calculation by arithmetic and mass curve method. types of pipes. types of valves, Functions and locations.
C: presence of heavy metals in water, their effects and remedy. Presence of nonbiodegradableorganics in water, their effects, halide formations. Their removal methods including osmosis, ultra-filtration, and adsorption. Basic idea of photocatalysis technology from removal of non-degradable organics.

CONTENTS

UNIT I

1. Introduction to Water Supply Schemes — 1.1 – 1.8
2. Water Intake Structures — 2.1 – 2.10
3. Conveyance and Pumping of Raw Water — 3.1 – 3.18
4. Population Forecast and Water Demand — 4.1 – 4.28

UNIT II

5. Quality of Water — 5.1 – 5.24
6. Water Treatment Processes : Aeration and Sedimentation — 6.1 – 6.50

UNIT III

7. Filtration — 7.1 – 7.26
8. Disinfection of Water — 8.1 – 8.12

UNIT IV

9. Miscellaneous Treatment Methods — 9.1 – 9.18

UNIT V

10. Water Distribution System — 10.1 – 10.44
11. Heavy Metals, Non-biodegradable Organics and Non-degradable Organics — 11.1 – 11.10

CHAPTER ONE

INTRODUCTION TO WATER SUPPLY SCHEMES

1.1 INTRODUCTION

Water is called "Jeevan" (i.e. life) in Sanskrit. It is basic need of all living beings. Other needs are air, food and shelter. Without water man cannot survive. In early days, water was primarily used for domestic needs like drinking, washing, bathing and cooking etc. But due to modernisation, water is also required for industrial, ornamental and sewerage purposes along with domestic needs. It is also required for parks, gardens, swimming pools etc. Water is also required for fire protection. Now-a-days, well designed and organized public water supply schemes are absolutely necessary to cater for various water requirements. Enormous quantity of water required for future industries is required to be taken into account for designing water supply schemes.

1.2 NECESSITY AND IMPORTANCE OF WATER WORKS

The main source of water is rainfall. When the rain falls from the clouds, it dissolves various impurities like gases and minute suspended particles present in the atmosphere. Rain water collects dust and other impurities present on the surface of the earth. Some part of rainfall evaporates and some part percolates in the earth, dissolving various soluble matter in it and ultimately joins the underground water raising its level. The balance amount of rainfall left after evaporation and percolation, flows over the surface of earth and joins nallas, streams and rivers. This flowing water is called as runoff or surface flow. It is impure as it collects lot of matter lying on surface of earth during its flow. Also surface water contains wastes discharged by various industries. Sometimes untreated sewages are also discharged in such flowing water, causing its pollution.

Hence, water, either from surface source or from underground source, is not suitable for drinking due to various impurities present in it. Also water may contain pathogenic bacteria leading to water borne diseases like cholera, dysentry and typhoid etc. Therefore, it is necessary to treat such water and make it fit for various purposes. Water is treated in treatment units (all called as water works) which require proper design and maintenance. These treatment units reduce impurities upto acceptable standards. Civil engineers must have thorough knowledge of planning, designing, estimation and construction of various treatment units, required to make the water available of acceptable standard.

1.3 USES OF WATER

1. Drinking, cooking and washing.
2. Bathing.
3. Swimming pools and water games.
4. Ornamental displays like fountains and cascades.
5. Watering lawns, gardens and roads.
6. For modern appliances like air conditioners, washing machines and dish washers.
7. For extinguishing fires.
8. Industrial processes and steam generation.
9. Irrigation purposes.
10. Sanitary purposes.

1.4 WATER SUPPLY SCHEMES

They essentially consists of the following phases :

1. Selection of source : The source may be surface source like river, canal, lake and reservoir or ground water source like wells and springs. The criteria in selecting the source is its reliability, minimum impurities and availability in the required quantity.

2. Collection and conveyance of raw water : The water from the source is required to be collected and conveyed to the treatment works for its purification. Depending upon the type of the source and its elevation, intake works, pump house and rising main etc. will be required. C.I. pipes are generally used. However, in case of gravity flow, open ducts or channels may be used to make the scheme economical.

3. Treatment of water : This depends upon the nature of impurities present in water, which are detected in the water testing laboratory. The usual process is sedimentation with or without coagulation, filtration and disinfection.

4. Pumping and storing water in elevated service reservoirs : The water after purification is required to be stored at higher elevation so that water is distributed to the public by gravity according to supply hours. This needs pumping of treated water, ventilation and protection during storing to avoid contamination. Additional storage of water is provided in case of breakdown of pumps. (Such additional storage is generally called as breakdown reserve.)

5. Distribution : For distribution of water, network of pipes is laid. It consists of mains, branches, distributries or feeders. Individual service connections are given from feeder lines.

The system of water supply adopted may be gravity or pumping or combination of the two, depending upon the topography of the town. Water supply to public may be intermittant (few hours in the morning and few hours in the evening) or continuous (twenty four hours).

1.5 DATA TO BE COLLECTED FOR WATER SUPPLY SCHEME

Water is prime necessity of every individual. For supplying water to the public, water supply projects are prepared and sent to proper authority for sanction of grants required for its execution. In the design of water supply project, the following data is collected :

1. **Source of raw water :** Various sources available, their reliability throughout the year, choice of the source between various alternatives available depends mainly upon the impurities present in them.

2. **Quantity of water required :** It depends upon :

    (a) **Population to be served :** This is decided by forecasting the population from sensus data.

    (b) **Water demands :** All types of demands like domestic public, industrial, fire etc. are sorted out.

    (c) **Design period :** Thirty years period is often considered.

    Finally total water demand per day for the city is worked out.

3. **Quality of water :** The samples of water from available sources are analysed in the laboratory to find out the various impurities present. This is essential to decide the line of treatment to be given to the raw water. This is also necessary to decide the best source out of the alternatives, if any.

4. **Survey data :** Surveys are carried out to prepare the topographical maps for intake works, rising main treatment site, location of elevated service reservoirs.

5. **Plan or Map of city or town :** The master plan containing existing roads, buildings and proposed developments along with the contours is procured, if available. If not available, plan table survey is carried out to obtain the city map. This map enables the design engineer to divide the city into various zones - low level, medium level and high level etc. and choose the position for locating distribution reservoirs with required capacity and to decide the layout of water distribution pipe network.

6. Aquisition of land and compensations to be paid to the land owners and legal complications etc.

7. Existing water supply position of the town and possibility of its expansion.

1.6 COMPONENTS AND LAYOUT OF WATER SUPPLY SCHEMES

Water is obtained from various sources. They are mainly classed into two categories :

(a) underground source, which consists of open well, tube well, artesian wells etc. and

(b) surface source which consists of streams, rivers, reservoirs, canals etc.

Depending upon the source of water supply the components of the water supply scheme will differ.

Following layouts are used :

1. For underground source, the components/layout involves provision of well, pump house, rising main, elevated service reservoir and water distribution pipelines. In such layout only chlorination treatment is done to supply disinfected water. It is very much suitable for village water supply schemes. [Fig. 1.2 (a)]

2. For surface source like river, canal etc., the components/layout consists of intake works, pumps, rising main, treatment units (like clarifiers, filters), elevated service reservoir and distribution system. This is a full fledged scheme and is used for town and cities.

Following is the flow diagram of water supply scheme.

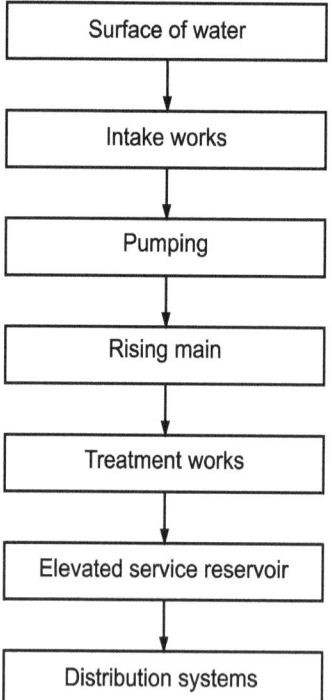

Fig. 1.1 : Flow diagram of water supply scheme

These layouts are shown in Fig. 1.2

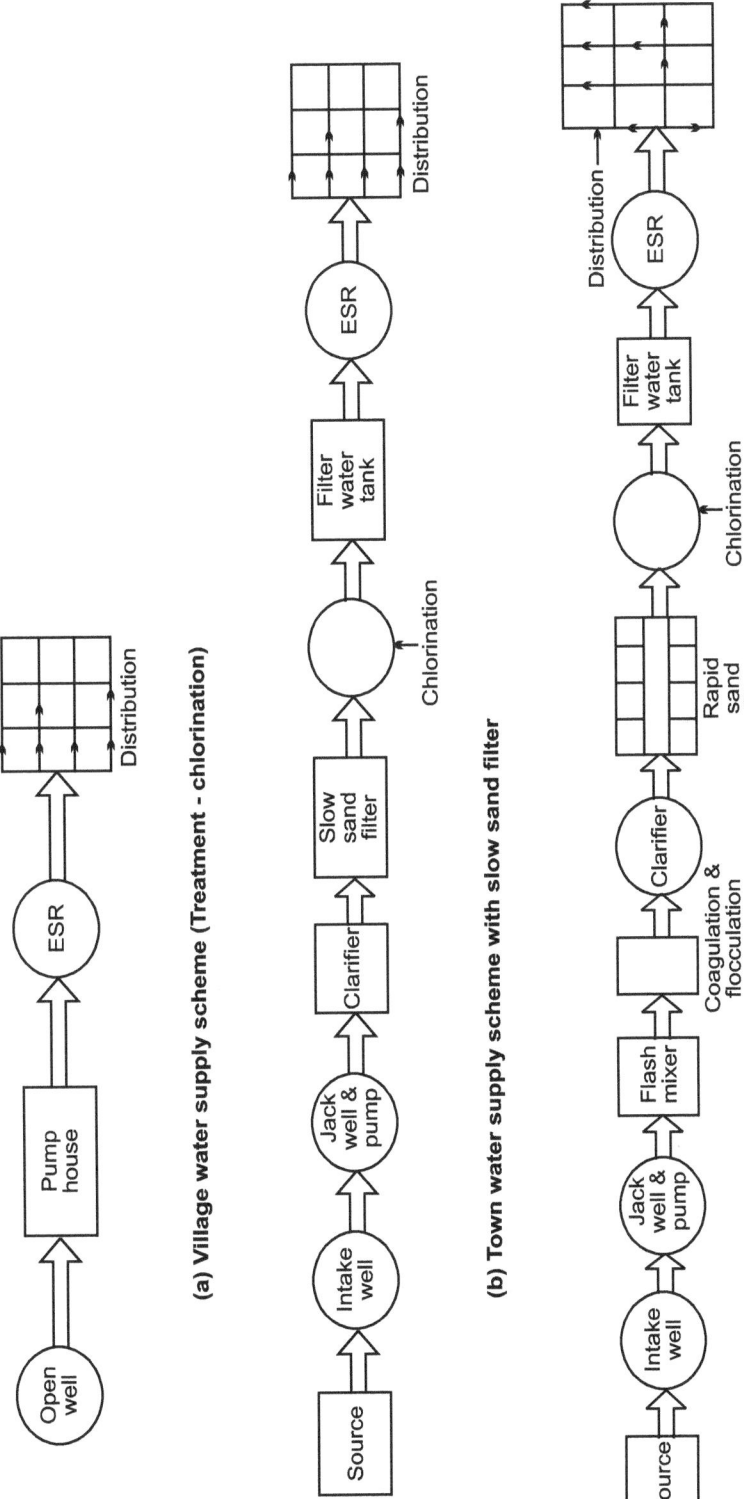

Fig. 1.2 : Layouts of water supply scheme

1.7 FINANCING WATER SUPPLY SCHEMES

For any water supply scheme, lot of money is required for planning, designing and construction of various components of the scheme. Also after the completion of the scheme, money is required for its proper running, maintenance and repairs and testing of day to day samples in the laboratory.

Local municipalities and city corporations are required to raise finances through Banks, State Governments in the form of loans for execution of water supply schemes.

For villages, State Governments generally provide 80 to 90% of the total cost of the project as assistance. The villages and town panchayats have to collect the remaining amount of 10%. Each State Government sets up the Environmental Engineering Department to look after the development and execution of such schemes. After completion of the schemes, they are handed over to local municipalities or village panchayats for running them. They charge consumers for water supplied to meet RMO (Repairing, Maintenance and Operation) expenses.

1.8 DESIGN PERIOD

Water supply scheme involves construction of intake structures rising main, pumps treatment units, raw or treated water storage tanks and network of pressure pipes for treated water distribution to the public. Many times weirs or dams are also required to be constructed in order to make the raw water available throughout the year. All these constructions involve huge expenditure. Moreover, these constructions when once carried out cannot be replaced or increased in their capacities easily and involve complications in case of their expansions. It is also desirable to use these constructed works till their useful life expires. If the water supply scheme is designed for the present population, it will fall short within coming few years as the population increases continuously. Hence, the various components of water supply schemes are made larger to fulfil the increasing water demands due to development and expansion of the town during the estimated life of the scheme. This future estimated period of number of years for which a provision is made in designing the capacities of various components of water supply scheme is called **Design Period.**

1.9 FACTORS AFFECTING DESIGN PERIOD

1. Useful life of components of water supply scheme will decide the design period.

2. Higher design period will have to be adopted if there are difficulties in future expansion.

3. Availability of funds affects the design period. Less amount of funds compels the designer to adopt smaller design period.

4. Rate of interest on loans for completion of water supply projects affects the design period. Larger the rate of interest on loan, smaller is the design period and vice versa.

5. If the rate of increase in population is lower, higher design period is adopted.

6. Quantity of water available from the source will have effect on the design period. Required quantity of water may not be available at the end of higher design period. In that case smaller design period will have to be chosen. In general, design period of 30 years is considered for water supply schemes.

1.10 DESIGN PERIODS FOR COMPONENTS OF WATER SUPPLY SCHEME

Sr. No.	Components	Suggested design period in years
1.	Dams, weirs, intake structures, reservoirs and penstock pipes	30 – 35 years
2.	Treatment units like clarifiers, filters etc.	(a) 15 – 20 years when interest rates on loans raised are higher. (b) 20 – 30 years when interest rates on loans raised are lower.
3.	Distribution system : (a) Pipes less than 300 mm diameter (b) Pipes larger than 300 mm diameter.	30 years 20 – 25 years

EXERCISE

1. What is the necessity of water supply schemes ? **(May 2010)**
2. What are the uses of water ?
3. Describe different phases involved in a water supply scheme.
(May 2006, 2008, 2009, 2010; Dec. 2009, 2010)
4. Draw a detailed flow chart of a conventional water treatment plant.
(Dec. 98, Nov. 97)

5. Enlist the data to be collected for any water supply project.

6. What is design period ? State the factors affecting the design period.

7. Suggest the design period for the following :
   (a) Intake structures
   (b) Treatment units and
   (c) Distribution system.

8. What are the objectives of treatment of water to be used for drinking purpose ? Draw flow diagram to treat surface water to make it fit for human consumption. **(May 2002, Dec. 2007)**

9. Draw a flow diagram of river water treatment process. **(Nov. 2002, May 2008)**

10. Explain the objectives of raw water treatment. Draw flow diagram to show various processes used to treat water in an urban area when the source of water is
    (i) Surface source, (ii) Sub-surface source. **(May 2005)**

◈ ◈ ◈

CHAPTER TWO

WATER INTAKE STRUCTURES

2.1 GENERAL

The entire water supply scheme, in short, consists of :

1. Collecting and conveying the raw water from the source to treatment plant.

2. Treatment of water in various units

3. Conveying the treated water to the town and distributing it amongst various consumers.

For collection and conveyance of raw water, intake structures, intake pipe, jack well and pump house and rising main are in general required. For efficient working and maintenance of rising main, different types of valves are provided on it. Collection works and pump house are described in the following articals.

2.2 INTAKE STRUCTURES

The raw water required for any water supply scheme is withdrawn from a surface source like river, reservoir, lake or canal, or from underground source like well or spring. When the withdrawal of water is from surface source, a construction called intake structure is provided to collect and drain water from the source over the range of fluctuating levels, and discharge it into pipe.

Intake structures mainly consists of : (i) conduit with protective works, (ii) screens at open ends, (iii) gates and valves to regulate the flow, and (iv) outlet pipe conveying water to sump.

The constructions may range from a simple concrete block supporting the end of conduit pipe to large concrete towers housing gates, valves and sometimes pump house also.

2.2.1 Factors Governing the Location of Intake

1. It should be near the treatment plant to cut down the cost of conveyance.

2. It should be located in the comparatively pure zone of water source to reduce the load on treatment works.

3. It should not be located on the downstream side of the sewage disposal.

4. It should not be located on curves.

5. It should be accessible even during floods.

6. It should be located at such a site from where it can draw water even during driest period of the year.

7. It should be away from navigation channels as it may admit raw water polluted by discharge of wastes by ships.

8. At site, sufficient quantity should be available for future expansion, if necessary.

9. At site, there should not be heavy current of water causing danger to intake structure.

10. It should be near the jack well as far as possible.

11. Power supply should be available at the site.

2.2.2 Types of Intakes

(I) Submerged intake or lake intake

(II) Exposed intakes

    (1) Canal intake

    (2) Reservoir intake

    (3) River intake : (a) Wet intake tower, (b) Dry intake tower

    (4) Movable intake.

2.2.3 Submerged or Lake Intake

It essentially consists of a pipe laid in the dredged channel along the bed of the lake. The depth of water is maximum at the centre of the lake. The dredged channel trench is refilled with soft material round the pipe and with hard material at the top of the trench. The pipes are laid usually with flexible joints. The inlet end, which is in the middle of the lake, is provided with bell mouth opening covered with a screen of steel bar or wire mesh and protected by a timber or concrete crib. The water enters the pipe through the bell mouth opening and flows under gravity to the bank where it is collected in a sump well and then pumped to convey it to treatment works. This type of intake is cheap to construct, and provides no obstruction to navigation. As it is submerged, there is no possibility for floating bodies and ice (in cold countries) to find entry into the inlet of pipe. To derive more discharge, two or even three pipes may be laid in parallel as per design.

There is one disadvantage that, for maintenance, they are not easily approachable. The following sketches show the submerged intakes with timber crib and also with concrete block (Fig. 2.1 and 2.2).

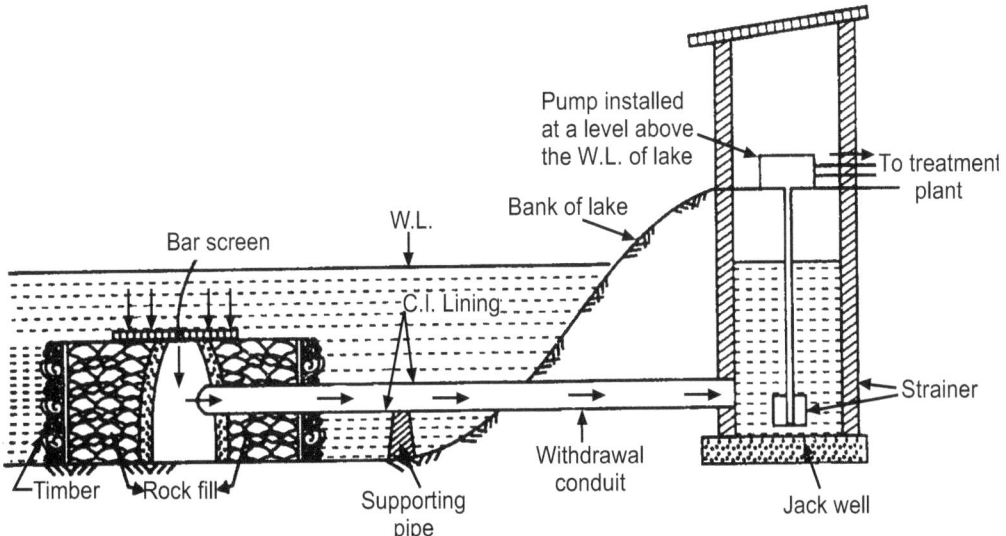

Fig. 2.1 : Rock filled timber crib - submerged intake

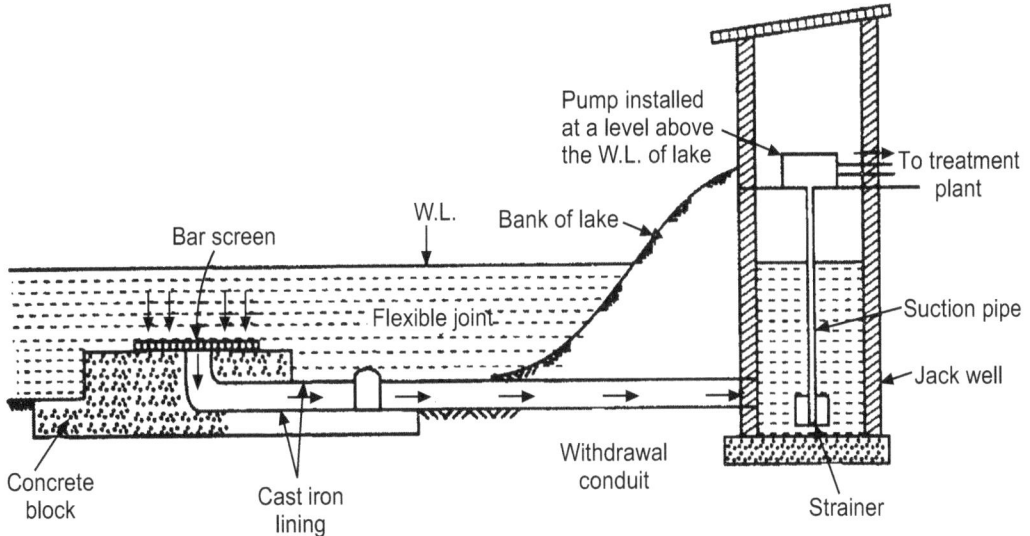

Fig. 2.2 : Simple concrete block - submerged intake

2.2.4 Exposed Intakes

1. Canal Intake :

It is a simple structure of either concrete or masonry constructed partly in the bank of the canal. A pipe with a bell mouth shaped inlet is placed in the chamber (as shown in the Fig. 2.3). Since, the water level in the canal is fairly constant, multiple inlet pipes are not required. A coarse screen is provided to the opening on one side of the chamber for debris-free entry of water in the chamber. In addition, hemispherical fine screen is also provided on the top of the bell mouth to exclude entry of fish and other matter. One sluice valve is provided to control the flow of water from intake through the outlet pipe going to treatment units. The valve is operated from the top of the canal bank. Near the intake, bed and banks are provided with stone pitching to protect them from erosion due to increased velocity of water near the intake.

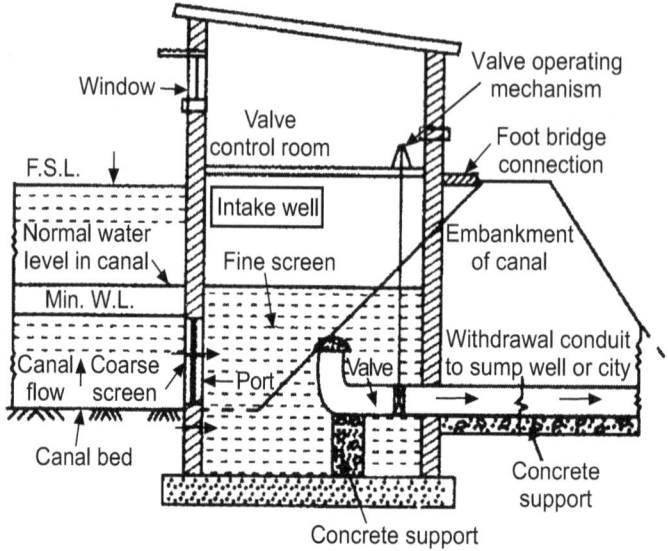

Fig. 2.3 : Canal intake

2. Reservoir Intake :

A reservoir is formed by constructing the dam or weir across the river. The dam may be a earth dam, masonry dam or concrete dam.

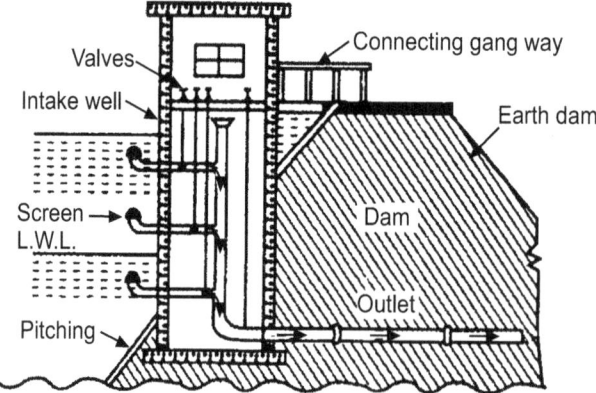

Fig. 2.4 : Reservoir intake

A reservoir intake consists of a circular well constructed in the body of the dam or on the upstream face of the dam. Many times it is also called as intake tower. It is located at such a place from where intake can draw adequate quantity of water even in the driest period of the year. Water level in the reservoir varies from season to season. Intake pipes are provided at different variations of water level. Screens are provided at the mouth of all inlet pipes to prevent entry of floating matter. Each inlet pipe is provided with a gate valve which is operated from top to admit water in the well. Access to valve room, if necessary, is provided by means of foot bridge.

In case of earth dams intakes are separately constructed and need provision of foot bridge (See Fig. 2.4). In case of masonry or concrete dam, intakes are constructed inside the dam itself with intake pipes coming out of the dam at various levels. (See Fig. 2.5).

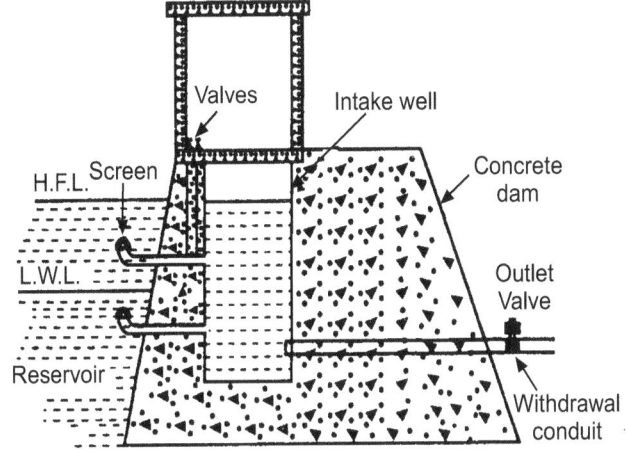

Fig. 2.5 : Reservoir intake constructed in the concrete dam

3. River Intake :

It is a circular well of 3 to 7 m in diameter constructed in masonry or concrete. In case of small rivers it is located along the bank of the river at such a place from where water is available even in the dry period of river (See Fig. 2.6). Since, it is located on the banks of river, it is also called as shore intake.

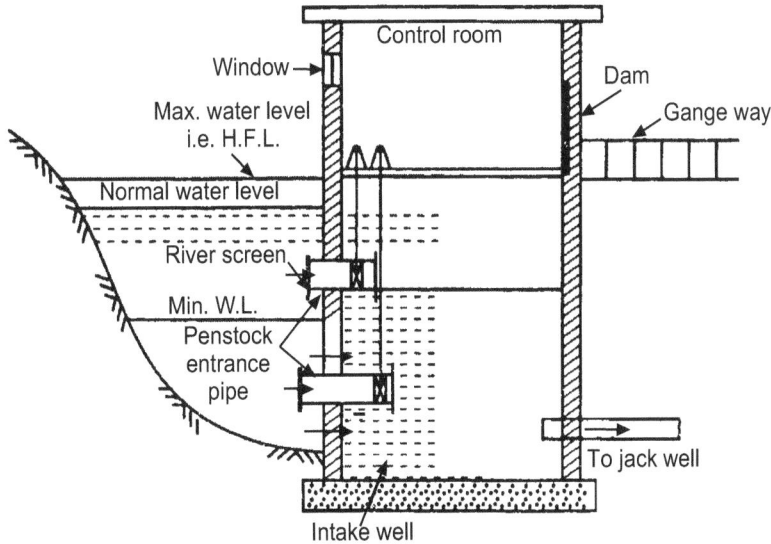

Fig. 2.6 : River intake

Intake towers : In some cases, intake is constructed in the river at suitable place away from the bank, in the form of island, connected by foot bridge (gangway) with the bank. Popularly such intakes are called as intake towers. Intake towers are also sometimes provided in the reservoirs. They are classified as : (i) Wet intake tower and (ii) Dry intake tower.

(i) Wet intake tower : In wet intake tower, there is a vertical circular shaft which draws water from its surrounding well. The well is provided with ungated openings as shown in the Fig. 2.7 and as such annular portion of the well is always filled with water and have the intake which is called as wet intake. The circular shaft located inside the well is provided with gated openings regulated from the control room at top. When gates are closed, shaft will remain dry. Shaft is connected to withdrawl pipe (conduit), which is embed below river bed and supply water to Jack well. Outside openings are provided with coarse type of screens. A typical section of wet intake tower is shown in the Fig. 2.7.

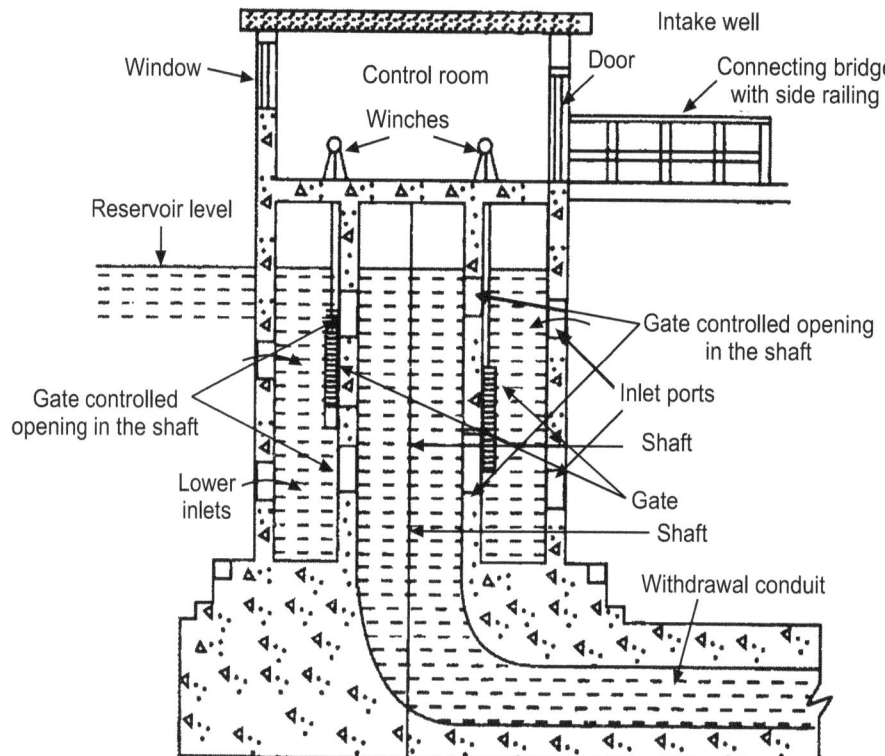

Fig. 2.7 : Wet intake tower standing in the river or reservoir

(ii) Dry intake tower : In this type, water is admitted in the well by operating the gates from control room. The water from the well is withdrawn through the well protected conduit placed on the bed of river. When the inlet openings are closed by the gates, there will not be any water inside the well and as such it is called as dry intake tower. Inlet openings are provided with proper screens to exclude entry of floating and unwanted matter. A typical dry intake tower is shown in the Fig. 2.8.

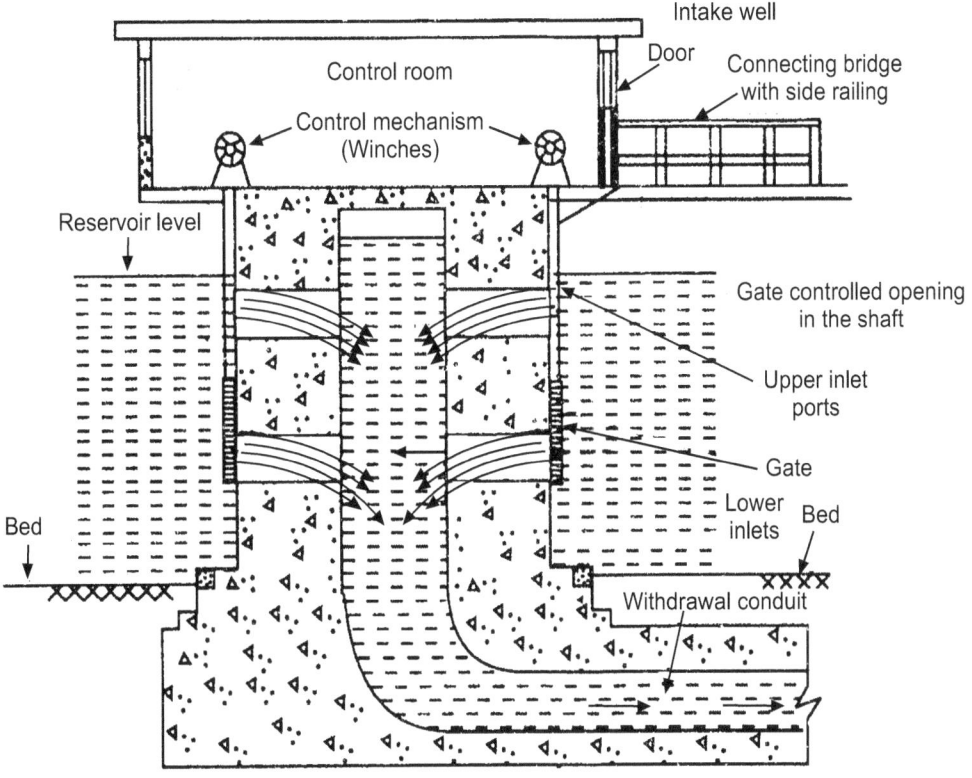

Fig. 2.8 : Dry intake tower standing in the river or reservoir

4. Movable Intake :

Such intakes are used as emergency measures particularly on the streams with sloping banks and having wide variations in their water surface elevations. On the sloping bank, a rail track as shown in the Fig. 2.9 is laid on the bank. The trolley carrying pumping set with suction pipe with strainer can be moved up and down the slope according to water level in the river. A delivery pipe is laid near but below the ground. A flexible house pipe is provided to connect outlet end of pump and the inlet end of usual delivery pipe. The water is pumped from river and is delivered to treatment plant.

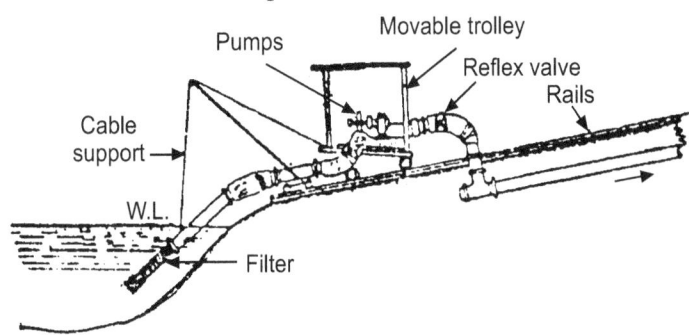

Fig. 2.9 : Movable intake

2.3 JACK WELL AND PUMP HOUSE

Many times site conditions do not permit the installation of pumping units on the top of intake. Hence, it becomes necessary to construct separate well in the bank of river which is called as Jack well. On the upper floor of the jack well, pump sets are housed and hence the upper room is called as pump house (often called as dry well). A raw water gravity main (pipe) is provided to convey water from intake well to jack well. Sufficient capacity is provided to jack well so that maximum designed water demand can be withdrawn from it by regulated pumping.

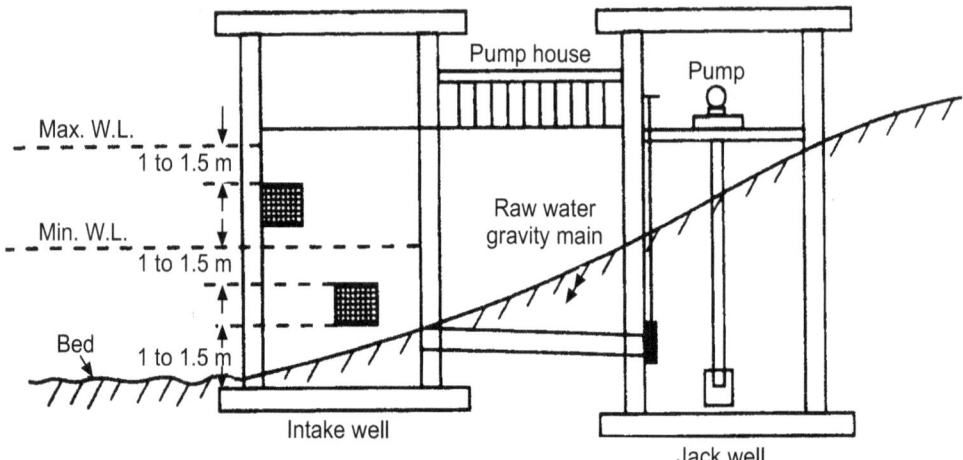

Fig. 2.10

2.3.1 Design Criteria

1. Intake well as well as jack well should be properly founded.
2. For structural stability the following forces are considered :
   (a) Action due to water currents and waves.
   (b) Blows from floating objects, including ice and also due to submerged objects.
   (c) Shifting of river banks.
   (d) Bouyant force.
3. Areas of inlet openings are worked out by considering the velocity of flow between 0.1 to 0.25 m/sec. To regulate flow, each opening is provided with valves or gates controlled from top.
4. Inlet openings should be 1 to 1.5 m below water level. Minimum three inlet openings should be provided at three different levels.
5. Each opening should be protected by providing fine screen and coarse screen from outside.
6. Diameter of intake well is about 3 to 5 m and its bottom should be at least 3 m below the minimum water level.

7. Capacity of jack well depends upon :
   (a) Pumping rate,
   (b) Pumping hours,
   (c) Inflow rate of water from intake well to jack well through connecting gravity main (pipe).

   Capacity of jack well = (Pumping rate − Inflow rate) Pumping hours

8. Raw water gravity main is designed by using Hazen William formula, with velocity of water through the main ranging between 0.9 to 1.5 m/sec. It is designed in such a way that the available pressure head between the source and its other outlet end, is just lost in overcoming friction in the mains. Its length is generally small.

Example 2.1 : Design screen and gravity main for Intake well for the following data :

Population = 60,000

Rate of water supply = 180 lit./h/day

Solution : Volume of water required per day = 60000×180 lit.

$$Q = \text{Rate of water supply required} = \frac{6 \times 18 \times 10^5}{24 \times 3600} \text{ lit./sec.}$$

$$= 125 \text{ lit./sec.}$$

$$= 0.125 \text{ m}^3/\text{sec.}$$

1. Design of Inlet openings :

Since, the screens are provided, assume the entering water through the inlet opening will have a velocity = 0.2 m/sec.

i.e. v = 0.2 m/sec.   ∴ Q = Area of inlet opening × Velocity

$$0.125 = A \times 0.2$$

∴ $A = 0.625 \text{ m}^2$

Make 100% allowance for bars of screen and its chocking

$$A = 2 \times 0.625 = 1.25 \text{ m}^2$$

Provide two openings each of area $\left[\frac{1}{2} \times (1.25)\right] = 0.625 \text{ m}^2$ at the same level.

Assume width of each inlet opening = 1 m

∴   Depth of each inlet opening = 0.625 m

∴   Provide two openings each of size 1×0.625 m at the same level. (Assuming water level remaining fairly constant)

OR provide similar set of two openings 3 m below normal level of water.

2. **Design of gravity main connecting intake and jack well :**

   Assume (a) Velocity of water through main = 1 m/sec.

   (b) Diameter of main = 1 m.

   ∴ $\quad Q = $ Cross-sectional area of pipe × Velocity

   $$0.125 = \frac{\pi}{4} \times d^2 \times 1$$

   Solving, $\quad d = 0.4 \text{ m} = 40 \text{ cm}$

   Applying Hazen William's formula,

   $$V = 0.85 \times C \times R^{0.63} \times S^{0.54}$$

   where, $\quad C = $ Constant depending on pipe material

   $\quad R = $ Hydraulic radius

   $\quad S = $ Head loss/unit length of pipe

   ∴ $\quad 1 = 0.85 \times 100 \times \left(\frac{0.4}{4}\right)^{0.63} \times S^{0.54}$

   Solving, $\quad S = 1 \text{ in } 254$

   $\quad\quad = 0.0039$

   $\quad\quad = 0.004$

EXERCISE

1. What is intake ? State the factors affecting location of intake.
2. Explain with sketches the following :
   (a) Canal intake
   (b) Reservoir intake
   (c) Lake intake
   (d) River intake
3. Explain in short the design criteria of intake well.
4. Design the intake well for the following data -
   Population = 75000, Rate of water supply = 180 lit./hr./day.

CHAPTER THREE

CONVEYANCE AND PUMPING OF RAW WATER

3.1 INTRODUCTION

Conveyance of water means carrying water from sources to the water treatment plant and from there to the consumers.

3.1.1 Schematic Arrangement of Water Supply Scheme

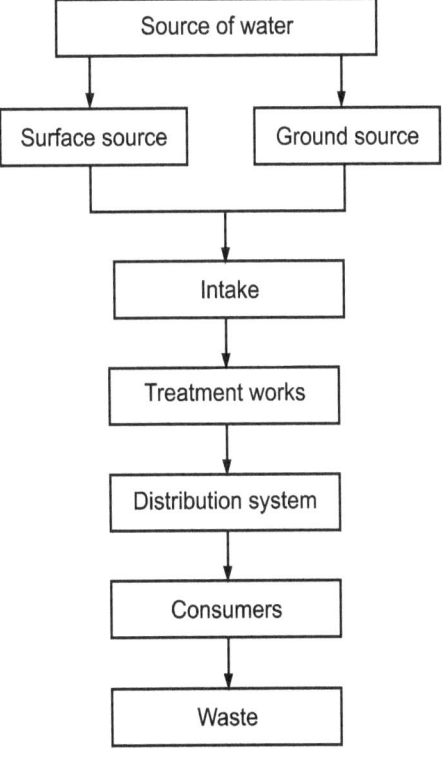

Fig. 3.1

3.2 PIPES

Pipes are circular conduits, in which water flows under pressure.

3.2.1 Selection of Material for Pipes

It depends upon :

1. Carrying capacity of the pipes.
2. Durability of pipe.
3. Type of water to be conveyed and its possible corrosive effects on the pipe material.
4. Availability of funds.
5. Maintenance cost, repairs etc.

3.2.2 Types of Pipes

1. Cost iron pipes :

Cast iron pipes are mostly used in water supply schemes. These are highly resistant to corrosion. They have life about 100 years.

Types :

(i) Horizontal cast iron pipes.

(ii) Vertical cast iron pipes.

Advantages :

Horizontal cast iron pipes are 100% stronger in tension and 50% stronger in rupture than vertical cast iron pipes.

Disadvantages :

(i) Heavy, therefore difficult to transport.

(ii) Brittle, therefore easily get cracks or breaks.

2. Wrought iron pipes :

Advantages over cast iron pipes :

(i) More lighter.

(ii) Easily cut, threaded, worked.

(iii) Gives neat appearance if used in interior works.

Disadvantages :

(i) More costly.

(ii) Less durable.

3. Steel pipes :

Uses :
- (i) Used for main lines.
- (ii) Where pressures are high and diameter is more.

Advantages :
- (i) Light in weight and withstand high pressure.
- (ii) Cheap and easy to construct.
- (iii) Easily transported than cast iron pipes.

Disadvantages :
- (i) Cannot withstand external load.
- (ii) Pipes are much affected by corrosion.
- (iii) Life period of steel pipes is 25 to 50 years.
- (iv) Difficult in making connections.

4. Concrete pipes :

Types :
- (i) Precast pipe.
- (ii) Cast in-situ pipe.

Uses :
- (i) It is used when water does not flow under pressure.
- (ii) Used upto 600 mm diameter.
- (iii) Pipes above 600 mm diameter are reinforced.

Mixture used for concrete pipes is 1 : 2 : 2.

Specifications :
- (i) Mixture = 1 : 2 : 2
- (ii) Aggregate size = 6 mm
- (iii) Reinforcement = 0.25%
- (iv) Thickness = 25 to 65 mm for 10 to 120 cm diameter.

5. Cement lined iron pipes :

Use :

When water contains corrosive elements, cement lined iron pipes are used.

Specifications :
- (i) Mortar = 1 : 1.
- (ii) Thickness = 5 to 6 mm.

Advantages :
- (i) Life is more than 75 years.
- (ii) Easily constructed on site and factories.
- (iii) Least coefficient of expansion.
- (iv) Unaffected by the force of buoyancy even if empty due to heavy weight.
- (v) Unaffected by atmospheric action or ordinary soil.

Disadvantages :
- (i) Affected by acids.
- (ii) Repairs are very difficult.
- (iii) Transportation and laying cost is high.
- (iv) Difficult to make connections.
- (v) Porosity may cause cracks.

6. **Asbestos pipes :**

Uses :

Small size distribution pipes.

Specification :

Diameter = 5 to 130 cm.

Advantages :
- (i) Light in weight.
- (ii) Easily cut, fitted, drilled, jointed.
- (iii) Unaffected by corrosive elements.

Disadvantages :
- (i) Brittle.
- (ii) Very costly.

7. **Copper and lead pipes :**

Uses :
- (i) Making goose neck in the house connection.
- (ii) Pipes carrying hot water inside building.

Advantages :
- (i) Not liable to corrode.
- (ii) They can be easily bent.
- (iii) Do not sag if hot water is used.

8. Lead pipes :

Uses :
- (i) Used in sanitary fittings.
- (ii) In water supply, these pipes are mostly used in chlorination and alum dosing.

Advantages :
- (i) Easily bent.
- (ii) Stand high pressure.

Disadvantages :
- (i) Cause poisoning.
- (ii) Sag when hot water is used.

9. Wooden pipes :

Specifications :
- (i) Manufactured upto length 7 m.
- (ii) Life 30-35 years.

Advantages :
- (i) These are easy to repair.
- (ii) Light in weight.
- (iii) Unaffected by corrosive water.
- (iv) Cheap and easily laid.

Disadvantages :
- (i) Collapse under external load.
- (ii) Decay due to wet rot.

10. Plastic pipes :

Types :
- (i) Low Density Polyethylene Pipe (LDPE).
- (ii) High Density Polyethylene Pipe (HDPE).
- (iii) Polyvinyl chloride pipe (PVC).

Advantages :
- (i) Plastic pipes are corrosive resistant.
- (ii) These pipes are light in weight.
- (iii) These pipes are very economical.

Disadvantages :
   (i)   Pipes are not to be used at high temperature (above 45°C).
   (ii) They are not strong as GI or CI pipes.
   (iii) Thermal expansion coefficient is higher than GI or CI pipes.

11. Vitrified clay pipe :

Use :

To carry sewage and drain water.

Advantages :
   (i)   Less corrosive.
   (ii) These pipes provide smooth surface for flow.

3.2.3 Joints in Cast Iron Pipes

1. Bell and spigot joint :

This is the most commonly used for cast iron pipes. Lead is used as filling material.

Hemp or yarn is wound round the spigot and inserted into the bell-end of the pipe already laid. The yarn is adjusted by means of a yarning tool. A gasket or joining ring is clamped around the joint to make a tight fitting. Molten lead is passed over the hemp to fill the remaining space in socket. The lead shrink on cooling, it is then calked i.e. made to fill the space with calking tool and hammer.

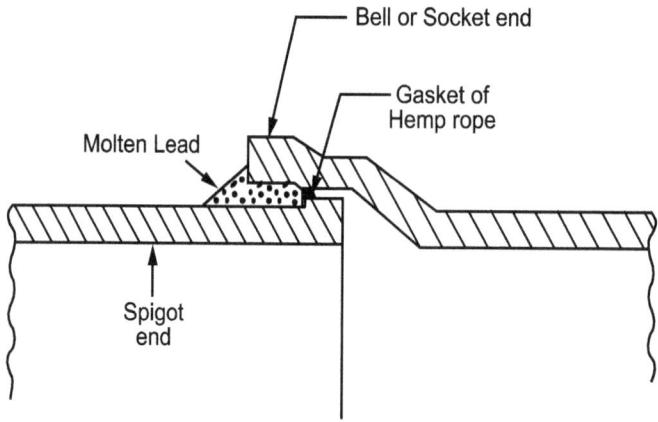

Fig. 3.2 : Bell and spigot joint

2. Expansion joint :

This is provided where pipes are subjected to high change in temperature. A rubber gasket is inserted in between the spigot and bell ends which makes the joint watertight. A flanged ring is bolted to the bell which expands and contracts along with the bell end.

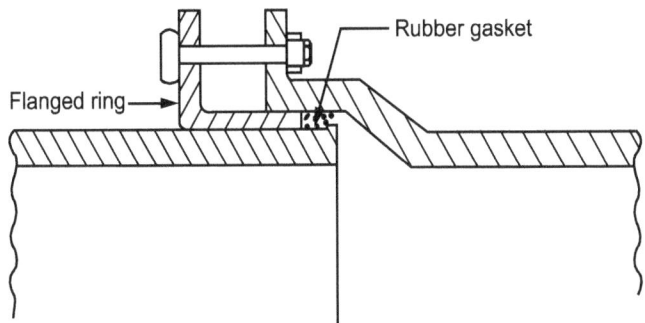

Fig. 3.3 : Expansion joint

3. Flanged joint :

This joint is used where the water pressure is light and diameter of pipe is more than 300 mm. The two ends of the pipes are provided with wide flange, which are bolted together. To make the joint watertight, a hard rubber gasket is inserted between the flanges which are bolted. This type of joint should not be used at places where it has to bear deflection or vibration.

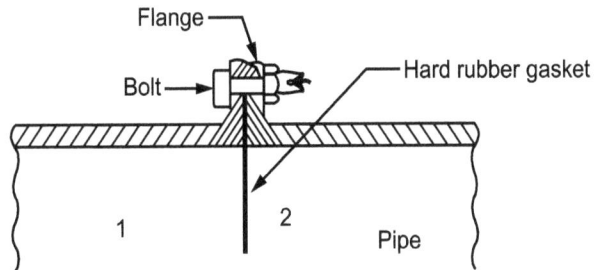

Fig. 3.4 : Flanged joint

3.2.4 Joints in Concrete Pipes

1. Cement collar joint :

These pipes are jointed by cement collar joint or by a spigot joint. Grooves provided to the ends are brought together. A collar made of concrete is slipped on. The space between the collar and the pipes is filled with C.M. (1 : 1) and finished to an angle of 45°.

Prestressed concrete pipes are provided with spigot at one end and socket at the other. The pipes are jointed with hemp of neat cement.

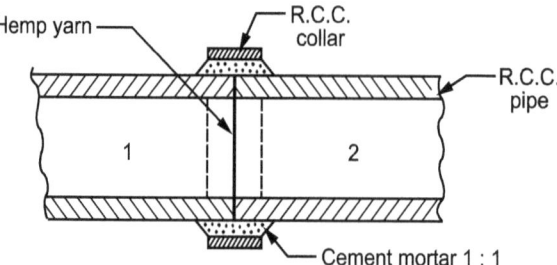

Fig. 3.5 (a) : Cement collar joint

2. Simplex joint :

This joint is used to concrete two asbestos cement pipes. A sleeve is provided over the abbatting ends in such a way that it fits over them. Two rubber rings are compressed between the sleeve and the pipe ends. The joint thus formed is called simplex joint.

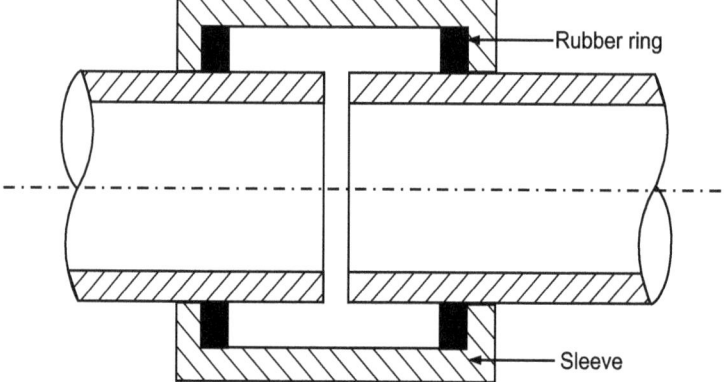

Fig. 3.5 (b) : Simplex joint

3.3 LAYING OF PIPES

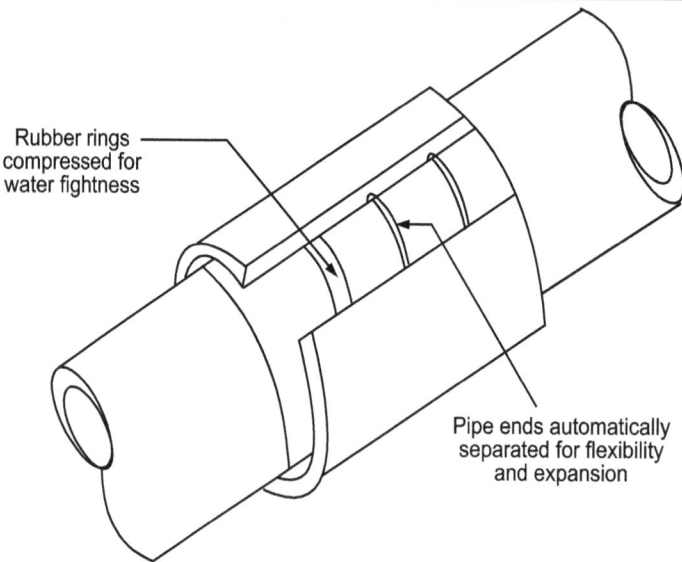

Fig.3.6 : Laying of pipe

Pipes are generally laid below the ground level, but sometimes they may be laid over the ground, when they pass in open areas.

Pipes are laid in the following ways :

1. First of all detailed map showing all roads, streets, lanes etc. is prepared.
2. On this map proposed pipeline with its sizes and length will be marked. The position of existing pipeline, curb lines, sewer lines, etc. will also be marked on it.
3. In addition to this, the position of valves and other pipe specials, stand post etc. will also be marked.
4. After planning, the centre line of the pipeline is marked on the ground by means of stakes driven at 30 m interval on straight lines and on curves they are at 7 m to 15 m spacing.
5. The excavation for the trenches will be done after centre line is marked on the ground.
6. The width of the trench will be 30 to 45 cm more than the external diameter of the pipe. At every joint depth will be 15 to 20 cm more than the actual depth. The pipeline should be laid more than 9 cm below the ground so that pipe may not break due to impact of heavy traffic load.
7. The trench should be protected by means of timber planks, so that it may not fall or collapse.
8. Heavy pipes are lowered by means of pulley blocks fixed on devices and lighter pipes are lowered manually.
9. The testing of pipes should also be done along with the laying of pipes.
10. Operation of filling up the trenches is carried which is also called as backfilling.

3.3.1 Testing of Pipeline

After laying work of pipeline they are tested by various methods. A pipeline section about 300 m length is tested for leakage, strength etc.

1. Pressure test :

Each valved section is filled with water and specified pressure applied by means of pump. All exposed pipe fittings, valves, hydrants and joints are examined carefully.

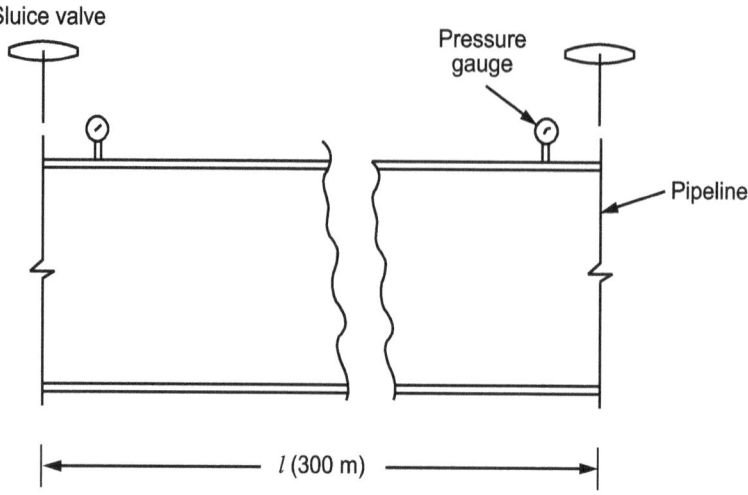

Fig. 3.7 : Pressure test

2. Leakage test :

Leakage is defined as the quantity of water to be supplied into the newly laid pipe or any valves section which does not reach the consumer and wasted. It is necessary to maintain the specified pressure after the pipe has been filled with water and the air is expelled.

Following are the steps for test :

1. The pressure on the water filled in each valve section is applied.
2. It is raised by means of a small hand pump upto 10 to 15% more than the maximum working pressure in that pipeline.
3. This pressure indicated on the pressure gauge is maintained for about 20 minutes.
4. If any leakage is present, this pressure will drop.
5. The amount of leakage should not be more than 20 litres per day per mm of diameter per km of pipe length.
6. The leakage is given by formula

$$Q = \frac{ND\sqrt{P}}{3.3}$$

where, Q = Allowable leakage in cm³/h

N = Number of joints in the length of the pipeline

D = Pipe diameter in mm

P = Average test pressure during the leakage test in kg/cm²

3.3.2 Corrosion Resistance of Pipe

Pipes get corroded under atmospheric action or under the action of water. The following adverse things happen because of corrosion :

1. Roughness of pipe is increased, hence discharge carrying capacity is decreased.
2. Pipe fittings fall.
3. Water, that flows through corroded pipes, get objectionable taste and odour.
4. Life of pipe gets reduced.

Corrosion can be prevented by applying protective anti-corrosive coating from outside. Thin film of calcium-carbonate is allowed to form, which prevents rusting action. Calcium carbonate is present in flowing water.

Corrosion is reduced also by giving treatment to water such as :

1. Removal of CO_2.
2. Adjusting pH values.

3.4 VALVES

The fixtures which are fixed along the distribution system are known as valves.

Purposes served :
1. Controls the rate of flow of water.
2. Releases or admits air into the pipeline.
3. Prevents or detects leakage.
4. Meets the demand during emergencies.
5. Makes the distribution system more efficient.

3.4.1 Sluice Valve

Also known as gate or stop valve. The entire distribution system is divided into blocks by providing these valves.

Small size sluice valves are enclosed in guard pipe around the spindle and supported over brick work. Larger valves are fixed in chamber. The entire distribution system is controlled by this valve.

These valves are provided in straight pipe length at 150-120 m interval and when pipeline is inserted, valves are fixed on both the sides of intersection.

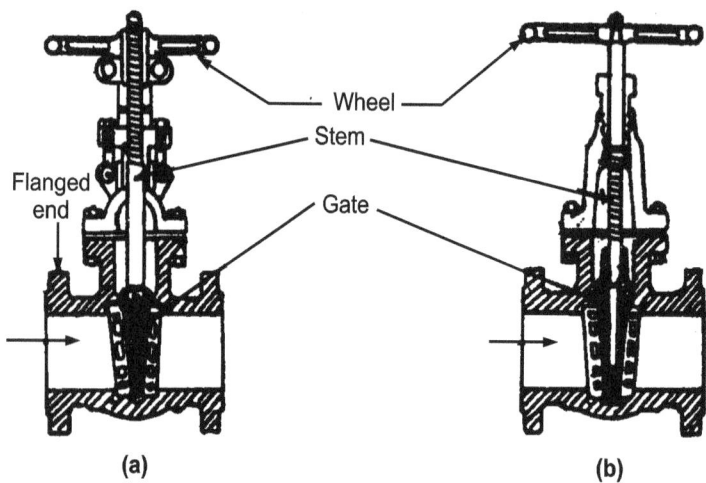

Fig. 3.8 : Sluice valve

3.4.2 Air Relief Valve

Water contains some quantity of air. When it flows, the air tries to accumulate at high point of pipeline, this may cause air lock reducing the discharge in the pipe. To avoid this, air valve is provided.

Use :

For automatic allowance of air to escape through it.

Location :

They are provided at summit points in the alignment of pipe.

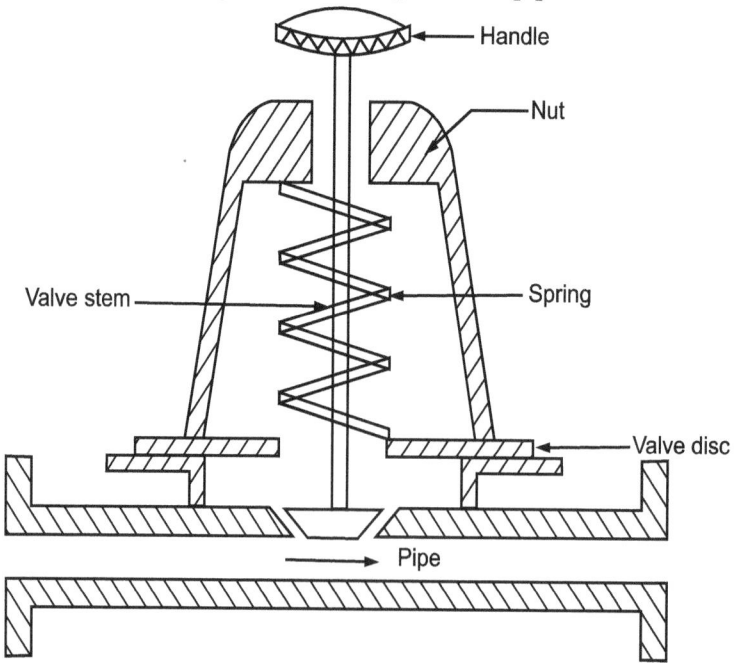

Fig. 3.9 : Air relief valve

3.4.3 Pressure Relief Valve

These are also called safety valves, provided at a point along the pipeline where pressure is likely to exceed permissible limit.

Use :

Relieves pressure automatically when it exceeds a fixed limit.

Location :

1. Two pipelines connecting pipe networks.
2. At two different elevations in pipeline.

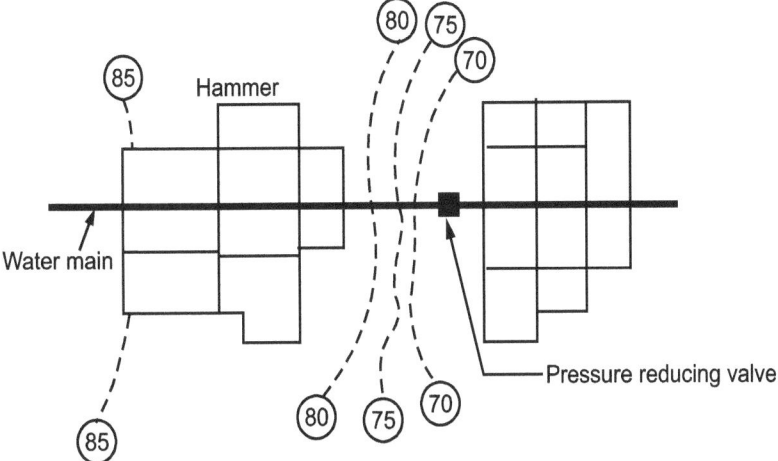

Fig. 3.10 : Pressure reducing valve

3.5 DESIGN OF THE RISING MAIN

3.5.1 Rising Mains

The water, after being pumped, is taken to the high levelled gravity pipe through the rising mains. The rising main may be of cast iron or asbestos cement pressure pipes. The velocity of flow in the rising main should not be less than 0.75 m/sec. at any time of flow.

3.5.2 Design Steps

Following are the steps for design of the rising main.

1. Assume the velocity of flow in the rising main.
2. Determine required cross-sectional area of the rising main.
3. Determine required diameter of the rising main.

3.6 HYDRAULIC DESIGN OF PUMPING STATION

3.6.1 Types of Pumping Stations

The pumping stations are classified as wet well and dry well. The wet well stations employ either suspended or submersible pumps.

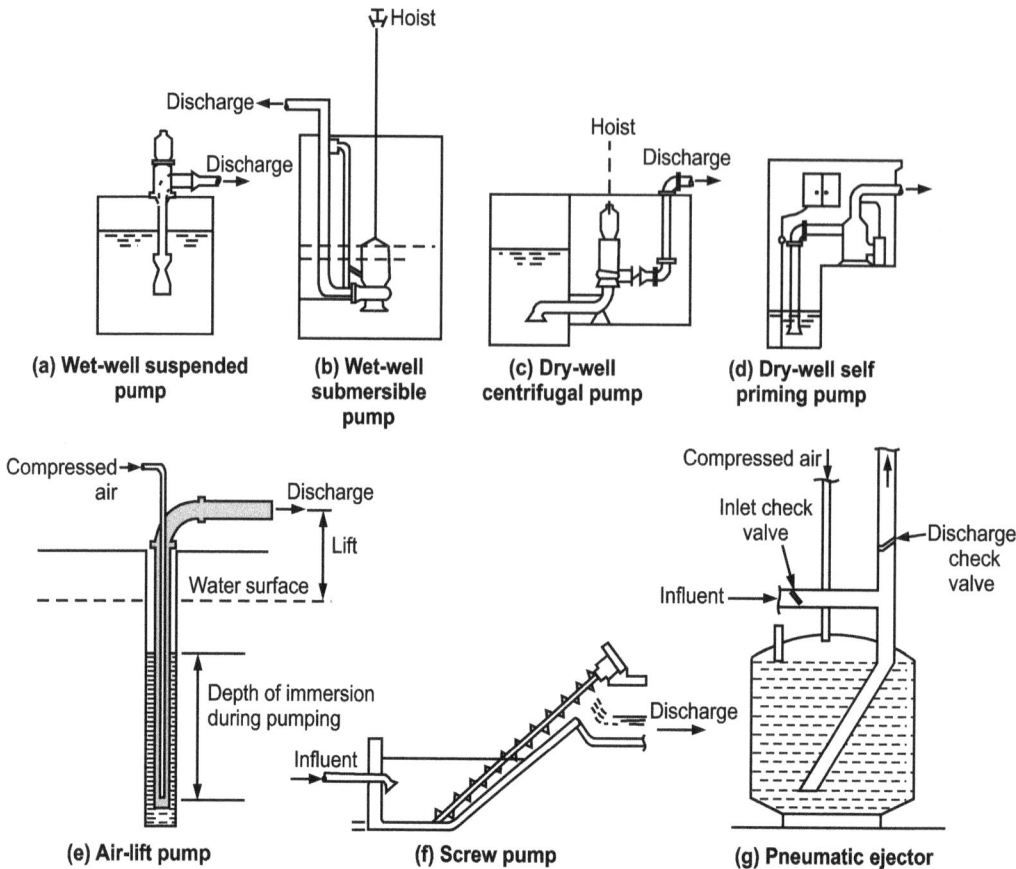

Fig. 3.11 : Types of pumps and pumping stations

Suspended pups have the motor mounted above the liquid level in the wet well while the pump remains submerged. Submersible pumps have integral motors with special seals suitable for operation below liquid level. The suspended and submersible pumping arrangements in wet well are illustrated in Fig. 3.11 (a) and (b).

3.6.2 Hydraulic Terms and Definitions Commonly Used in Pumping

Common terms sued in pumping and pump analysis include (1) head, (2) capacity discharge or flow rate and (3) work power and efficiency. These terms are briefly discussed in this section.

(a) Head :

Head describes hydraulic energy (kinetic or potential) equivalent to a column of liquid of specified height above a datum. Head and pressure may be expressed in terms of the other (1 m of water = 0.91 kPa; or 1 ft of water = 0.433 psi). Many head terms in pumping include static suction lift (or static suction head), static discharge head and total static head. These terms are illustrated in Fig. 3.12.

The total dynamic head (TDH) of a pump is the sum of total static head, the friction head (including minor losses) and the velocity head. The friction head consists of loss of head in piping (suction and discharge). It is calculated from Darcy-Weisbach or Hazen-Williams equations. The minor losses are produced due to fittings, valves, bends, entrance, exit etc., and are normally calculated as a function of velocity head. Some of these terms are defined as given below.

$$TDH = H_{stat} + h_f + h_m + h_v$$

$$h_f = f\frac{LV^2}{2gD} \quad \text{(Darcy-Weisbach)}$$

$$h_f = 6.82 \left(\frac{V}{C}\right)^{1.85} \times \frac{L}{D^{1.167}} \quad \text{(Hazen-Williams, SI units)}$$

$$h_m = K\frac{V^2}{2g}$$

$$h_v = \frac{V^2}{2g}$$

$$h_L = h_f + h_m + h_v$$

The Hazen-Williams equation is most commonly used for force mains. This equation in various forms is given below :

$$V = 0.355 \, C \, D^{0.63} \left(\frac{h_f}{L}\right)^{0.54} \quad \text{(SI units)}$$

$$V = 0.550 \, C \, D^{0.63} \left(\frac{h_f}{L}\right)^{0.54} \quad \text{(U.S. customary units)}$$

$$Q = 0.278 \, C \, D^{2.63} \left(\frac{h_f}{L}\right)^{0.54} \quad \text{(SI units)}$$

$$Q = 0.432 \, C \, D^{2.63} \left(\frac{h_f}{L}\right)^{0.54} \quad \text{(U.S. customary units)}$$

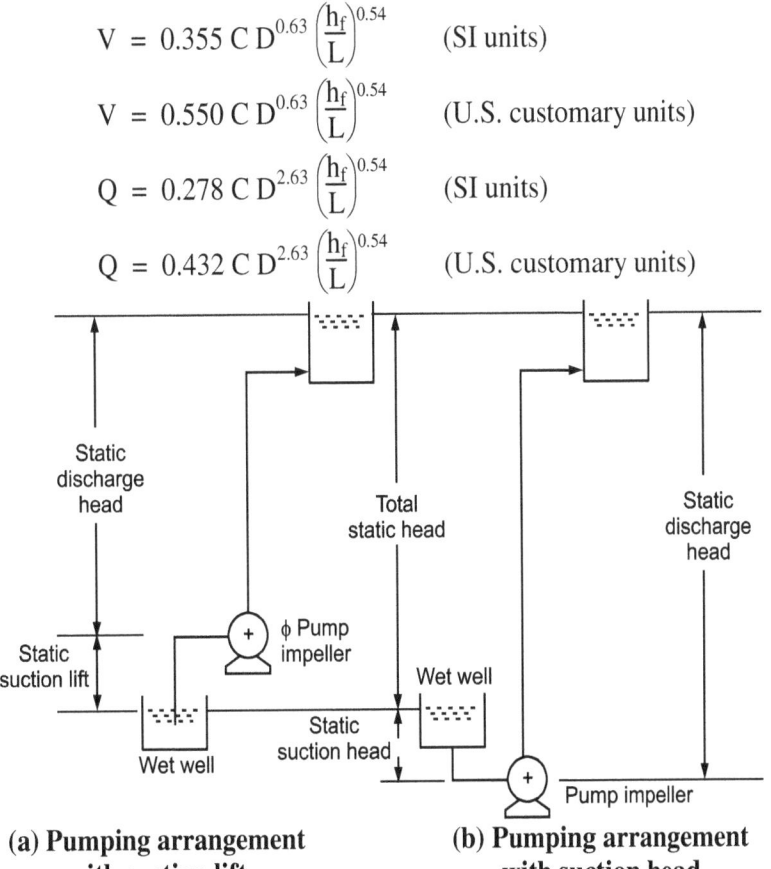

(a) Pumping arrangement with suction lift

(b) Pumping arrangement with suction head

Fig. 3.12 : Head terms used in pumping

where, TDH = Total dynamic head (or total head, TH), m (ft)
H_{stat} = Total static head, m (ft) (see Fig. 3.12)
h_f = Total friction head loss in suction and discharge pipes, m (ft)
h_L = Total head loss, m (ft)
h_m = Minor losses, m (ft)
h_v = Velocity head, m (ft)
V = Velocity in the pipe, m/s (ft/s)
Q = Flow rate, m^3/s (ft^3/s)
f = Coefficient of friction (the value of f depends on the Reynold's number and the relative roughness and diameter of the pipe. It may range from 0.01 to 0.10)
C = Coefficient of roughness (the value of C depends on the material and age of the pipe. It may range from 60 to 140)
D = Equivalent diameter of the pipe, m (ft)
g = Acceleration due to gravity, 9.81 m/s^2 (32.2 ft/s^2)
K = Head loss coefficient
L = Length of pipe, m (ft)

3.6.3 Design of Pumping Station

The design of a pumping station involves selection of site, pumping station and pumps and controls. Each of these considerations is briefly discussed below.

(a) Selection of site : Proper site selection for a pumping station is essential for good design and operation of the facility. Important site considerations include (1) all weather roads and parking, (2) protection from 100 year flood stage, (3) location relative to population areas due to odor problems (provision for odor control facilities, such as aeration, chlorination or hydrogen peroxide treatment, should also be made) and (4) dual-power source for continuous operation in the event of a primary power failure.

(b) Selection of pumping station : Wet well and dry well pumping stations were discussed in earlier section. Wet well pumping stations utilize suspended and submersible pumps, while dry-well stations utilize self-priming pumps or pumps positioned below the liquid level in the wet well. Basic design considerations for wet and dry-well pumping stations are given below :

1. The wet and dry wells should be separated by a water and gas-tight wall with separate entrances provided to each well.
2. Stairway should have non-slip steps and should be provided in dry well and in wet well where bar screens or other equipment requiring routine inspection and maintenance may be located. Manhole steps with an entrance hatch should be avoided. Circular or spiral stairway with walk-in door should be preferred.

3. As much as possible, all equipment requiring routine inspection should be installed in the dry well.
4. Ventilation should be provided for all dry wells below ground surface and in all wet wells housing equipment.
5. As a general rule, ventilation equipment should provide at least six air changes per hour or the minimum standard of the application building codes.
6. The bottom of the wet well should have a minimum slope of 1 : 1 to the pump intake. There should be no projections which may allow solids accumulation. Antivortex baffling should be considered for the pump suction in large pumping stations.

3.6.4 Criteria for Pump Selection

Prior to the selection of a pump for a pumping station, detailed consideration has to be given to various aspects, viz. :

(a) Nature of liquid, may be chemicals or if water, then whether raw or treated.
(b) Type of duty required, i.e. whether continuous, intermittent or cyclic.
(c) Present and projected demand and pattern of change in demand.
(d) The details of head and flow rate required.
(e) Type and duration of the availability of the power supply.
(f) Selecting the operating speed of the pump and suitable drive/driving gear.
(g) The efficiency of the pump/s and consequent influence on power consumption and the running costs.
(h) Various options possible by permuting the parameters of the pumping system, including the capacity and number of pumps including stand byes, combining them in series or in parallel.
(i) Options of different modes of installation, their influence on the costs of civil structural constructions, on the ease of operation and maintenance and on the overall economics.

EXERCISE

1. Explain the function of Jack well.
2. Give schematic arrangement of water supply scheme.
3. What is rising main ?
4. State the advantages and disadvantages of laying of rising main on the surface and underground.
5. What are different types of pump ?
6. Give criteria for selection of pipe.
7. Name different types of pipes used in water supply.

8. Explain the procedure of laying of pipes.
9. List various types of joints in pipe.
10. Give the definition of valves and state its purpose.
11. Draw a labelled sketch of bell spigot joint.
12. State where flanged joint is used.
13. State situation where flexible joint is provided.
14. Name the test for newly laid pipeline.
15. Enlist different types of joints in pipes with one purpose of each in water supply scheme.
16. Enlist any four types of valves used on rising main with their location and use.
17. Enlist any four types of joints used in water mains.
18. Enlist different types of valves. Explain any one of them with neat sketch giving function and principle of working.
19. State the functions of air relief valve.
20. Enlist the different types of joints used in water supply scheme. Explain any one of them with neat sketch giving function, location and use in scheme.
21. Draw a labelled sketch of 'air relief valve' provided on a water main.
22. State four sequential steps to be adopted for laying of 1.5 m diameter R.C.C. pipes.
23. State four advantages of R.C.C. pipes over other pipes.
24. Compare expansion joint and flanged joint.
25. Why the corrosion of pipes affects their carrying capacity ?
26. Why steel pipes are not suitable for distribution pipes ?

CHAPTER FOUR

POPULATION FORECAST AND WATER DEMAND

4.1 NEED FOR FORECASTING POPULATION

The population of every town or city goes on increasing every year. If water supply scheme is designed for the present population, it will be inadequate within few coming years, as the population increases continuously. All components of water supply scheme when once constructed cannot be made larger or replaced easily in future. Hence, various components of the water supply scheme are designed to supply water to the population which will be existing at the end of design period. Therefore, it is necessary to find the population of the town or city at the end of the design period (generally 30 years). It is done from the past census data generally available with the local bodies like punchayat, municipality or corporation.

In short *"Finding probable population of a city at a future date, from census data of previous decades is known as forecasting of population"*.

4.2 METHODS OF POPULATION FORECAST

Following methods are generally used to estimate the future population :

1. Arithmetical Increase Method

2. Geometrical Increase Method

3. Incremental Increase Method

4. Declining growth or Decrease Rate of Growth Method

5. Simple graphical or Graphical Extension Method

6. Graphical Comparison Method

7. Zoning Method or Master Plan Method

8. The Logistic Curve Method

9. The Ratio Method or Apportionment Method.

4.2.1 Arithmetical Increase Method

It is based on the assumption that the average rate of increase in population from decade to decade is constant. Mathematically, it can be expressed as $\frac{dP}{dT}$ = constant, where, $\frac{dP}{dT}$ is the rate of change of population. From the previous census data, the increase in population between consecutive decades is found and from this average increase per decade is worked out. Future population, as shown below, is then worked from the present population.

Let 'P' be the present population, 'd' is the average increase per decade and P_n is the future population after the period of 'n' decades (1 decade = 10 years). It is given by the following relation.

$$P_n = P + nd$$

This method is suitable when (a) The design period for the town is small and (b) When the town is old and large and also reached its saturation population due to maximum development.

This method is unsuitable for towns which are developing at a faster rate as compared to its past development. It gives lower results of future population. The following example will illustrate this method.

Example 4.1 : Following is the population data for a town. Water supply scheme is to be designed for this town with a design period of 30 years. Find the population at the end of the year 2020 by arithmetical method.

Year	1950	1960	1970	1980	1990
Population	35,000	37,500	43,500	52,000	57,500

Solution :

Year	Population	Increase in population
1950	35000	
1960	37500	2500
1970	43500	6000
1980	52000	8500
1990	57500	5500
	Total	22,500

$n = \frac{1}{10}(2020 - 1990)$
= 3 decades
P = 57,500

$$\text{Average increase in decade} = \frac{22500}{4} = 5625$$

Therefore, Population at the end of 2020 = P_n = P + nd

$$= 57,500 + 3 \times 5625 = 74,375$$

Hence, population at the end of year 2020 will be 74,375.

4.2.2 Geometrical Increase Method

This method is also called as uniform percentage method. It is based on the assumption that the average percentage increase in population from decade to decade is constant. From the census date of previous four, five decades the percentage increase between consecutive decade is found out and then its average is worked out.

If 'P' is the present population, 'r' is the average percentage increase per decade, then 'P_n' the population after n decades is given by the relation

$$P_n = P\left[1 + \frac{r}{100}\right]^n$$

Derivation of the formula :

$$\text{Population after one decade} = P_1 = P + \frac{r}{100} \times P = P\left[1 + \frac{r}{100}\right]$$

$$\text{Population after two decades} = P_2 = P_1 + \frac{r}{100} \times P_1$$

$$= P_1\left[1 + \frac{r}{100}\right]$$

$$= P\left[1 + \frac{r}{100}\right]\left[1 + \frac{r}{100}\right]$$

$$= P\left[1 + \frac{r}{100}\right]^2$$

Similarly, population after three decades $= P_3 = P\left[1 + \frac{r}{100}\right]^3$

Hence, population after 'n' decades $= P_n = P\left[1 + \frac{r}{100}\right]^n$

This method is suitable for towns having large scope of expansion and a fairly constant rate of growth is expected.

This method gives higher results, as compared to arithmetical method. It will be clear from the next example.

Example 4.2 : Solve the previous example by geometric increase method.

Solution :

Year	Population	Increase in population	Percentage increase in population
1950	35,000	2500	$\dfrac{2500 \times 100}{35,000} = 7.14\%$
1960	37,500	6000	$\dfrac{6000 \times 100}{37,500} = 16.00\%$
1970	43,500	8500	$\dfrac{8500 \times 100}{43,500} = 19.5\%$
1980	52,000	5500	$\dfrac{5500 \times 100}{52,000} = 10.5\%$
1990	57500		

Total percentage increase = 53.26

$\therefore$ Average percentage increase, $r = \dfrac{1}{4} \times 53.26 = 13.315\%$

$\therefore$ Population in the year 2020 = $P_{2020} = P\left[1 + \dfrac{r}{100}\right]^3$

$= 57,500\left[1 + \dfrac{13.315}{100}\right]^3 = 83,662$

By arithmetical method population in the year 2020 = 74,375.

Hence, it will be seen that this method gives higher results.

4.2.3 Incremental Increase Method

The benefits of arithmetical as well as of geometric method is included in this method. Similar to arithmatic method average increase per decade (d) is found out. Then increase or decrease in the population change for each decade is found out and from these average incremental increase is worked. Let us call it as 't'. Then, population at the end of nth decade is given by the following relation.

$$P_n = P + nd + (1 + 2 + 3 \ldots n)t$$

or

$$P_n = P + nd + \dfrac{n(n+1)}{2} \times t$$

where, P = Present population
  d = Average increase per decade
  t = Average incremental increase
  n = Number of decades

The method is recommended to be used for towns whose population is varying at a progressive rate and not at constant rate.

The method will be clear from the following solved example.

Example 4.3 : Solve the previous example by Incremental Increase method.

(8 Marks, Nov. 2001)

Solution :

Year	Population	Increase in population	Incremental increase
1950	35,000		
1960	37,500	2500	–
1970	43,500	6000	+ 3500
1980	52,000	8500	+ 2500
1990	57,500	5500	– 3000
		Total 22500	+ 3000

$$\text{Average per decade, d} = \frac{22500}{4} \qquad t = \frac{3000}{3}$$

$$= 5625 \qquad\qquad = 1000$$

∴ Population in the year 2020 $= P_{2020} = P + nd + \frac{n(n+1)}{2} \times t$

$$= 57500 + 3 \times 5625 + \frac{3(3+1)}{2} \times 1000$$

$$= 57500 + 16875 + 6000$$

$$= 80,375$$

Note : By comparing the results of the population for the same town by above three methods, it is seen that arithmetic method gives low population, whereas the geometrical method gives higher population. The incremental increase method gives medium population (future).

Example 4.4 : With the help of following data, estimate the future population of a town in the year 2001, using incremental increase method.

Year	1911	1921	1931	1941	1951	1961
Population (in thousands)	350	466	994	1560	1623	1839

Solution :

Year	Population	Increase in population	Incremental increase
1911	350		
1921	466	116	
1931	994	528	+ 412
1941	1560	566	+038
1951	1623	063	− 503
1961	1839	216	+ 153
	Total	1489	+ 100

$n = \frac{1}{10}(2001 - 1961)$ = 4 decades

Average per decade, $d = \frac{1489}{5} = 297.8$

$t = \frac{100}{4} = 25$

∴ Population in the year 2001 = $P_n = P + nd + \frac{n(n+1)}{2} \times t$

$= P_{2001} = 1839 + 4 \times 297.8 + \frac{4(4+1)}{2} \times 25$

$= 1839 + 1191.2 + 250$

$= 3280.2$ Thousand

∴ Population in the year 2001 = 3280.2 Thousand

Example 4.5 : Estimate forecast population by 2011, 2021 with following data from census report :

Year	1961	1971	1981	1991	2001
Population	25000	28000	32000	40000	49000

Use incremental increase method.

Solution :

Year	Population	Increase in population	Incremental increase
1961	25000		
1971	28000	3000	
1981	32000	4000	+ 1000
1991	40000	8000	+ 4000
2001	49000	9000	+ 1000
	Total	24000	6000

$n = \frac{1}{10}(1961 - 2001)$ = 4 decades

Average per decade, $d = \dfrac{24000}{4}$, $t = \dfrac{6000}{3}$

$= 6000$ $= 2000$

∴ Population in the year 2011 $= P_n = P + nd + \dfrac{n(n+1)}{2} \times t$

$= P_{2011} = P_{2001} + 1 \cdot d + \dfrac{1(1+1)}{2} \times t$

$= 49000 + 1 \times 6000 + \dfrac{1(1+1)}{2} \times 2000$

$= 49000 + 6000 + 2000$

$= 57000$

∴ Population in the year 2011 $= 57000$

Now, Population in the year 2021 $= 49000 + 2 \times 6000 + \dfrac{2(2+1)}{2} \times 2000$

$= 49000 + 12000 + 6000$

$= 67000$

∴ Population in the year 2021 $= 67000$

4.2.4 Declining Growth Method or Decrease Rate of Growth Method

The method assumes that the town has some limiting saturation population. From the past census data, it is seen that early growth of the town is at an increasing rate (faster) and latter growth is at a decreasing rate, indicating saturation limit. The method involves calculation of percentage increase for every decade and then working out the decrease in the percentage increase. The average of decrease in percentage increase is deducted from the latest percentage increase for each successive future decade.

The method is suitable for the town whose rate of increase in population is decreasing. The method will be clear from the following solved example.

Example 4.6 : The following is the census data for a town.

Year	1941	1951	1961	1971	1981
Population (in thousands)	90	130	184	253	326.68

Estimate the future population of the town for the year 2011 by declining growth method.

Solution :

Year	Population	Increase in population	Percentage increase in population	Decrease in % increase
1941	90			
1951	130	40	$\dfrac{40 \times 100}{90} = 44.44\%$	
1961	184	54	$\dfrac{54 \times 100}{130} = 41.54\%$	2.90%
1971	253	69	$\dfrac{69 \times 100}{184} = 37.50\%$	4.04%
1981	326.68	73.68	$\dfrac{73.68 \times 100}{253} = 29.12\%$	8.38%
			Total	15.32%

$\therefore$ Average decrease in % increase $= \dfrac{15.32}{3} = 5.1067$

The population at the end of 1991, 2001 and 2011 is worked out as follows :

Year	Net percentage increase in population	Probable population at the end of
1991	29.12 – 5.1067 = 24.013%	$326.68 + \dfrac{326.68 \times 24.013}{100} = 405.126$
2001	24.013 – 5.1067 = 18.906%	$405.126 + \dfrac{405.126 \times 18.906}{100} = 481.719$
2011	18.906 – 5.1067 = 13.8%	$481.719 + \dfrac{481.719 \times 13.8}{100} = 548.2$

Hence, the population at the end of the year 2011 will be 5,48,200.

4.2.5 Simple Graphical Method or Graphical Extension Method

In this method, a graph is plotted before the population and time in decades from the records of past census. The curve so obtained is extended further in the same manner to get the future population. The method gives approximate results as the extension of the curve depends upon the skill and experience of the person. The method may be used to apply a check on the results obtained by other methods.

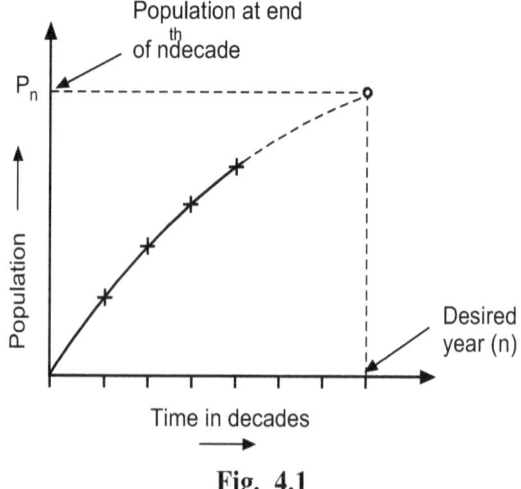

Fig. 4.1

Example 4.7 : (a) Following is a census data for the city. Forecast its population for the year 2011 (i) Using incremental increase method and (ii) by simple graphical method.

Year	1931	1941	1951	1961	1971	1981
Population in thousands	50	55	66	78	90	110

Solution : (i) **By incremental increase method :** Here n = 3 decades

Year	Population	Increase in population	Incremental increase
1931	50		
1941	55	5	
1951	66	11	6
1961	78	12	1
1971	90	12	0
1981	110	20	8
Total average		60	15
		$d = \dfrac{60}{5} = 12$	$t = \dfrac{15}{4} = 3.75$

$$\text{Population } P_{2021} = P + nd + \dfrac{n(n+1)}{2} \times t$$

$$= 110 + 3 \times 12 + \dfrac{3(3+1)}{2} \times 3.75$$

$$= 168.5 \text{ thousands}$$

(ii) **By graphical method :**

Population from graphical extended curve = 180 thousands.
Coment - initially slope of curve is gentle. From 1961, the curve is steeper

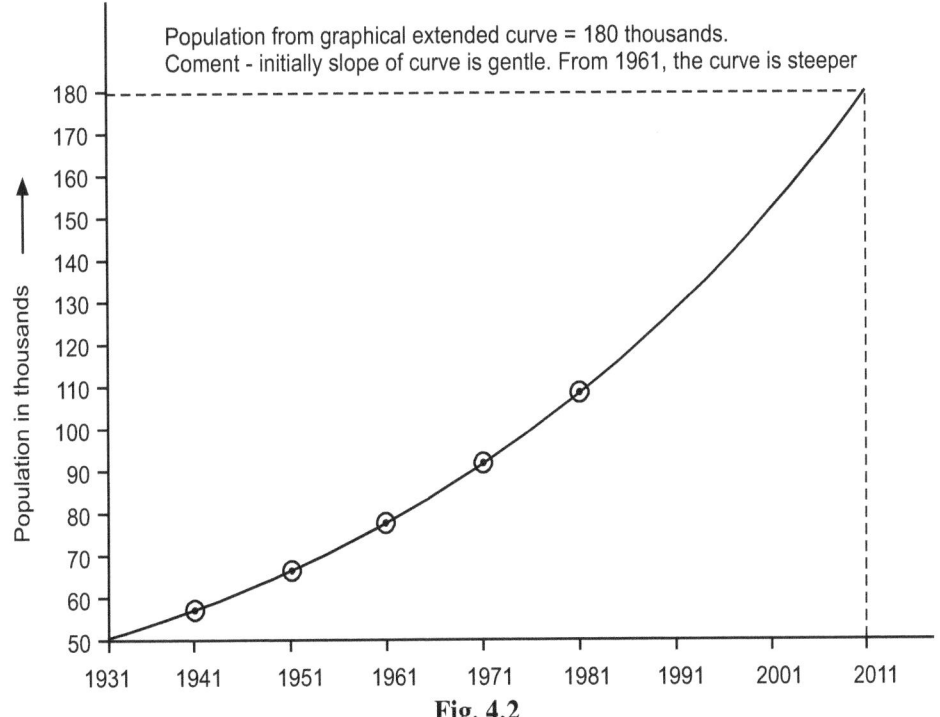

Fig. 4.2

4.2.6 Graphical Comparative Method

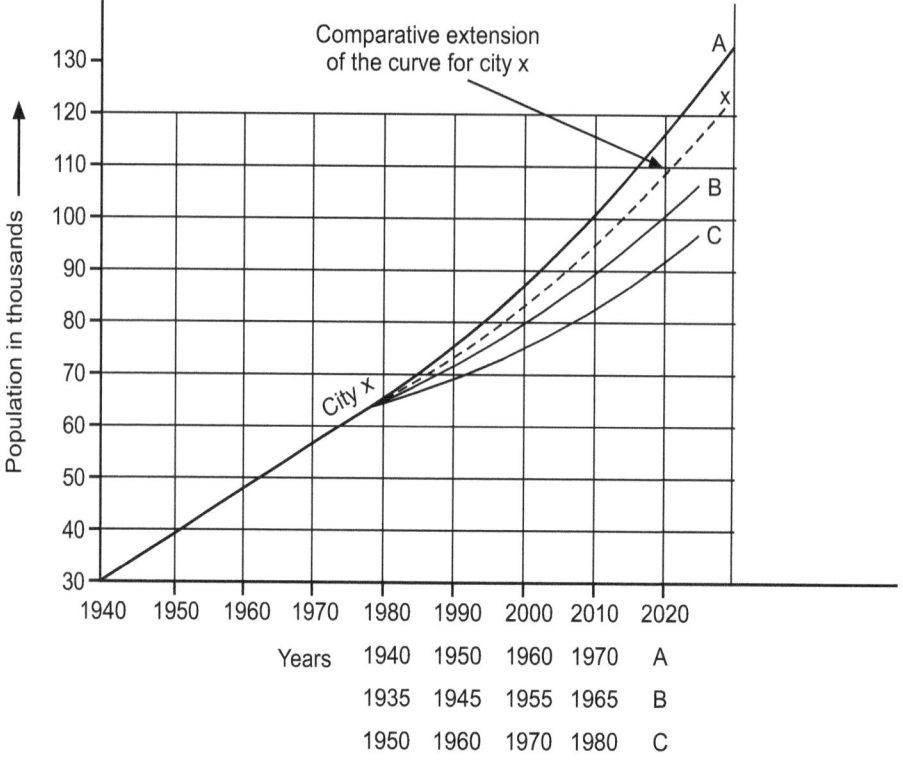

Fig. 4.3

First cities having similar characteristics as that of the city under consideration are selected. It is then assumed that the city in question will develope similarly as per selected cities.

Let 'x' be the city whose population at the end of 2020 is to be estimated and whose graph is plotted from the previous census data as shown above upto 1980 with population 62,000. Let selected city A reached the population 62,000 in the year 1940 and its curve is plotted from the same point. Similarly, curves are plotted for other cities B and C whose population reached upto 62,000 in the years 1935 and 1950 respectively. The curve of city x is then extended as shown by dotted line by comparison with cities A, B and C.

In practice it is not easy to find identical cities with respect to population growth.

4.2.7 Zoning Method or Master Plan Method

Now-a-days development of towns and cities is not allowed in haphazard manner. For their proper development, master plans are prepared according to bylaws and regulations of the local bodies or State Governments. For this, the city is divided into various parts often called as 'zones' such as commercial, industrial, residential, educational, parks and gardens. Future development is allowed to take place according to this master plan.

The master plan for the city is prepared for at least 30-40 further years. The population densities for these various zones to be developed are also fixed. From the densities and the areas of the zones, it is easy to work out the future population for the city whose master plan is prepared.

The following Table 4.1 gives the zonewise population densities.

Table 4.1

Sr. No.	Type of zone	No. of people per hectare
1.	Residential zone	
	(i) Large plots with single bunglow	10 - 40
	(ii) Small plots with single bunglow	50 - 90
	(iii) Row houses, single or two stories	100 - 250
	(iv) Multistoried buildings with apartments	300 - 2500
2.	Commercial zone	40 - 80
3.	Industrial zone	
	(i) Small scale	50 - 100
	(ii) Big industries	100 - 200
4.	Public parks, gardens	50 - 100
5.	Educational complexes	200 - 300

4.2.8 Logistic Curve Method

Under normal conditions, the population of a city shall grow according to the shape of the 'S' curve. In the beginning rate of growth of population is proportional to the population $\left(\frac{dP}{dt} \propto P\right)$. Later on rate of growth is constant and prior to saturation stage, the rate of growth is proportional to the difference between saturated population (P_s) and population P $\left[\frac{dP}{dt} \propto (P_s - P)\right]$.

The 'S' shaped curve is often called logistic curve. P.F. Ver Halst gave the following mathematical relation

$$\log_e \left(\frac{P_s - P}{P}\right) - \log_e \frac{P_s - P_0}{P_0} = -KP_s t$$

where, P_0 = The population at the starting point of the logistic curve

P_s = Saturated population

P = Population at any time from origin A

K = Constant

The above equation can be modified and put in the following form.

$$P = \frac{P_s}{1 + \frac{P_s - P_0}{P_0} \log_e^{-1}(-KP_s t)}$$

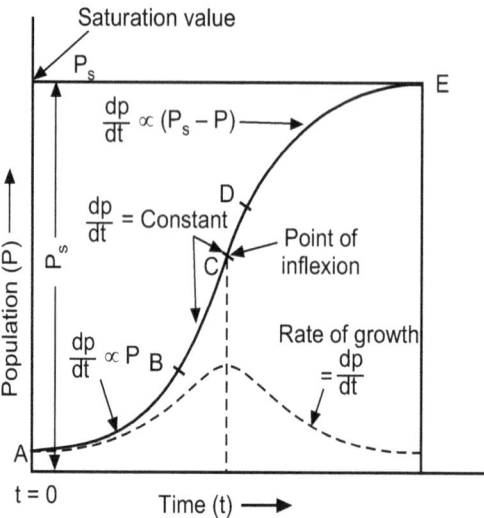

Fig. 4.4

Assume $\frac{P_s - P_0}{P_0} = m$ (a constant) and $-KP_s = n$ (a constant)

The above equation reduces to

$$P = \frac{P_s}{1 + m \log_e^{-1}(nt)} \qquad \ldots (4.1)$$

Mr. Mc Lean suggested that if three pairs of characteristics P_0, P_1 and P_2 at time $t = 0$, t_1 and $t_2 = 2t$, are chosen, the saturation value P_s and constants m and n can be worked out from the following three equations :

$$P_s = \frac{2 P_0 P_1 P_2 - P_1^2 (P_0 + P_2)}{P_0 P_2 - P_1^2} \qquad \ldots (4.2)$$

$$m = \frac{P_s - P_0}{P_0} \qquad \ldots (4.3)$$

$$n = \frac{2.3}{t_1} \log_{10}\left[\frac{P_0 (P_s - P_1)}{P_1 (P_s - P_0)}\right] \qquad \ldots (4.4)$$

Knowing P_0, P_1 and P_2 from census data, above equation will give values of R_s, m and n. These values when substituted in the equation (4.1) of logistic curve will give the population at any time 't'.

4.2.9 The Ratio Method or Apportionment Method

In this method, the population figures for the past 5 to 6 decades are obtained from the census records for the required city as well as of the whole country. This population for the city under consideration is expressed as the percentage of the population of the whole country for every past decade. e.g. the population of a city under consideration was say 50 lakhs and country's population is say 1000 lacks in 1970, the ratio or percentage will be 0.05 or 5%. Such ratio or percentages are worked for past 5, 6 decades. A graph is then plotted between time and these ratios and the curve so obtained is then extended upto design period, to get the corresponding ratio. This ratio is then multiplied by the expected national population at the end of design year. The expected national population in the coming years is generally with Government of India Census Department.

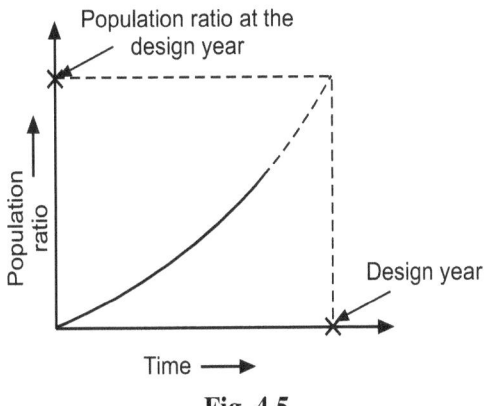

Fig. 4.5

Remarks :
1. Suitable for cities having population growth parallel to national growth.
2. Not suitable for cities having abnormal conditions.

4.3 FACTORS AFFECTING GROWTH OF POPULATION

The change in population of any town is mainly depending upon birth, death and migration from other town or villages. Generally, now-a days, death rate is low and hence the population of any town increases due to birth and migration. Following factors considerably affect the estimated population.

1. **Social facilities :** Medical, educational, recreational and cultural facilities.
2. **Development programmes :** Development of projects like Express Highways (e.g. Pune - Mumbai), Railways (e.g. Konkan Railway), river valley projects.
3. **Community life :** Standard of the people, living habits, social customs.
4. **Tourism :** Towns of historic importance like Pune, Aurangabad, Kolhapur, Ahmednagar. Religious places like Alandi, Pandharpur, Tuljapur, Nashik Trimbakeshwar etc. Tourist facilities like good hotels, parks, gardens, and availability of local conveyance etc.

5. **Economic considerations :** Development of new industries, discovery of oil or establishment of atomic, thermal and gas based power projects. Presence of minerals in the vicinity of the town.

6. **Agricultural based industries :** Sugar mills, dairies, cotton, lather, edible oils, food packaging etc.

7. **Disastorous factors :** Floods, epidemics, earthquake, frequent draughts etc.

Example 4.8 : A town has got the following census data :

Year	1930	1940	1950	1960	1970	1980	1990
Population	9600	12,700	18,300	22,650	27,000	31,000	34,500

Estimate population in the year 2020, by any three different methods.

Solution : The example is solved by arithmetic, geometric and incremental increase method.

Year	Population	Increase in population	Percentage increase in population	Incremental increase in population
1930	9600			
1940	12,700	3100	$\frac{3100}{9600} \times 100 = 32.29\%$	
1950	18,300	5600	$\frac{5600}{12700} \times 100 = 44.09\%$	+ 2500
1960	22,650	4350	$\frac{4350}{18300} \times 100 = 23.77\%$	– 1250
1970	27,000	4350	$\frac{4350}{22650} \times 100 = 19.20\%$	000
1980	31,000	4000	$\frac{4000}{27,000} \times 100 = 14.81\%$	– 350
1990	34,500	3500	$\frac{3500}{31,000} \times 100 = 11.29\%$	– 500
	Total	24900	145.45	+ 400
	Average per decade	$d = \frac{24900}{6} = 4150$	$r = \frac{145.45}{6} = 24.24$	$t = \frac{400}{5} = 80$

1. Population by arithmetic method after 3 decades (n = 3) :

    $P_{2020} = P + nd = 34,500 + 3 \times 4150 = 46,950$

2. Population by geometric increase method :

$$P_{2020} = P\left[1 + \frac{r}{100}\right]^3 = 34500\left[1 + \frac{24.24}{100}\right]^3 = 34500\,(1.2424)^3 = 66161$$

3. Population by incremental increase method :

$$P_{2020} = P + nd + (1 + 2 + ... n)\,t$$
$$= 34500 + 3 \times 4150 + 6 \times 80$$
$$= 47430$$

Example 4.9 : (a) Under what conditions would you recommend the arithmetical method of forecasting future population of a town ?

(b) The following figures represent the census data of a town. **(Dec. 1992)**

Year	1940	1950	1960	1970	1980	1990
Population	1,50,000	1,80,000	2,34,000	3,27,600	4,58,640	6,87,960

Forecast the future population of the town for the year 2020 by geometrical increase method.

Solution : Increase in population from decade to decade and also percentage increase in population is shown in the table below.

Year	Population	Increase in population	Percentage increase in population
1940	1,50,000		
1950	1,80,000	30,000	$\frac{30,000}{1,50,000} \times 100 = 20\%$
1960	2,34,000	54,000	$\frac{54,000}{1,80,000} \times 100 = 30\%$
1970	3,27,600	93,600	$\frac{93,600}{2,34,000} \times 100 = 40\%$
1980	4,58,640	1,31,040	$\frac{1,31,040 \times 100}{3,27,600} = 40\%$
1990	6,87,960	2,29,320	$\frac{2,29,320 \times 100}{4,58,640} = 50\%$
		Total = 180	
		Average percentage increase (r) = $\frac{180}{5}$ = 36	

Population in the year 2020 $= P_{2020} = P\left[1 + \dfrac{r}{100}\right]^n$

$= 6,87,960\left[1 + \dfrac{36}{100}\right]^3$

$= 687960 \times (1.36)^3$

$= 17,30,533.1$

Example 4.10 : The population of a town for the past census data is given below. Estimate the population after 3 decades by (1) Arithmetical, (2) Geometrical and (3) Incremental increase method.

Year	1940	1950	1960	1970
Population in thousands	50	58	67	89

Solution :

Year	Population	Increase in population	Percentage increase	Incremental increase
1940	50			
1950	58	8	$\dfrac{8 \times 100}{50} = 16.00\%$	–
1960	67	9	$\dfrac{9 \times 100}{58} = 15.52\%$	1
1970	89	12	$\dfrac{12 \times 100}{67} = 17.91\%$	3
	Total	29	49.43%	4

Average per decade, $d = \dfrac{29}{3} = 9.67$, $r = \dfrac{49.43}{3} = 16.48$, $t = \dfrac{4}{2} = 2$

Population after 3 decades i.e. in year 2000 :

1. By arithmetical increase method :

$P_{2000} = P + nd = 89 + 3 \times 9.67 = 118.01$ thousand

2. By geometric increase method :

$P_{2000} = P\left[1 + \dfrac{r}{100}\right]^n = 89\left[1 + \dfrac{16.48}{100}\right]^3 = 140.65$ thousand

3. By incremental increase method :

$P_{2000} = P + nd + \dfrac{n(n+1)}{2} \times t$

$= 89 + 3 \times 9.67 + \dfrac{3(3+1)}{2} \times 2$

$= 118.01 + 12 = 130.01$ thousand

4.4 INTRODUCTION

For designing the water supply for any town the design engineer has to work out the total quantity of water required for various purposes of the town. He then finds the suitable source of water to meet this total demand. In big cities, two or three sources may be adopted to meet the large demand of the city.

4.5 RATE OF WATER DEMAND

The quantity of water required for a city is affected by the 'Rate of demand'. It is the rate of water to be supplied per head per day. It is always expressed as so many litres/head/day. Sometimes it is also expressed as so many litres/person/ day or litres/capita/day. Total water demand depends upon the consumption for various purposes like domestic, commercial, industrial and fire demand etc. The rate of demand for all these purposes is worked out on per capita basis by dividing the total demand by the number of persons served. If 'V' is the quantity of water required per year in litres and 'P' is the estimated population to be served, then per capita demand is given by $\dfrac{V}{P \times 365}$ litres per day.

4.6 VARIOUS WATER DEMANDS

Water is used for the following purposes :

1. Domestic demand
2. Public demand
3. Commercial, institutional and industrial demand
4. Fire demand
5. Loss and wastage

1. Domestic demand : It includes water needed for drinking, cooking, washing, bathing, lawn sprinkling, gardening, sanitary purposes and air conditioning etc. This demand depends upon habits, living conditions and standards of the people. This demand may lie between 50 to 350 lit/capita/day. The higher demand is due to use of air coolers, air conditioners, automatic household appliances such as dish washers, washing machines for clothes and car washing etc. As per I.S., for residences, domestic demand is about 135 lit/capita/day. This demand is about 55 to 60% of total demand.

The break up of 135 lit/capita/day is approximately as follows :

1.	Drinking	5 lit/capita/day
2.	Cooking	5 lit/capita/day
3.	Bathing	55 lit/capita/day
4.	Washing clothes	20 lit/capital/day
5.	Washing utensils	10 lit/capita/day
6.	House washing	10 lit/capita/day
7.	Toilet flushing	30 lit/capita/day
	Total	135 lit/capita/day

2. Public demand : It includes water needed for washing streets, swimming pools, public parks, fountains and ornamental displays, flushing of public toilets and intermittent flushing of underground sewers etc. This demand may range from 20 to 70 lit/capita/day. Average demand may be taken as 25 lit/capita/day. In India, this demand is about 5 to 10% of the total consumption. Approximate values of water consumption for some municipal purposes are given in Table 4.2.

Table 4.2 : Consumption of water for municipal purposes

Purpose	Water consumption
1. Public parks	2.5 lit/sq.m/day
2. Road washing	1 to 1.5 lit/sq.m/day
3. Sewer flushing	4.5 lit/hr/day
4. Road side trees	28,150 lit/km/day

3. Commercial and industrial water demand : It includes water demand for offices, shopping centres, hotels, cinema halls, schools, colleges, hostels, hospitals, railway and bus stations and various industries. As per I.S. 1172 – 1983, water requirements for buildings other residences are given in the Table 4.3. Approximate consumption may be taken as 40 – 45 lit/capita/day.

For industries, actually there is no direct relation of this consumption with population. Also water demand varies from industry to industry. Moreover certain industries may have their own water supply source and the scheme. Such information is required to be collected and water demand is estimated. Approximate demand of water for few industries is given in the Table 4.4.

In general this demand may be taken up about 20 to 25% of the total consumption.

Table 4.3 : Table showing the water requirements for buildings other than residences

Sr. No.	Classification of building	Water requirement in litres per day
1.	Hospitals (including laundry) :	
	(a) Having number of beds < 100	340 per bed
	(b) Having number of beds > 100	455 per bed
2.	Nurse's and Doctor's quarters	135 per head
3.	Hotels	180 per bed
4.	Restaurants	70 per seat
5.	Schools :	
	(a) Day schools	45 per head
	(b) Residential schools	135 per head
6.	Hostels	135 per head
7.	Offices	45 per head
8.	Theatres and concert halls	15 per seat
9.	Factories in general :	
	(a) Where bathrooms are provided	45 per head
	(b) Where bathrooms are not provided	30 per head

Table 4.4 : Table showing water requirements for few industries

Type of industry	Unit of production	Water requirement in kilolitres/unit
1. Sugar	One bag of 100 kg	0.1 to 0.2
2. Textile	100 kg	8 to 14
3. Paper	tonne	200 to 400
4. Fertilizer	tonne	80 to 200
5. Automobile	per vehicle	40
6. Leather	100 kg	4
7. Glass	tonne	68
8. Artificial silk	tonne	2000
9. Wool	tonne	150 - 500
10. Gold	tonne of ore	1 - 1.5
11. Iron	tonne of ore	4 - 5

4. Fire demand : In cities, most of the areas are thickly populated. Also in the industrial zones, there may be number of industries using inflamable materials. Fire may break in any area at any time causing serious damage to the property and loss of life. There are various reasons for breaking the fire like short circuiting due to faulty wiring, improper storing and handling of inflammable articles, explosions of gas cylinders and chemical containers, intensional lighting of fires by dissatisfied workers or criminal people. For fire fighting, most of the cities have their own squad with necessary equipment. Large quantity of water is required for extinguishing fire.

Fire demand is the quantity of water required for extinguishing fire. The total demand for fire, in a year may be small, but the rate of consumption of a time is very large. It is difficult to estimate when the fire will break and what will be its extent. Hence, the fire demand is generally calculated based on some empirical formulae as given below :

(i) **Kuichling's formula :** $Q = 3182 \sqrt{P}$

(ii) **Freeman's formula :** $Q = 1136 \left(\dfrac{P}{5} + 10 \right)$

where, Q = Fire demand in lit/minute, P = Population in thousands.

(iii) **Government of India recommendation** (for cities having population more than 50,000) : $Q = 100 \sqrt{P}$,

where, Q = fire demand in kilolitres/day and P = Population in thousands.

(iv) **Buston's formula :** $Q = 5663 \sqrt{P}$ lit/min.

(v) **National Board of fire under writer's formula :**

$$Q = 4637 \sqrt{P} \ (1 - 0.01 \sqrt{P}) \text{ lit/min.}$$

Example 4.11 : Find out the 'Fire Demand' for the town having population 4,00,000 using various formulae.

Solution : Population in thousands = P = 400

(i) Buston's formula :

$$Q = 5663 \sqrt{P}$$
$$= 5663 \sqrt{400}$$
$$= 5663 \times 20 = 113260 \text{ lit/min.}$$

(ii) Kuichling's formula :

$$Q = 3182 \sqrt{P}$$
$$= 3182 \sqrt{400}$$
$$= 3182 \times 20 = 63640 \text{ lit/min.}$$

(iii) Freeman's formula :

$$Q = 1136\left[\frac{P}{5} + 10\right]$$

$$= 1136\left[\frac{400}{5} + 10\right]$$

$$= 1136 \times 90 = 102240 \text{ lit/min.}$$

(iv) National board of fire underwriters formula :

$$Q = 4637\sqrt{P}\left[1 - 0.01\sqrt{P}\right]$$

$$= 4637 \times \sqrt{400}\left[1 - 0.01\sqrt{400}\right]$$

$$= 4637 \times 20\left[1 - 0.01 \times 20\right]$$

$$= 4637 \times 20 \times 0.8 = 74192 \text{ lit/min.}$$

(v) Government of India recommendation for towns having population more than 50,000.

$$Q = 100\sqrt{P} \text{ kilolitres/day}$$

$$= 100\sqrt{400} = 100 \times 20 = 2000 \text{ kilolitres/day}$$

5. **Loss and wastage :** Loss of water in the distribution system may be due to

(a) Leakages in household plumbing as well as in the main and submarine due to faulty joints.

(b) Unauthorised water connections.

(c) Slippage in motor and pump.

Wastage is caused by the residential consumers by throwing stored water for collecting fresh water, when the water is supplied on intermittent basis. Many times householders leave their taps open during non-supply hours.

This quantity may be about 20 to 25% in material and well maintained distribution system. This quantity may be as high as 50% of the supply in badly maintained and unmetered water supply system, in the localities where the people do not understand importance of treated water.

4.6.1 Total Water Demand for a City

The total water demand for a city is the sum of all the demands mentioned above. However, the demands vary from city to city depending upon the number of factors explained in the next article.

For average India city the average break up of total demand of water in litres per capita per day is given below in Table 4.5.

Table 4.5

	Type of demand	Demand in lit/capita/day
1.	Domestic use	135
2.	Public use	25
3.	Commercial and Industrial use	40
4.	Fire demand	15
5.	Loss and wastage	55
	Total demand	270

Daily water demand for a city is obtained by multiplying this per capita rate by the population.

If 'P' is the population of the city, the daily water demand (consumption) = $270 \times P$ litres.

4.7 FACTORS AFFECTING WATER DEMAND

1. Size of city : The per capita demand is generally more for large cities, since commercial and industrial developments take place in them. In large cities, lots of quantities of water are consumed in parks, gardens, public toilets and also by the rich communities using modern amenities. In short, larger the size of city, more is the per capita demand.

The following Table 4.6 clearly shows the increase in water demand with the increase in population.

Table 4.6

	Population	Water demand in lit/capita/day
1.	Less than 20,000	110
2.	Between 20,000 – 50,000	110 – 150
3.	Between 50,000 – 2 lakhs	150 – 180
4.	Between 2 lakhs – 5 lakhs	180 – 210
5.	Between 5 lakhs – 10 lakhs	210 – 240
6.	More than 10 lakhs	240 – 270

2. Habits of people : The use of water depends upon the living standard of the consumer. This depends upon the economic status of the people. The consumption of water varies widely in different localities in the same city. In posh localities the demand per capita will be more, whereas in slum area it will be less as the water is supplied through common tap.

3. Climatic conditions : At places where summers are hot and dry, the consumption of water is more as more quantity is used for bathing, sprinkling on house floors, air coolers, air conditioner's, sprinkling lawns and gardens. Also in extreme cold countries, taps are kept open, in winter season, to prevent freezing of pipes, leading to more consumption.

4. Cost of water : If the cost of water is more, the consumption will be less and vice versa. This may not be true in highly polished areas.

5. Commerce and industry : Presence of industry increases per capita demand. It also varies with the type of industry, e.g. industries like dairy and paper mill require more quantity of water.

Demand in commercial establishments is affected by the number of establishments, number of people working in each concern and whether air conditioning is provided in them or not.

6. Quality of water : If the quality and taste of water is good, consumption will be more. The people will not use other sources like well water, having brackish taste.

7. Efficiency of the water supply system : If the system is efficient, the pressure in the distribution pipes will be high, causing more consumption. Losses through faulty plumbing will also be more.

8. System of sanitation : If the underground drainage system is provided in the town, more quantity of water is used in flushing water closets and urinals.

9. System of supply : The water supply to a city may be intermittent or continuous. In general, the consumption is less in intermittent system. In continuous system, the water is lavishly used. Consumers became carders forgetting the importance of water. In slum areas, common taps always run open causing lot of wastage.

10. Metering of supply : Metering consists of providing a meter to every house water connection (often called as house service connection) for measuring the quantity of water supplied. The consumer is charged according to meter reading. Metering reduces the consumption, since the people know that they will have to pay more for the losses and wastages caused by them. So the people develop a tendency to use the water economically.

There are certain drawbacks of metered supply of water. Every consumer has to bear cost of meter and its insulation. Poor and low income group people use less water causing unhygenic environment. Also meters cause obstruction to the flow of water resulting in loss of pressure. This ultimately increases the cost of pumping. Many times meters go out of order, need repairs for putting them into reuse. Meter readers are required to be employed for taking monthly or bi-monthly readings. Clerical staff is required for billing, dispatching of bills and receiving cash and maintaining accounts. Sometimes meters are stolen and replacement of another meter provides high burden on the consumer.

4.8 VARIATIONS OR FLUCTUATIONS IN DEMAND

The per capita demand is the average of daily consumption of the year. This demand does not remain constant throughout the year. It varies from season to season, month to month and also hour to hour. Hence, the variations may be classified as :

(1) Seasonal variations

(2) Monthly variations

(3) Daily and hourly variations.

1. **Seasonal variations :** The demand varies from season to season. The demand is more in summer than in winter. During rainy season demand may be still less. During summer the demand increases because the people consume more water for bathing, watering lawns and gardens, washing and sprinkling purposes. The average daily demand may increase by 40 to 50%.

2. **Monthly variations :** From the records of monthly consumption, it will be seen that, even in the same season demand varies from month to month. In big cities and hill station towns, consumption increases in May, June and July when the people visit such places to enjoy their holidays. Monthly variations are not useful for design purposes.

3. **Daily and hourly variations :** Day to day variations are called daily variations. These variations depend upon various factors such as habits of the consumers, climatic conditions and type of area i.e. industrial, residential or commercial. The consumption of water will be more on Sundays and holidays, due to washing of clothes, floorings and comfortable bathing as compared to the consumption on working days.

If the records of hourly consumption are observed it is seen that there is hour to hour variations which is called as hourly variation. A typical hourly demand graph is shown in the following Fig. 4.6.

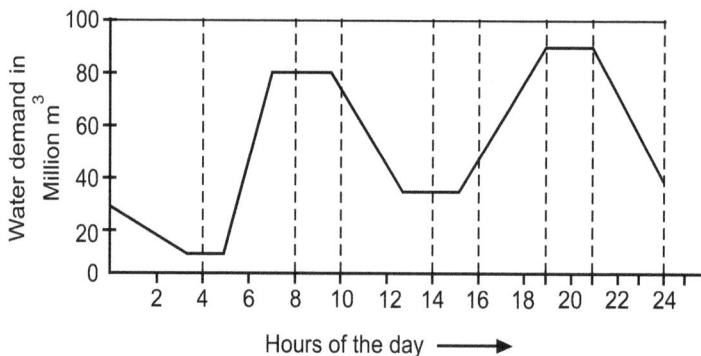

Fig. 4.6 : Typical graph showing hourly variations

From the graph it is seen that the maximum (peak) demand is during 7 am to 9 am and steadily falls down and reaches a minimum between 11.00 to 3 pm and again reaches the peak between 7 pm to 9 pm. The minimum demand of the water is in the late hours of night. The flow of water at night excluding industries generally represent the amount of losses and wastages as the domestic demand is practically nil during this time.

4.9 ASSESSMENT OF VARIATIONS

The demand is more variable in case of small towns. The maximum demand, either hourly, daily or monthly, is generally expressed as the ratios of their means. These figures also vary from town to town or zone to zone in the same town.

The average daily demand is calculated by dividing the total annual consumption by the number of days in a year. (= $\frac{V}{365}$ where, V is the volume of water consumed in a year.)

The rate of demand of the peak hour of the peak day of the maximum demand season is called as the absolute maximum hourly demand.

Following figures are generally adopted for various peak demands :

1. Hourly peak demand = 150% of its average demand.
2. Daily peak demand = 180% of its average demand.
3. Weekly peak demand = 150% of its average demand.
4. Monthly peak demand = 128% of its average demand.

If Q is the average daily demand,

Maximum hourly consumption of the maximum demand/day

$$= 150\% \times \text{Average hourly consumption of the maximum day}$$

$$= 1.5 \times \frac{\text{Maximum daily demand}}{24}$$

$$= 1.5 \times \frac{180\% \text{ of average daily demand}}{24}$$

$$= \frac{1.5 \times 1.8 \times Q}{24}$$

$$= 2.7 \times \frac{Q}{24} = 2.7 \times \text{Annual average hourly demand}$$

Many times, for finding out the ratios of peak demand to their corresponding average, the formula given by Goodrich is used.

$$P = 180 \, t^{-0.10}$$

where,   P = Percent of the average draft (flow) for time 't' in days

$$t = \text{Time in days from } \frac{2}{24} \text{ to 365 days}$$

Applying the above formula for daily variations by putting t = 1,

$$P = 180 \times (1)^{-0.10} = 180\%$$

Hence, maximum daily demand = 180% of average daily demand.

Similarly, for monthly variations, t = 30 days

$$P = (180)(30)^{-0.10} = 128\%$$

Hence, maximum monthly demand = 128% of average monthly demand.

Draft : The flow of water is called as draft.

Total draft : It is maximum of the following :

(i) Sum of maximum daily demand and fire demand.

(ii) Maximum hourly demand.

Coincident Draft : The maximum daily demand together with fire draft is called as coincident draft.

4.10 EFFECTS OF VARIATIONS IN DEMAND ON WATER SUPPLY UNITS

The various units in the water supply scheme are required to be designed to serve the maximum demand as well as for the variation in the demand. Following are the recommendations for various units :

1. When well is a source of supply of water, it is designed for maximum daily demand.

2. Pipes conveying water from source to reservoirs are designed for maximum daily demand.

3. Treatment units like filters are generally designed for maximum daily demand (i.e. 1.5 times the average daily demand).

4. Pumping units, distribution mains are designed for maximum hourly demand (i.e. about 2.7 times annual average hourly demand.)

5. Service pipes and feeders are designed for twice the average demand.

6. The sedimentation tanks and filters are usually designed for the average daily rate of demand.

7. While designing the service reservoir, considerations are made for hourly variations, emergency reserve, fire demand and pumping hours. Sometimes 2 hours storage is taken for fire demand. The total storage (for all demands) of the service reservoir is equal to one day's consumption.

4.11 FACTORS AFFECTING LOSSES AND WASTAGES IN WATER SUPPLY

It is already seen that huge quantity of water is lost through leakages in pipe joints, valves and consumer's individual faulty plumbing.

Factors affecting losses and their control are given below :

1. System of supply : The system of water supply may be continuous or intermittent. In the intermittent systems, the losses are reduced and are directly proportional to supply hours. However, if the people are throwing the old stored water and also keeping the tap open, wastages may be more.

It is necessary to confirm that the distribution system is leakage proof by periodical checking.

2. Policy of metering : When the consumers are charged according to their consumption, they will be careful in using the water economically, otherwise they will have to pay more for their wastages. Tendency to waste the water is reduced. For continuous system (i.e. 24 hours supply), metering is generally made compulsory for consumers.

3. Pipe joints : Since, the water supply pipe network consists of pipes, joints and valves for the control of flow, there is large possibility of their leaking causing wastage of water. Regular inspection and repairing the leaky joints and valves may reduce water losses.

4. Pressure in the system : If the water pressure is high in the system, leakages in pipe joints, valves and house hold taps will also be high leading to more loss of water. But if the pressure is low, certain areas may receive less amount of water leading to unrest amongst them. Normal pressure should be maintained in the system.

5. Unauthorised connection : Some people take illegal connections of water, causing loss of water and also the loss of revenue to the water supply authority. Periodical inspection for locating such connections may be carried out and such people should be fined heavily.

6. Mentality of the consumer : The people should be educated to understand the importance of water, through T.V. and Radio programmes. Water works should kept open for visit to the public once or twice a year to understand as how the water is purified and cost incurred to make it available in their houses, so that people will be mentally prepared to use water carefully.

EXERCISE

1. Name the different mathematical methods of forecasting of population and describe any one of them. **(Dec. 2006, 2007)**

2. What is the need of forecasting population while designing a water supply scheme for a town ? **(Nov. 93)**

3. State the character of town according to which you would consider one of the following methods particularly suitable :
   (i) Arithmetical Increase Method
   (ii) Geometrical Increase Method
   (iii) Incremental Increase Method. **(Nov. 93)**

4. Following is the census data of a town. Calculate prospective population in the year 2020. Use both arithmetical and incremental increase method.

Year	1930	1940	1950	1960	1970	1980	1990
Population in thousands	13	19	22	30	37	43	57

5. Enumerate different methods of forecasting population and explain 'Incremental Increase Method'. **(Jan. 92)**

6. What is demand of water ? What are various demands of a growing town ? Mention these demands per capita basis. **(May 1993, 2008; Dec. 2006)**

7. Forecast the future population of a town for the year 2021 by incremental increase method using the following census data:

Year	1931	1941	1951	1961	1971	1981	1991
Population in thousand	24	28.5	34.8	41.9	46.7	51.5	56.6

(May 93)

8. Estimate the population for the year 2010 by any method for the data as follows.

Year	1950	1960	1970	1980	1990
Population in thousand	65	85	90	96	110

(**Ans.** By Arithmetic method, Population = 132.5 thousands)

9. What do you understand by 'per capita demand of water'? How it is determined?

(May 1996)

10. Explain in short factors affecting the growth of population. **(Nov. 2000, May 2002)**

11. Discuss various factors that affect the rate of demand.

(Nov. 2002, 2009; May 2006, 2008, 2009, 2010)

12. Write a note on variations in rate of demand.

13. Explain in short how variations in the demand affect the design of various units.

14. Discuss the factors affecting losses and wastages in water supply.

15. How can fire demand be estimated?

16. Find out the 'Fire Demand' for the town having population 2,25,000 using various formulae.

17. How is the provision made for fire demand in water supply scheme? **(Nov. 2001)**

18. Explain any two formulae to calculate fire demand. **(May 2004)**

19. Explain fluctuations in demand of water. **(May 2004)**

20. Describe various water requirement categories which are used to calculate total demand of water. **(May 2006)**

21. Write a note on variations in rate of demand. Explain clearly how you take into account these variations in the design of various units.

(May 2006, 2008, 2009)

22. How is the provision made for fire demand in water supply scheme?

(Dec. 2006, 2007, 2010)

CHAPTER FIVE

QUALITY OF WATER

5.1 INTRODUCTION

Pure water is a chemical compound H_2O. However, such pure water is not available in nature. The main source of water is precipitation. The precipitation at the time of its formation does not contain any impurities, but traces of minerals and other matter present in the atmosphere. When this precipitation reaches the earth's surface, additional impurities are introduced. These impurities may be physical, chemical or bacteriological form.

As the precipitation flows over the earth's surface, it collects particles of soil, tree leaves, garbage, pesticides and other human, animal or chemical wastes and also other decayed organic matter. Such water flowing on the surface is called as surface source. Nallas, streams and rivers are the forms of surface source. Sewage and industrial effluents are often discharged in surface waters causing further pollution of water.

Now, when surface water percolates, underground suspended matters are filtered out. But dissolved minerals and salts remain in the percolated water. Finally this percolated water joins the underground water and raises its level, often called as water table. Open wells, tube wells and artesian wells are the forms of underground or subsurface source.

Water, either from surface source or underground source, contains various impurities which change the quality of water.

5.2 IMPORTANT QUALITIES OR REQUIREMENTS OF WATER FOR DOMESTIC USE

1. It should be colourless, good to taste, free from odour and sparkling clear.

2. It should be free from pathogenic bacteria or organisms.

3. It should be soft and free from harmful salts.

4. It should contain sufficient amount of dissolved oxygen and should be free from objectionable gases like H_2S etc.

5. It should be available in sufficient quantity at reasonable cost.

6. It should be free from radioactive matter, phenolic compounds, iodine, fluoride and chlorine.

7. It should be free from objectionable minerals like iron, manganese, arsenic and lead, and other poisonous metals.

8. It should be non-corrosive and free from scale forming compounds.

5.3 WATER CYCLE

The global system that supplies and removes water from the surface of earth is known as water cycle or hydrological cycle. It has no beginning or end as the water is continuously kept in motion in the nature. It consists of various processes of precipitation, interception, evaporation, transpiration, infiltration, percolation storage and surface run off. Schematically, the water cycle is shown in Fig. 5.1.

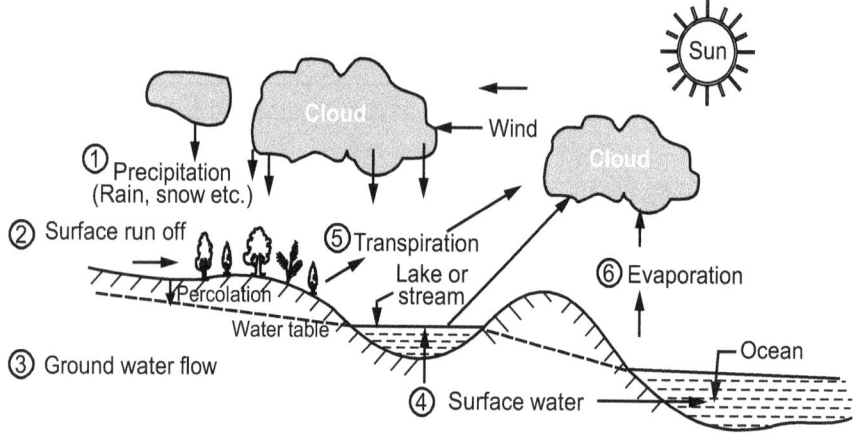

Fig. 5.1 : Water cycle or Hydrological cycle

5.4 SOURCES OF WATER AND THEIR QUALITY

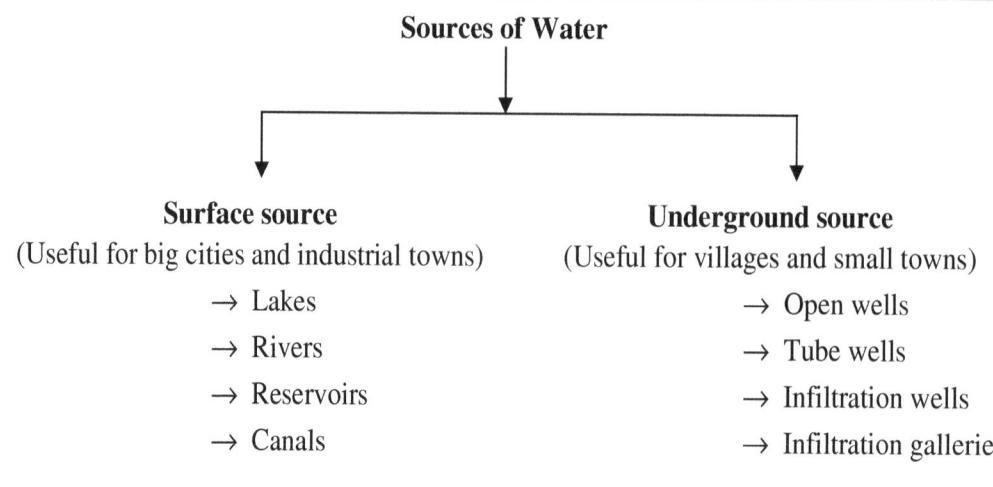

Quality	Quality
1. Impurities present : (a) Inorganic - silt, clay etc. (b) Organic - Plants, dead organic materials and animals algae and weed growth in still water.	1. Impurities present : Dissolved salts, minerals and gases etc.
2. Generally soft and less corrosive.	2. Generally hard due to dissolved salts of Ca and Mg.
3. Contaminated due to admittance of sewage	3. Less contaminated due to percolation through strata of soil.
4. Turbidity is more.	4. Turbidity is less.
5. pH ranges between 6.5 to 7.5.	5. pH is more than 7.
6. Hardness ranges between 30 to 150 mg/l.	6. Hardness ranges between 100 to 600 mg/l.

5.4.1 Impurities in Water

Water, either from surface source or underground source, contains number of impurities in varying amounts. Impurities are classified as follows :

1. Suspended impurities.
2. Colloidal impurities
3. Dissolved impurities.

1. Suspended impurities : These impurities are in the form of suspension/dispersion of solid particles which can be removed by sedimentation or filtration. Suspended impurities include clay, algae, fungi, organic and inorganic matters. These macroscopic impurities cause turbidity in the water. Hence, it is customary to measure the concentration of suspended impurities by its Turbidity.

2. Colloidal impurities : These impurities are in the form of very finely divided dispersion of particles in water. These impurities being very small, cannot be removed by ordinary filters. These are not visible to naked eye. All colloidal impurities are electrically charged and repel one another and hence remain in continuous motion and do not settle. Therefore, their removal is very difficult. Colloidal organic matters present in water are often associated with bacteria which may become the chief source of epidermics.

Colloidal impurities often impart colour to water. Hence, their concentration is measured by colour tests. The size of the colloidal particles ranges between 1 micron to 1 millimicron.

3. Dissolved impurities : These impurities may be in the form of solids, liquids or gases. This type of impurities may contain organic and inorganic compounds. The concentration of total dissolved solids is usually expressed in mg/l or p.p.m.

The following Table 5.1 shows various impurities and their effects.

Table 5.1 : Various impurities and their effects

Sr. No.	Classification	Name of the impurity	Effects of the impurity
1.	Suspended impurities	(a) Silica, clay, silt and other inorganic soils. (b) Algae and protozoa (c) Bacteria - Pathogenic	(a) Cause turbidity (b) Cause turbidity, colour and odour (c) Cause diseases
2.	Colloidal impurities	(a) Vegetables and organic wastes (b) Viruses and other minute dead animals (c) Colouring matters	(a) Cause colour, taste and acidity (b) Produce harmful disease germs (c) Colour
3.	Dissolved impurities	**(a) Salts :** (i) Carbonates and bicarbonates of calcium and magnesium (ii) Sulphates and chlorides of Calcium and Magnesium (iii) Sodium - bicarbonate and Sodium - carbonate (iv) Sodium fluorides (v) Sodium chloride	 (i) Cause hardness and alkalinity. (ii) Cause hardness and corrosion. (iii) Cause alkalinity and softening. (iv) Dental flurosis or mottled enamel. (v) Taste.

... Contd.

	(b) Metal and compounds :	
	(i) Manganese	(i) Black or brown colour.
	(ii) Silver	(ii) Discolouration of skin, eyes
	(iii) Iron oxide	(iii) Hardness, corrosiveness, taste, red colour
	(iv) Nitrates (NO_3)	(iv) Methaemoglobinemia.
	(c) Poisonous metals :	
	(i) Lead	(i) Cumulative poisoning
	(ii) Arsenic	(ii) Slow poison, carcenogenic
	(iii) Barium	(iii) Toxic effect on heart, nerves
	(iv) Boron	(iv) Affect central nervous system
	(v) Cyanide	(v) Immediate poisoning, Fetal
	(vi) Cadmium	(vi) Kidney damage (Nephrotoxic)
	(vii) Chromium	(vii) Poisonous, Carcenogenic
	(viii) Mercury	(viii) Cumulative poison
	(ix) Selenium	(ix) Toxic to animals, fish
	(x) Nitrites (NO_2)	(x) Poisonous blue baby sickness carcenogenic
	(d) Gases :	
	(i) Carbon dioxide	(i) Acidic, corrosion of metals
	(ii) Hydrogen sulphide	(ii) Bad odour, acidic and corrosion
	(iii) Oxygen	(iii) Corrosion of metals

5.5 ANALYSIS OF WATER

Water in its pure form is rarely available on the surface of the earth. It contains various types of impurities which can be determined in the laboratory. This analysis is carried out on raw water, water undergoing various stages of treatment and on purified or treated water before it is supplied to public.

5.5.1 Objects or Purposes of Water Analysis

(i) To classify the quality of raw water by analysing various impurities present, which helps in the selection of a raw water source.

(ii) To decide the outline of purification/treatment process.

(iii) To determine the chemical and bacteriological pollution of water.

(iv) To determine the nature of matter in suspension.

(v) To determine the level of organic impurities.

(vi) To check up the quality achieved during various phases and adjust the optimum dose of chemicals to be used in the treatment.

(vii) To check up the final quality of water and ascertain whether it has achieved the required standard or not, as specified by I.S. or W.H.O. (World Health Organisation) before it is fed into distribution system.

5.5.2 Collection of Samples

Analysis or examination of water is done on the samples brought from the source. The sample collected and brought in the laboratory should represent truly the quality of source. Generally, 2 - 5 litres of water sample is required for analysis. Polythene bottles are generally used for collecting samples.

Grab or catch sample : A single sample of water collected from the sampling spot any instant, to find the character of the sample at that particular instant is known as *grab or catch sample*. The frequency of grab sampling depends upon the magnitude of fluctuation in the quality of source.

Composite samples : Composite samples are mixture of grab samples collected at the same sampling point at different times. Grab samples at predecided interval of 30 minutes, 60 minutes or 120 minutes proportional to flow are collected and mixed or composited over a period of 24 hours, contents are thoroughly mixed and the average sample is taken for analysis. Such a composite sample of 24 hour period is considered as a standard for analysis.

5.6 CLASSIFICATION OF ANALYSIS OR EXAMINATION OF WATER

Testing or examination of water is divided into following three categories -

1. Physical examination,
2. Chemical examination and
3. Biological examination.

5.6.1 Physical Examination or Analysis

Physical examination carried out in the laboratory include the following :

(1) Colour
(2) Taste and odour
(3) Temperature
(4) Turbidity
(5) Specific conductivity.

1. Colour : Colour of water is generally due to the presence of fine particles of organic matter in suspension. Sometimes it is due to certain mineral matter in solution. Excessive growth of algae and aquatic micro-organisms also impart colour to water.

Colour is measured with a **tintometer**. The instrument has a eyepiece with two holes. A sample of water under examination is compared with known value of standard coloured water.

The unit of colour is measured on 'Platinum-cobalt scale'. The colour produced by dissolving 1 mg of platinum cobalt in one litre of distilled water is called as *one unit*.

Standard limits : For public water supply, the number of units on cobalt scale should not exceed 20. It should be preferably 5 to 10 units.

Significance :

(i) No health significance unless the colour is produced by toxic elements like Cr^{+6} and Cr^{+3} (Cr^{+6} produce orange colour, while Cr^{+3} produce green colour).

(ii) From aesthetic point of view, colour is objectionable to consumers.

(iii) Coloured water cause discolouration and stains to clothes.

2. Taste and odour : These are caused due to the presence of one or more of the following :

(i) Domestic and Industrial wastes and decomposing organic wastes.

(ii) Dissolved gases like carbon dioxide, hydrogen sulphide, methane etc.

(iii) Chemical compounds like phenols, sodium chloride, iron compounds, carbonates and sulphates of some elements.

(iv) Certain types of micro-organisms, either alive or dead.

The odour of water changes with temperature and it may be classed as earthy, grassy, fishy, sweetish and vegetable etc. Odour of water sample is at 20 to 25°C by using the instrument called **'Osmoscope'**. The odour reduces with rise in temperature due to escape of dissolved gases.

Unit of odour is **'Threshold odour number'**. Odour is measured by adding small quantity of water sample to be tested at a time to 100 cc of fresh odour free water and the quantity of water sample added at which the odour is just detectable is called *'threshold odour number.'* For example, suppose 2 cc of water to be tested is added to 100 cc of fresh odour free water and the mixture is smelled, odour is not perceived. Now, higher quantity say 3 cc of water sample is added to 100 cc of fresh odour free water and mixture is smelled and odour is now detected. The threshold odour number is 3. For public water supply, Threshold odour number should not be more than 3. Desirable odour number is between 1 to 3.

3. **Temperature :** Test or examination of water for temperature has no significance because practically the temperature of water can be changed. The desirable temperature of water supplied should be between 10°C to 20°C and temperature higher than 25°C is objectionable.

4. **Turbidity :** It is imparted to the water by a large amount of colloidal and suspended matter like clay, silt or finely divided organic matter present in it. Water appears turbid and turbidity depends upon fineness and concentration of particles present in water. Turbidity is defined by the obstruction that is caused to the passage of light through the sample of water.

Unit of turbidity : Unit of turbidity is ppm or mg/litre on silica scale. One mg of colloidal silica suspended in one litre of distilled water, produces one unit of turbidity. (Sometimes Fuller's earth is used). The permissible turbidity in domestic water is between 5 to 10 mg/l. Cause rejection of water if the turbidity is above 25 mg/l.

Measurement of turbidity : Turbidity of water is measured by the following instruments/methods : (i) Turbidity rod, (ii) Nephelometer, (iii) Jackson's turbidimeter and (iv) Baylis turbidimeter.

(i) **Turbidity rod :** It is used to measure turbidity of water in the field. It consists of graduated aluminium rod to give turbidity values directly. A graduated non-stretchable tape is attached to the upper end of this rod to help lowering of the rod in water. A screw containing a platinum needle of 1 mm diameter and 25 mm long is inserted at the lower end of the rod. A vertical rod or a stick is inserted in the nickel ring so as to support and keep the rod in a vertical position. A eye mark is provided on graduated tape for viewing during the test.

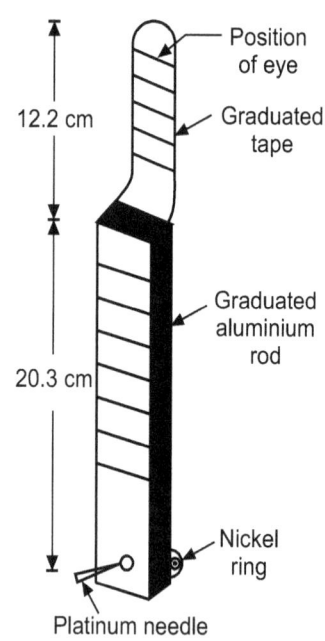

Fig. 5.2 : **Turbidity rod**

For measurement of turbidity, the lower end of the rod is gradually immersed in water and the depth at which the platinum needle ceases to be seen, by keeping the eye at the eye mark, under standard light conditions is read on the graduated scale, which directly gives the turbidity in mg/l.

(ii) **Nephelometer :** It is the modern commercial turbidimeter. Here the light intensity is measured at right angle to the incident ray, by use of photometer. It measures the intensity of light passing through the turbid water sample, after the same is scattered at right angles to the incident ray. The turbidity measured by nephelometer is generally expressed as NTU

(Nephelometric Turbidity Unit). Now-a-days, Formazin polymer is used as reference turbidity standard suspension, nephelometric turbidity units are also sometimes referred to as FTU (Formazin Turbidity Unit).

(iii) Jackson's turbidimeter : This is a laboratory instrument used to measure turbidity when it is higher than 50 mg/l. It consists of a metal stand holding a metal container and a graduated glass tube in it. A standard candle is placed below the stand as shown in the Fig. 5.3. Water is added into the glass tube, a small quantity at a time and the image of the flame of the candle is observed from top. The level of water in the glass tube is slowly increased till the image of the flame cannot be seen. The height of water level measured in the graduated glass tube gives the turbidity of water in ppm or mg/l or JTU (Jackson's Turbidity Unit).

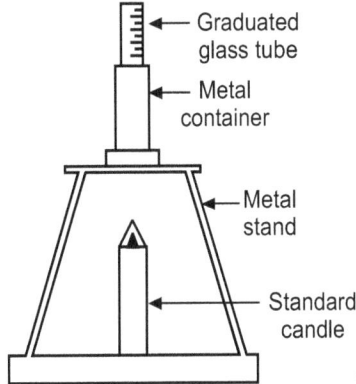

Fig. 5.3 : Jackson's turbidimeter

(iv) Baylis turbidimeter : This is an accurate instrument used to measure the turbidity of sample less than 5 units. It consists of a metal box in which two glass tubes are kept at one end and a 250 W bulb with reflector is placed at the other end as shown in Fig. 5.4. The tubes at their bottom are supported on white opal glass plate and are surrounded by blue cobalt plates which can be seen in the figure.

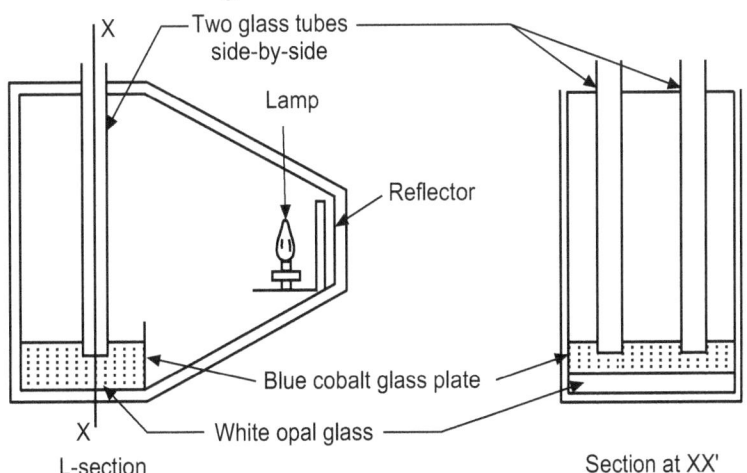

Fig. 5.4 : Baylis turbidimeter

One tube is filled with the sample water, whose turbidity is to be found out. Second tube is filled with standard water of known turbidity. In the light of the lamp, both tubes appear blue due to blue cobalt plates and the comparison is made. If the light differs another tube containing standard solution of different turbidity is kept in place of the previous tube and again comparison is made. This replacement of standard solution of various known turbidity and their comparison is continued till the colour of both tubes match. The standard solution of known turbidity at this stage gives the turbidity of the given sample. This turbidity is in ppm or BTU (Baylis Turbidity Unit), both being same.

Turbidity unit	Short form	Equivalent to
Nephelometric Turbidity Unit	NTU	mg/l or ppm
Formazin Turbidity Unit	FTU	mg/l or ppm
Jackson's Turbidity Unit	JTU	mg/l or ppm
Baylis Turbidity Unit	BTU	mg/l or ppm

Effects of excess turbidity :
1. It causes gastrointestinal irritation.
2. Decrease in disinfection efficiency as turbid particles provide shelters to viruses and bacteria.

Controlling turbidity : (I) Primary Treatment : (i) Alum dosing, (ii) Flocculation.
(II) Secondary Treatment : (i) Desalination, (ii) Softening.

5. **Specific conductivity :** The amount of dissolved salts present in water can be easily estimated by measuring the specific conductivity of water. It is determined with the help of a portable dionic water tester. The unit of specific conductivity is micro-mhos per cm at 25°C. The specific conductivity value when multiplied by a particular coefficient gives dissolved salt concentration in mg/l in the given sample. The rough value of the multiplying coefficient is 0.65. The exact value of this coefficient depends upon the type of salts present in water sample.

5.6.2 Chemical Examination / Analysis of Water :

It is carried out to find out chemical characteristics like :

(1) Total solids, (2) Hardness, (3) pH and Alkalinity, (4) Chlorides, (5) Dissolved gases, (6) Sulphates, (7) Nitrogen and its compounds, (8) Metals and other chemical substances and (9) Poisonous elements.

1. **Total solids :** These are classified as follows :
(I) Suspended solids :
   (a) Colloidal matter - causes turbidity.
   (b) Settleable matter - causes turbidity but coarser particles get settled in sedimentation tanks.

(II) Dissolved solids : Depending upon the type of salts, these solids may cause hardness, alkalinity or salinity.

Measurement of total solids : The amount of total solids present in water is determined by evaporating a known volume of sample water and weighing the dry residue left. Since, the volume of sample is known, total solids present can be converted into mg/l. To find the suspended solids a known volume of water sample is filtered by using filter paper and weighing the residue left on filter paper. This amount of suspended solids can be expressed in mg/l. The difference between total solids and suspended solids will give the amount of dissolved solids present in sample.

Permissible standard : Total solids in potable water should be limited to 500 mg/l. They should not exceed 1000 mg/l.

2. **Hardness :** It is the characteristic which prevents the formation of lather with soap. Hardness is expressed in mg/l as of $CaCO_3$.

Total hardness comprises of two components :

(i) Temporary hardness or carbonate hardness,

(ii) Permanent hardness or non-carbonate hardness.

- Temporary hardness is caused due to the presence of bicarbonates of calcium and magnesium in water.

- Permanent hardness is caused due to the presence of sulphates, chlorides and nitrates of calcium and magnesium.

Standards - Total hardness as $CaCO_3$ - Acceptable - 200 mg/l

- Maximum permissible - 600 mg/l

Classification of Hardness :

Amount of Hardness in mg/l as of $CaCO_3$	0 – 75	75 – 150	150 – 300	above 300
Classification of water	Soft	Moderately hard	Hard	Very hard

Standards for drinking water :

Authority	Acceptable limit in mg/l as $CaCO_3$	Maximum permissible limit in mg/l as $CaCO_3$
BIS	300	600
GOI	200	600
WHO	100	500

Effects of hardness when in excess :

1. Inconvenience during cooking due to scale formation.
2. More soap consumption during washing.
3. It causes bad taste.
4. It causes discolouration of clothing in dyeing industries.

5. It causes more consumption of fuel in boilers and hot water heating systems due to scale formation.

6. Corrosion and incrustation of pipelines and plumbing fixures is caused to a great extent.

7. It may cause Gastro-Intestinal Irritation (G.I.I.) and purging.

Determination of hardness :

(a) Complexometric titration method or EDTA method.

(b) Clark's method.

(c) Hehner's method.

(a) Complexometric method : It is also known as 'Versenate method.' In this method, hardness is determined by titrating against EDTA solution (Ethylene Diamine Tetra Acetic Acid), using Eriochrome black T as indicator, in the laboratory.

(b) Clark's method : It is assumed that hardness causing salts react with soap and form insoluble compounds before lather is produced. Total hardness is found by knowing the amount of soap solution required to obtain permanent lather with water sample of known volume with constant shaking. This method is not used at present.

(c) Hehner's method : Temporary hardness is determined by titration with a standard solution of sulphuric acid by using methyl orange as indicator. To find permanent hardness, standard sodium carbonate solution is added to the water sample and evaporated to get dry residue. The amount of sodium carbonate in excess over that required to convert the sulphates and chlorides into carbonates, gives the permanent hardness.

Method to find components of total hardness :

To find the carbonate and non-carbonate components of hardness, help of the knowledge of alkalinity is taken. It is known that hydroxyl (OH) alkalinity do not produce hardness. But carbonate (CO_3) and bicarbonate (HCO_3) alkalinity produce hardness.

This fact is used to find out the two components of hardness as follows :

(a) Let total hardness = T mg/l

(b) Let CO_3 and HCO_3 alkalinity = A mg/l

(c) If A ≥ T, carbonate hardness (CO_3) = T mg/l

and in this case non-carbonate hardness = Nil

(d) If A < T, carbonate hardness (CO_3) = A mg/l

and in this case non-carbonate hardness = (T − A) mg/l.

Example 5.1 : Following results were obtained during laboratory analysis of water for hardness and carbonate and bicarbonate alkalinity. Find the components of hardness.

(1) Total hardness = 80 mg/l

(2) CO_3 and HCO_3 alkalinity = 55 mg/l

Solution : Since, alkalinity is less than total hardness, both carbonate and non-carbonate hardness are present.

$\therefore$ $\quad\quad\quad\quad CO_3$ hardness = A mg/l = 55 mg/l

$\quad\quad\quad\quad$ Non CO_3 hardness = (T – A) = 80 – 55 = 25 mg/l

3. pH and alkalinity : (i) pH : Here p stands for potezo meaning power and H stands for hydrogen ion concentration. Hence, pH is nothing but hydrogen ion concentration of water. pH is defined as the logarithm of reciprocal of H^+ ion concentration.

pH is a measure of acidity or alkalinity of water. Acidity is caused by mineral acids, free carbon dioxide, sulphates of iron and aluminium.

Alkalinity in water is caused by hydroxides or bicarbonates of sodium, potassium, calcium and magnesium.

When electric charge is passed through water, it dissociates itself into positively charged and negatively charged ions. As per law of mass action, the product of the two types of ions is always constant. For water, concentration of H^+ ions × concentration of (OH^-) ions = constant = 10^{-14}. But water is electrically neutral. Hence, the H^+ ion concentration = OH^- ion concentration.

$\therefore$ H^+ ion concentration = $10^{-7} = \dfrac{1}{10^7}$ and OH^- ion cconcentration = $10^{-7} = \dfrac{1}{10^7}$

For pure water (H) = 10^{-7}, hence pH = $\log_{10} \dfrac{1}{(H)} = \log_{10} \dfrac{1}{10^{-7}} = 7$

pH scale : When hydrogen ion concentration increases, water becomes acidic and pH value reduces.

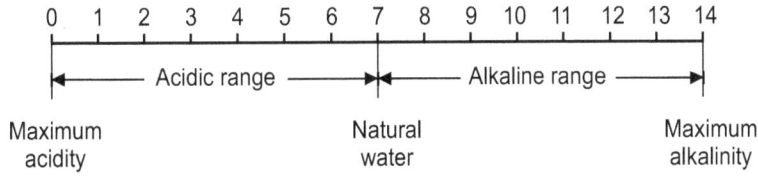

Fig. 5.5

Measurement of pH :

pH value is determined by the following methods :

(a) Electrometric method : A pH metre is used in this method. A water sample to be tested is kept in beaker and the two electrodes of the instrument are dipped in water and connected to a dry cell. The current is passed through the circuit and pH value is read on the dial directly. Recent pH meters display pH readings electrically on digital dial upto two decimals.

(b) Colourimetric method : In this method, chemical reagents or indicators are added to the sample of water. The colour produced is compared with the standard coloured water kept in sealed tubes of known pH values. This is the simplest test and is commonly used.

(c) pH paper : They are available in the market in the form of small strips like litmus paper. The pH paper is dipped in the sample of water which turns into some colour. This colour is compared with the printed colour range giving values of pH of sample. Each pH bundle is provided with printed colour range along with pH values. For laboratory work, pH paper is very useful.

Standards for drinking water :

Authority	Acceptable range	Maximum permissible range
World Health Organisation (WHO)	7 – 8.5	6.5 – 9.2
Government of India (GOI)	7 – 8.5	6.5 – 9.2
BIS	6.5 – 8.5	6.5 – 8.5

Effects when pH is more or less :

1. When the value of pH of water is outside permissible range, that water is objectionable for use. Also it causes taste and corrosion.
2. If water having pH > 9.2 is consumed, it causes bleeding in the stomach, which is dangerous.
3. If pH < 6.5 and if PVC pipes are used to carry such water, the lead is extracted from PVC material and goes to consumers along with water and forms a slow cummulative poison.

Importance of pH in water supply :

1. If the source of water is having pH between 6 to 8.5, the quality of that water is considered to be excellent and acceptable.
2. **Importance of pH in coagulation :** For effective coagulation, it is necessary to maintain pH range between 6.5 to 8.
3. **Importance in chlorination :** $HOCl^-$ component is said to be 80 times more powerful than OCl^- component. This formation of components is related with pH value.

   At pH = 7, 80% applied chlorine is HOCl and 20% is OCl

   At pH = 8, 20% applied chlorine is HOCl and 71% is OCl.

   Hence, for effective disinfection, pH should be 7 to have higher efficiency.
4. **Corrosion control :** Water below 6.5, is highly corrosive. Alkaline waters are less corrosive. At pH 7, corrosion is absent. Corrosion of iron pipes and valves occurs if treated water passing through them has pH less than 6.5.
5. Iron precipitates if pH > 6.5 and manganese precipitates when pH > 8.5 during aeration.

(ii) Alkalinity : It is the capacity of water to neutralise acid. It is caused by the presence of carbonates, bicarbonates and hydroxides of Ca, Mg, Na and K. It is caused by weak acid and strong base.

Distribution forms of alkalinity :

pH		Forms of alkalinity
	> 11.3	OH^- only
> 8.3	10.57 – 11.30	($OH^- + CO_3^{--}$) predominantly or CO_3^{--} only.
	8.3 – 10.56	($CO_3^{--} + HCO_3^-$) predominantly or CO_3^{--} only.
< 8.3	4.5 – 8.3	HCO_3^- predominantly
	< 4.5	Nil

Unit of alkalinity : Alkalinity is expressed in mg/l as $CaCO_3$.

Standards for drinking water :

As per BIS (i) HDL value = 200 mg/l as $CaCO_3$

(ii) Maximum Permissible Level (MPL) = 600 mg/l as $CaCO_3$

Effects of alkalinity :

1. When alkalinity is more than 200 mg/l, taste of water becomes unpleasant.

2. When hydroxide alkalinity exceeds 0.8 mg/l, water becomes highly unsuitable due to caustic taste. Bleeding of tongue and gullet may occur if such water is consumed. Also water will be highly corrosive.

3. Coagulation becomes efficient if raw water is naturally alkaline.

4. Chlorides : Chlorides are present in all natural waters. Fresh water sources contain chlorides ranging from 100 to 2000 mg/l. Surface waters may derive large amounts of chlorides from - (a) Sewage effluents, (b) Industrial effluents and (c) Sea water infiltration.

Unit of chlorides : Chlorides are expressed in mg/l.

Standards for drinking water :

Authority	Acceptable limit in mg/l	Maximum permissible limit in mg/l
WHO	200	600
GOI	200	1000
BIS	250	1000

Effects of chlorides :

1. When chlorides are present in water, taste and corrosion is imparted.
2. Excess chlorides present in water indicate possibility of contaminated and likely to cause diseases.
3. If such water is used in boilers, scale formation and sometimes boiler explosion may take place.

Determination of chlorides in lab : Amount present in the water sample is found out by adding silver nitrate of known concentration and potassium chromate to the water to be tested. Silver nitrate is added till reddish brown precipitate is formed.

5. Dissolved gases : Surface waters contain dissolved oxygen which is derived either from atmosphere or due to the activities of algae and other plant life in water. Also amount of gases like hydrogen sulphide, methane, carbon dioxide, chlorine may be there depending upon the amount and character of unstable organic matter. As the temperature increases, the gases, particularly oxygen contents, in water reduces.

6. Sulphates : Natural waters contain varying amounts of sulphates. Sulphates are found in water due to leaching from sulphate minerals and oxidation of sulphides. They also exist due to aerobic oxidation of organic matter in sulphur cycle. Industrial waste waters from paper, textile, tanneries, pesticides etc. contribute sulphates to receiving bodies of water. Sulphates are generally associated with Ca, Na and Mg.

Effects of sulphate :

1. Sulphate in drinking water causes laxative effect.
2. If such water is used in boilers, scale formation takes place.
3. It also causes odour and corrosion under aerobic conditions.

Standards for drinking water :

Authority	Acceptable limit in mg/l	Maximum permissible level in mg/l
WHO, GOI and BIS	200	400

For some industries, sulphate concentration less than 50 mg/l is required.

7. Nitrogen and its compounds : Nitrogen may be present in water in the following forms :

(a) Free ammonia, (b) Albuminoid nitrogen, (c) Nitrite and (d) Nitrate.

(a) Free ammonia : Its presence indicates the first stage decomposition of nitrogenous organic matter arising from the excremental discharges of human and animal. Free ammonia is estimated in the laboratory, by distillation of water sample. Ammonia released is collected and the quantity is measured. Permissible value of free ammonia in potable water is limited to 0.15 mg/l.

(b) **Albuminoid nitrogen or organic nitrogen :** It is normally derived from the animal and plant life associated with aquatic environment. Its presence indicates organic pollution in water supply. Its quantity is found out by adding sulphuric acid or alkaline solution of potassium permanganate to water sample and boiling the mixture. This liberates ammonia gas which is measured and expressed in mg/l.

The sum of ammonia nitrogen and albuminoid nitrogen is called Kjedahl nitrogen.

(c) **Nitrites (NO_2) :** Nitrites are produced by oxidation of ammonia. They indicate incomplete oxidation of organic matter. The amount of nitrites present in a water sample is determined by adding sulphonic acid and naphthamine which gives red colour. The colour formed is compared with standard coloured solutions to determine its value in mg/l. Nitrites must be absent in potable water.

Effects when present : It causes blue baby sickness, as it is a poisonous substance. Also it may produce cancer.

(d) **Nitrate (NO_3) :** It is the end product of decomposition of organic matter in the water, indicating completion of oxidation of organic matter and is no more harmful.

The amount of nitrates is determined by adding phenol-di-sulphonic acid and potassium hydroxide which gives colour. The colour so formed is matched with standard colours to ascertain the contents in mg/l.

8. **Metals and other chemical substances :**

They are tabulated below. Permissible standard and effects are quoted.

	Element / Substance	H.D.L.	M.P.L.	Effect when in excess
1.	Iron (Fe)	0.1 mg/l	1 mg/l	Imparts taste to water. It stains clothes and causes discolouration.
2.	Manganese (Mn)	0.05 mg/l	0.5 mg/l	Causes organic growth. Blocks pipes and valves.
3.	Magnesium (Mg)	30 mg/l	150 mg/l	Cause corrosion, hardness and purging.
4.	Calcium as Ca	75 mg/l	200 mg/l	Cause hardness, cooking and washing inconvenience.
5.	Fluorides **	1.0 mg/l	1.5 mg/l	Causes dental fluorosis chipping of teeth in children.
6.	Phenols	0.001 mg/l	0.002 mg/l	Causes taste and odour particularly after chlorination. Bactericidal in higher concentration.
7.	Sulphates	200 mg/l	400 mg/l	May cause purging and Gastro-intestinal irritation.

[**Note :** ** Presence of fluorides in water in small concentration upto 1 mg/l is desirable because such water improves dental health by hardening the enamel of teeth and also prevents dental caries.]

9. **Poisonous elements :**

Name	M.P.L. in mg/l	Effects when in excess	Source
1. Lead	0.10	It is cumulative poison.	Lead fittings, plastic pipes in which lead is used as stabilizer.
2. Arsenic	0.05	It is slow poison. It is suspected to be carcinogenic.	Waste waters from nitrogenous fertilizer industries.
3. Chromium	0.05	Poisonous. It is suspected to be carcinogenic in high concentrations.	Waste waters from electroplating industries.
4. Cynide	0.05	Immediately poisoning.	Waste water from electroplating industries.
5. Cadmium	0.01	It is nephrotoxic, i.e. it causes kidney damage. Also it causes cardio-vascular disturbances.	Waste water from electroplating and plastic industries.
6. Mercury	0.001	It is cumulative poison.	Waste water from mercury cell process, Cl_2 manufacturing process.

5.6.3 Biological Examination

Bacteria are the minute single cell organisms. They are produced by binary fission and may have various shapes. They are so small, required to be examined under microscope. They are present in raw or contaminated water.

Some varieties are harmless and are known as non-pathogenic or non-pathogens.

Some varieties are deadly harmful causing water borne diseases. They are known as pathogenic bacteria or pathogens. Most of the varieties of bacteria require oxygen for their survival. These bacteria consume oxygen which is dissolved in water.

Depending upon the way of satisfaction of oxygen, they are classified as :

(a) **Aerobic bacteria :** They survive by using dissolved oxygen in water.

(b) **Anaerobic bacteria :** They are not dependent on dissolved oxygen. In the absence of dissolved oxygen they derive their oxygen requirement by decomposing organic matter and extract chemically bound oxygen.

(c) **Facultative bacteria :** They can survive with or without free oxygen.

Pathogenic organisms cause water borne diseases and many non-pathogenic bacteria like E. coli, a member of coliform group, also live in the intestine of warm blooded animals and human beings. It is difficult to conduct specific tests for the identification of specific pathogens. Hence, the coliform group of bacteria can serve as indicators of the contamination of water with domestic and industrial waste. The 'coliform group density' which is a criteria of the degree of pollution, is used as the basis for standards of bacterial quality of water supplies.

Following methods are used to analyze bacterial quality of water :

(a) Standard Plate Count (SPC) or Total count test :

In this test, bacteria are made to grow as colonies, by innoculating a known volume of sample into a nutrient AGAR medium. This is kept in an incubator at 20°C for 48 hours or 37°C for 24 hours. The colonies of bacteria grow, which are seen and counted. The bacterial density is expressed as number of colonies per 100 ml of sample. The total count should not be greater than 100 per cc of water.

(b) Membrane Filter Technique (M.F.) :

This method is superior and less cumbersome. In this test, a known volume of water sample is filtered through a membrane of glass filter paper or cellulose acetate, with pores less than 0.5 microns. The bacteria present in the sample will be retained on this membrane. This filter paper membrane is put in contact with nutrient M-Endo's medium which permits the growth of only coliform, (The process is often called as culturing) in an incubator for 20 - 24 hours at 35°C. The coliform colonies are developed and these visible colonies are counted. Each colony represents one bacteria of the original sample. The bacterial count is expressed as number of colonies per 100 ml of sample.

(c) E. coli test or Coliform test :

It is noticed that coliform organisms in contact with lactose medium ferment within 48 hours with formation of gas.

The test is carried in the following three stages :

(i) Presumptive test (Medium - MeConky broth)

(ii) Confirmatory test (Medium - Brilliant Green Bile broth)

(iii) Completed test (Medium - Eosin methyl blue agar)

(i) Presumptive test : The sample of water is placed in sterile tubes and MeConky broth is added. The tubes are incubated for 24 hours at 37°C. If no gas is formed then coliform and E. coli are absent. The test is continued and it is again examined at the end of 48 hours. If no gas is formed, the test is negative and water is safe.

If the gas is formed, the test is positive indicating presence of bacteria and water is not safe for drinking. Now, the next stage test is carried out.

(ii) Confirmatory test : The culture from the positive test carried out above is incubated into two tubes (I and II) containing B.G.B broth. Tube I is incubated at 37°C for 24 to 48 hours. If gas is formed, coliform is indicated.

Tube II is incubated at 44°C for 12 hours. If the gas is formed, E. coli is indicated.

(iii) Completed test : Here the nutrient medium used is Eosin Methyl Blue Agar (EMBA). Here culture from tube I and II are streaked on two different plates say B and C respectively containing EMBA. Both plates are incubated at 37°C for 24 hours.

On plate B, if observed under microscope, large, moist and convex colonies with dark centres are seen, it confirms presence of coliform.

On plate C, if observed under microscope, small, dry and flat colonies with metallic lustre are seen, it confirms the presence of E. coli bacteria.

If the test is negative, the water is safe for drinking.

(d) Most Probable Number (M.P.N.) :

The most probable number is a number which represents the bacterial density which is most likely to be present. This M.P.N. is based on the application of laws of statistics to the results of a number of tests and is more accurate than coliform index. Here number of tests are conducted on portions of sample using different dilutions, for E-coli identification. The standard samples consist of five 10 ml portions. If in examination of E. coli, all portions are negative, M.P.N. is nil. If only one is positive, M.P.N. value from standard M.P.N. table is 2.2 per 100 ml.

5.7 RECOMMENDATIONS OF MINISTRY OF URBAN DEVELOPMENT (MUD)

The manual on Water Supply and Treatment prepared by the Central Public Health and Environmental Engineering Organisation, under the Ministry of Urban Development (MUD) India, lays down the following standards for water.

(a) Physical and chemical standards :

The physical and chemical quality of water should not exceed the limits shown in Table 5.2.

Table 5.2 : Physical and chemical standards (MUD, India)

Sr. No.	Characteristics	Acceptable*	Cause for** rejection
1.	Turbidity (units on J.T.U. scale)	2.5	10
2.	Colour (units of platinum cobalt scale)	5.0	2.5
3.	Taste and odour	Unobjectionable	Unobjectionable
4.	pH	7.0 to 8.5	6.5 to 9.2
5.	Total dissolved solids (mg/l)	500	1500
6.	Total hardness (as $CaCO_3$) (mg/l)	200	600
7.	Chlorides (as Cl) (mg/l)	200	1000
8.	Sulphides (as SO_4) (mg/l)	200	400
9.	Fluorides (as F) (mg/l)	1.0	1.5
10.	Nitrates (as NO_3) (mg/l)	45	45
11.	Calcium (as Ca) (mg/l)	75	200
12.	Magnesium (as Mg) (mg/l)	♭ 30***	150
13.	Iron (as Fe) (mg/l)	0.1	1.0
14.	Manganese (as Mn) (mg/l)	0.05	0.5
15.	Copper (as Cu) (mg/l)	0.05	1.5
16.	Zinc (as Zn) (mg/l)	5.0	15.0
17.	Phenolic compounds (as Phenol) (mg/l)	0.001	0.002
18.	Anionic detergents (as MBAS) (mg/l)	0.2	1.0
19.	Mineral oil (mg/l)	0.01	0.3
	Toxic Materials		
20.	Arsenic (as As) (mg/l)	0.05	0.05
21.	Cadmium (as Cd) (mg/l)	0.01	0.01
22.	Chromium (as hexavalent Cr) (mg/l)	0.05	0.05
23.	Cyanides (as CN) (mg/l)	0.05	0.05
24.	Lead (as Pb) (mg/l)	0.1	0.1
25.	Selenium (as Se) (mg/l)	0.01	0.01
26.	Mercury (total Hg) (mg/l)	0.001	0.001
27.	Polynuclear Aromatic Hydrocarbons (PAH)	0.2 µ (g/l)	0.2 µ (g/l)
	Radioactivity		
28.	Gross Alpha activity	3 pci/l	3 pci/l
29.	Gross Beta activity	30 pci/l	30 pci/l
	pci = pico Curie		

Notes :

1. *   The figures indicated under the column *acceptable* are the limits upto which the water is generally acceptable to the consumers.

2. ** Figures in excess of these mentioned under *acceptable* render the water not acceptable, but still may be tolerated in the absence of alternative and better source but upto the limits indicated under the column 'cause for rejection,' above which the supply will have to be rejected.

3. *** If there are 250 mg/l of sulphates, Mg content can be increased to a maximum of 125 mg/l with the reduction of sulphates at the rate of 1 unit per every 2.5 units of sulphates.

4. It is possible that some mine and spring water may exceed these radioactivity limits and in such cases it is necessary to analyse the individual radio-nuclides in order to access the acceptability or otherwise for public acceptance.

(b) Bacteriological standards : (See Table 5.3)

Table 5.3 : Guideline values for bacteriological quality

Organism	Unit	Guideline value	Remarks
(A) Piped water supplies :			
1. Treated water entering the distribution system :			Turbidity < 1 NTU for disinfection with chlorine; pH preferably 8.0; free chlorine residual 0.2 - 0.5 mg/l following 30 minutes (minimum) contact.
(i) Faecal coliforms	Number/100 ml	0	
(ii) Coliform organisms	Number/100 ml	0	
2. Untreated water entering the distribution system :			
(i) Faecal coliforms	Number/100 ml	0	
(ii) Coliform organisms	Number/100 ml	0	In 98% of samples examined throughout the year, in the case of large supplies when sufficient samples are examined.
(iii) Coliform organisms	Number/100 ml	3	In an occasional sample but not in consecutive sample.
3. Water in distribution system :			
(i) Faecal coliforms	Number/100 ml	0	
(ii) Coliform organisms	Number/100 ml	0	In 98% of samples examined throughout the year, in the case of large supplies when sufficient samples are examined.
(iii) Coliform organisms	Number/100 ml	3	In an occasional sample but not in consecutive sample.
(B) Unpiped water supplies			
(i) Faecal coliform	Number/100 ml	0	
(ii) Coliform organisms	Number/100 ml	10	Should not occur repeatedly; if occurrence is frequent and if sanitary protection cannot be improved, an alternative source should be found, if possible.
(C) Emergency water supplies			
(i) Faecal coliforms	Number/100 ml	0	
(ii) Coliform organisms	Number/100 ml	0	Advise public to boil water in case of failure to meet guide line values.

(c) Virological aspects :

0.5 mg/l of free chlorine residual for one hour is sufficient to inactive virus, even in water that was originally polluted. This free chlorine residual is to be insisted in all disinfected supplies in areas suspected of endemicity of infectious hepatitis to take care of safety of the supply from virus point of view which incidentally takes care of safety from the bacteriological point of view as well. For further areas, 0.2 mg/l of free chlorine residual for half an hour should be insisted.

5.8 WATER BORNE DISEASES AND THEIR CONTROL

Water is a good carrier of disease germs which are responsible for water borne diseases. These diseases fall into different categories according to the nature of organisms causing diseases. Such organisms may be bacteria, protozoa viruses, worms and fungi.

Following diseases are caused by the respective organisms :

(I) Diseases caused by bacteria :

    (a) Cholera - by - vibrio - cholerae   (b) Typhoid fever

    (c) Paratyphoid fever   (d) Bacillary dysentery

    (e) Gastro-enteritis.

(II) Diseases caused by viral infection :

    (a) Poliomyelitis   (b) Infectious hepatitis (Jaundice).

(III) Diseases caused by protozal infections - Amoebic dysentery.

(IV) Diseases caused by Helminthic (Worm).

The micro-organisms responsible for spreading these diseases, enter the human body with food and water which might have been contaminated by the patients with the disease or of carriers of the germs.

Shallow well waters in villages often get such contamination due to leakage of waste water from nearby cesspools. In cities sewer pipeline may leak near the water carriage line and leakage may find entry through faulty and leaky joints thereby contaminating the water supply.

Preventive measures :

1. Water supply lines and sewage pipelines should not be laid on the same side of the road.
2. Water supplies of the town should be thoroughly checked and disinfected before supplying to public.
3. Distribution pipe network of water supply should be often inspected, tested and repaired for leakages.
4. The general habit of cleanliness must be inculcated amongst the people.
5. The fly nuisance in the town should be controlled and kept minimum by general cleanliness and spraying insecticides from time to time.

EXERCISE

1. Give the significance of the following in the drinking water :
   (i) Turbidity (ii) Fluorides (iii) Hardness (iv) MPN. **(Nov. 97)**
2. What are the standards of Government of India for drinking water for the following -
   (i) pH (ii) Fluorides (iii) Nitrites (iv) Iron (v) Manganese (vi) Bacteria.
   (May 97)
3. What is the significance of chloride test ? Explain how chlorides are determined in the laboratory. **(May 96)**
4. What are Indian standards for quality of potable water for Iron, Fluoride, Residual chlorine, Bacteria, Hardness, Nitrates, pH and Turbidity. **(Dec. 98)**
5. Answer the following in brief : **(May 93)**
   (a) What is turbidity ? **(May 2000)**
   (b) What forms of alkalinity exist - (i) Above pH = 10, (ii) Above pH = 8.3, (iii) Between pH = 8.3 and 4.5, (iv) Below pH = 4.5.
   (c) State MPL for the following parameters in drinking water - pH, Hardness, Fluorides, Nitrites, Iron, Chlorides.
6. State the reasons for the following : **(May 93)**
   (a) When water is acidic, plastic pipes are not suitable for domestic water supplies.
   (b) Traces of fluorides are desirable in drinking water. **(May 2000)**
   (c) E. coli must be absent in drinking water. **(May 2000)**
7. State the permissible limits of the following in drinking water and the effects, if they are present in excess : **(Nov. 93)**
   Turbidity, Sulphates, Chlorides, Nitrates, Iron, Fluorides, Total hardness, Lead, Cynide, E. coli.
8. Explain the effect of fluorides in drinking water giving Indian standards. **(May 94)**
9. Define M.P.N. Why E. coli is chosen as indicator organism ? **(May 94)**
10. Explain laboratory method of finding turbidity of water sample.
    (Dec. 90, May 2007)
11. Write a note on common impurities noticed in water.
12. Write short notes on :
    (a) Temporary and permanent hardness   (b) pH and its determination
    (c) M.P.N.   (d) E. coli test
    (e) Free ammonia and albuminoid ammonia
13. Enumerate in brief the various impurities of physical, chemical and bacterial characteristics of testing of raw water supplies.
14. Write a brief note on water borne diseases.
15. Write down the Indian standards for the drinking water for (1) Chlorides, (2) Sulphates, (3) Hardness, (4) Nitrates, (5) M.P.N. index.
    What are the ill effects on human health if above impurities are in excess ?
    (May 2004)
16. Give reasons :
    Excess hardness of water is undesirable in industrial water supply. **(May 2005)**
17. Write distribution forms and effect of alkalinity. **May 2007, 2008, 2009)**

CHAPTER SIX

WATER TREATMENT PROCESSES : AERATION AND SEDIMENTATION

6.1 INTRODUCTION

It is already seen that raw water belonging to any source may contain various impurities which are grouped as : (i) Physical impurities, (ii) Chemical impurities and (iii) Bacteriological impurities.

Physical impurities impart turbidity, taste, odour and colour to the water. Chemical impurities, depending upon their nature and extent of amount present may impart pH, alkalinity, hardness, toxicity etc. Excess amounts of some metals and dissolved gases cause corrosion to pipes, valves and fittings. Bacteriological impurities, particularly pathogenic bacteria spread water borne diseases. These impurities will be present in water in suspended, colloidal or dissolved form.

The object of water treatment is to remove or reduce these impurities upto acceptable standard, before the water is supplied to the public.

6.2 TREATMENT OF WATER

The complete process of removal of undesirable matter (various impurities), in order to make the water acceptable for domestic or industrial use, is commonly termed as *treatment of water* or *purification of water*. Since, treatment is a costly affair, various purification (treatment) units are constructed and maintained by Public bodies like municipality, corporations, industrial development boards or government.

6.3 OBJECTIVES OF TREATMENT OF WATER

The following are the objectives of treatment of water :

1. To make water odour free and tasty.
2. To make it colourless.
3. To make the water safe and sparkling for drinking and domestic purposes.
4. To remove dissolved gases and turbidity of water.
5. To make it free from all objectionable impurities present in suspension, colloidal or dissolved form.
6. To remove harmful bacteria.
7. To remove hardness of water.
8. To make the water suitable for a wide variety of industrial purposes like dyeing, brewing, soft drinks, steam generation etc.

6.4 VARIOUS PROCESSES AND IMPURITIES REMOVED

Process	Impurities removed
1. Screening	It is adopted to remove floating matter. It is provided at the intake point.
2. Aeration	It removes objectionable tastes, odour and dissolved gases like CO_2 and H_2S. Dissolved oxygen is increased.
3. Plain sedimentation	It is adopted for removing settleable suspended impurities like silt, sand etc. which are heavier than water.
4. Sedimentation with coagulation	It is used to cause the sedimentation of colloidal and very fine suspended particles. Some bacteria are also removed.
5. Filtration	It is the most important stage in the treatment. Colloidal and very fine particles escaped from sedimentation tank are removed. Micro-organisms are removed to a large extent.
6. Disinfection	All remaining organisms including pathogens are destroyed.
7. Miscellaneous	
(a) Softening	Hardness is removed.
(b) Activated carbon treatment	Matters causing taste and odour.

It should be noted that all the processes given above may not be required. Depending upon the analysis of raw water regarding its quality, suitable treatment processes are used.

6.5 LAYOUT AND COMPONENTS OF WATER TREATMENT PLANT

The layout of a typical water treatment plant is shown in Fig. 6.1.

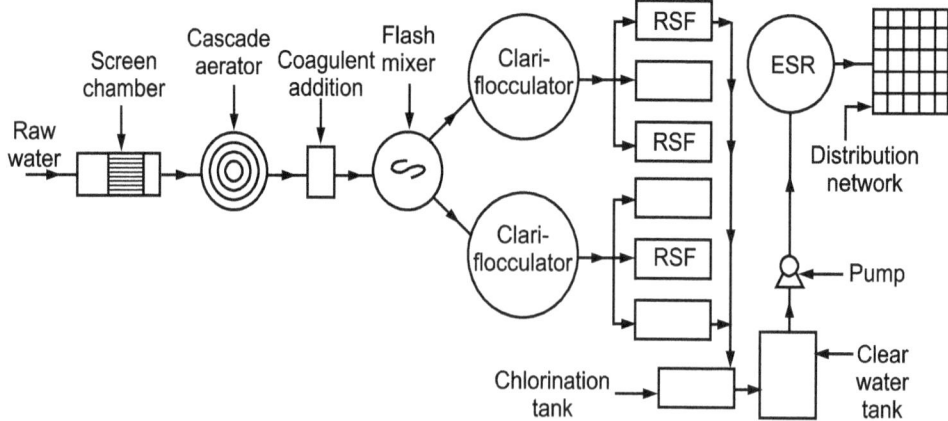

Fig. 6.1

6.5.1 Components of Water Treatment Plant

A typical water treatment plant consists of the following components :

1. **Intake well, jack well and a pump house :** The raw water is admitted from the source in these wells through inlet openings fitted with coarse screen to exclude floating matter.
2. **Screen chambers :** Raw water brought through rising main is admitted in screen chamber provided with bar screens and/or fine screen to exclude remaining floating matter.
3. **Aerators :** Through aerators the water is exposed to atmospheric air to eliminate gases like H_2S, CO_2 and mineral matters like Fe, Mn.
4. **Coagulant tank :** Here the desired coagulant is added in the water.
5. **Flash mixer :** Water containing coagulant is intimately mixed in this unit.
6. **Clariflocculator :** This is a combined unit doing the operations of flocculation and also sedimentation (often called as clarification). Water from flash mixer is admitted in the flocculation zone where with the help of moving paddles, suspended particles come together (agglomerate) and form compact settleable mass called *floc*. The water containing this floc moves to a portion of unit where sedimentation of the floc occurs.
7. **Filter beds :** These are in the form of tanks rectangular in shape. Number of such beds often called as battery of filters are provided in the big building. This building is called as filter house.

    Very fine particles and colloidal matter which have refused to settle earlier are removed through filtration.
8. **Chlorination or Disinfection unit :** Here generally chlorine is applied to filtered water to completely distroy the micro-organism escaped through filtration. This confirms the purity of water. This is the last unit of water treatment.
9. **Pumping, Elevated Service Reservoir (ESR) :** Pure water is admitted in a protected clear water tank. This water is then pumped and fed to ESR through a rising main.
10. **Distribution system :** The treated water from this overhead reservoir is fed into distribution system for consumption.

Note :
1. In case of ground water source, sedimentation and filtration may not be required because the ground water is already filtered during its percolation through various layers of the soil. In such case, the disinfection through chlorination may be sufficient.
2. The nature and degree of treatment depends upon the source and some units mentioned above may not be required.

Various processes adopted in water treatment are explained in details in the next articles.

6.6 AERATION

Aeration is an important unit operation in which the principle of gas transfer is used. The process of exposing large surface of water to the atmospheric air is called *aeration*. Its main purpose is to absorb more oxygen and let out unpleasant odours and gases and oxidise Fe and Mn in water.

Objectives of aeration :

1. To increase oxygen contents in water for imparting freshness.
2. To expell volatile substances and gases like H_2S, CO_2 causing bad taste and odour.
3. To oxidise iron and manganese so that these can be precipitated and removed.
4. To destroy bacteria to some extent, by agitation of water during aeration.

Methods of aerations :

I. By using fountains, spray nozzles : Water is discharged under the effect of fountain action, in the form of fine spray. Spraying results in the formation of extremely minute droplets of water. This increases its surface area of contact with air.

Spray nozzles are located in a pool of water. They involve considerable loss of head. The pressure required to operate spray nozzles is about 0.7 to 1.4 kg/cm^2. This removes CO_2 and H_2S to the extent of 90%. Spray nozzles may be of fixed type or movable type as shown in the Fig. 6.3.

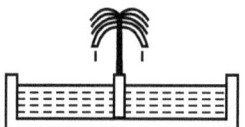
Fig. 6.2 : Fountain

Fig. 6.3 : Spray nozzles (movable type)

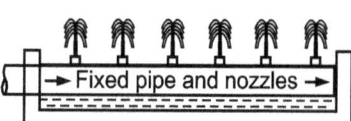
Fig. 6.4 : Spray nozzles (fixed type)

II. Gravity or free fall aerators :

(a) Cascade aerators : They are the simplest free fall aerators. A simplest cascade consists of a series of 3 or 4 steps, either circular or straight type as shown in Fig. 6.5. Water is allowed to fall through a height of 1 to 3 metres. These may be in the open air or under shelter.

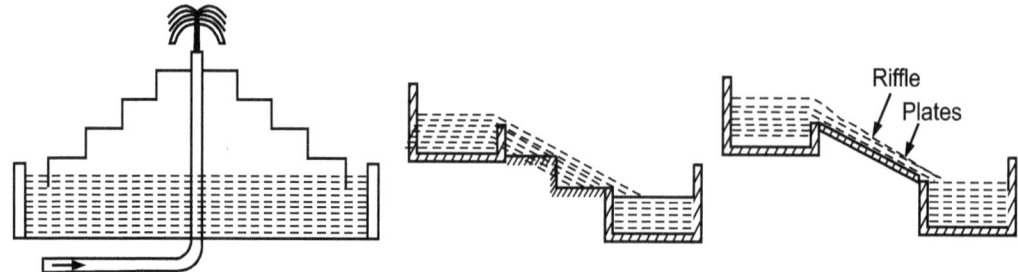

Fig. 6.5 : Circular type   Fig. 6.6 : Straight steps   Fig. 6.7 : Inclined apron aerator

Example 6.1 : The maximum daily demand of water is 114 MLD. Design aeration fountain (cascade aerator).

Solution : Data : $Q = 114$ MLD

(1) Diameter of bottommost cascades :

Design flow, $Q = 114$ MLD $= 114 \times 16^6$ lit/day $= 4750$ m³/hr.

Loading rate $= 0.03$ m²/m³/hr.

∴ Area required $= 4750 \times 0.03 = 142.50$ m²

Assume size of central shaft $= 1200$ mm diameter

∴ Total area of unit required $= 142.50 + \frac{\pi}{4} \times (1.2)^2 = 143.63$ m²

∴ Outer diameter of unit required $= \sqrt{\frac{143.63 \times 4}{\pi}} = 13.52$ m

Provide 5 cascades with tread and rise of 1.25 m and 0.2 m each respectively, given diameter of bottommost cascade as 13.70 m.

(2) Size of collecting channel outside the aeration fountain :

Design flow (peripheral) $= \frac{114000}{2} = 57000$ m³/day $= 0.66$ m³/sec.

Adopt velocity of 1 m/sec., the area of aeration launder $= \frac{0.66}{1} = 0.66$ m².

∴ Provide a launder of 1.0 m $\times 0.66$ m.

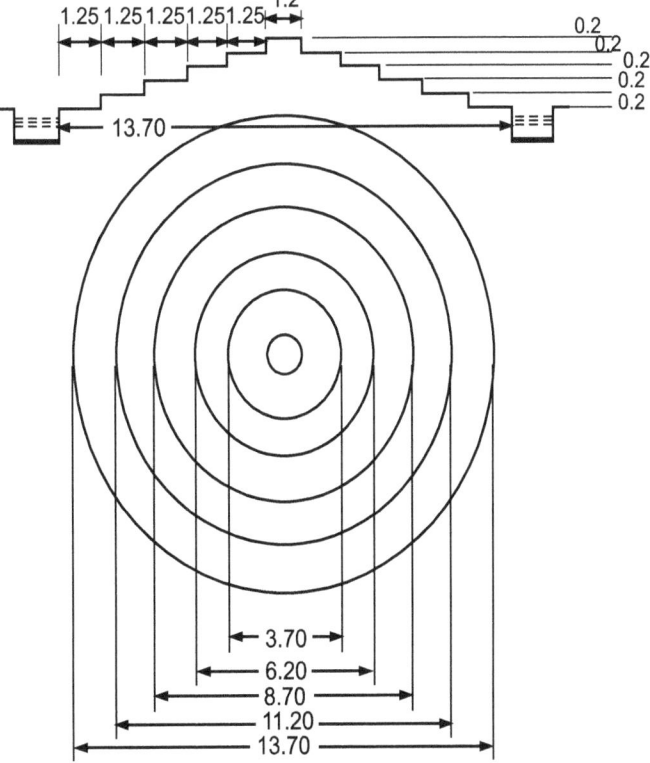

Fig. 6.8 : Aeration fountain (cascade aerator)

(b) Inclined apron aerator : As shown in the Fig. 6.7, water is allowed to fall along an inclined apron (plane) with riffle plates to cause breaking up of the flowing sheet of water, for agitation and aeration.

III. Trickling beds or multiple trays : In this method, water is pumped into a feeding tank placed at a height and allowed to trickle down through a perforated pipe on the beds or trays.

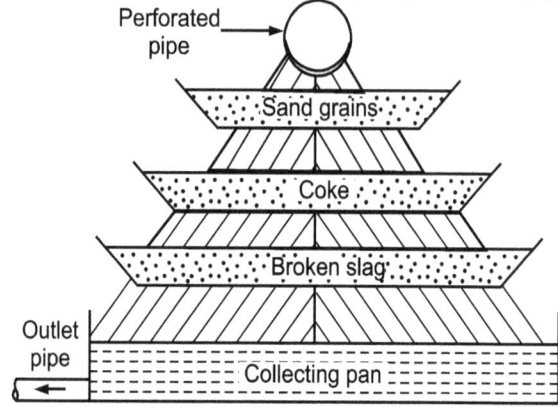

Fig. 6.9 : Trickling beds or multiple trays

Three or four perforated trays filled with sand, broke coke or slag of size 5 to 7.5 cm. The trays are arranged serially one over the other vertically. Each horizontal bed is of 25 cm height. A vertical clearance of 15 cm is kept between the consecutive trays. Water trickles down from one bed to another and is collected finally at the bottom collecting pan. This method gives better results of removal of iron and manganese than cascade method.

IV. By air diffusion : In this method, network of compressed air pipes is placed at the bottom of the water tank. Compressed air is blown through the perforations in these pipes against diffuser plates. The air bubbles travel upwards through water, cause turbulence and bring about the aeration. Suitable nozzles are fitted on the compressed air pipe to control the size of air bubbles produced. This diffusion tank (basin) has a detention period of 15 minutes and a depth of 3 to 5 metres and is of continuous flow type.

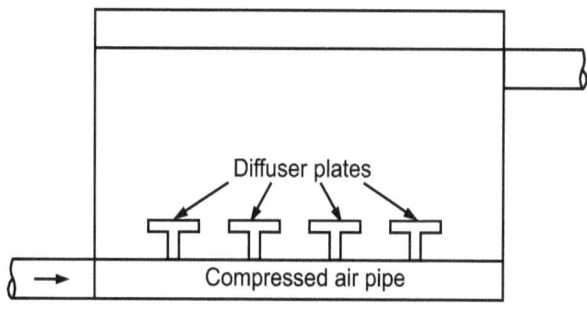

Fig. 6.10 : Continuous flow type diffusion tank

Limitations of aeration :
1. It is inefficient to remove or reduce tastes and odours caused by
   (a) Non-volatile substances like oils of algae.
   (b) Chemicals discharged in industrial wastes.
2. Due to over oxygenation, water becomes corrosive and de-aeration may be required.
3. Aeration is economical only in warmer climate months.
4. Possibility of air-borne contamination in water.
5. Iron and Manganese can be precipitated by aeration only when organic matter is absent.

6.7 SEDIMENTATION

The water contains variety of particles, mineral as well as organic. Some particles may be colloidal, very fine or coarse. Also, the specific gravity of the particles may range from 1.01 to 2.65. This indicates that different particles will require different time for their settlement.

Sedimentation is a process of removal of suspended particles of impurities by gravitational settling. It occurs when particles are heavier than water. This process takes place in a basin or tank usually known as sedimentation tank. Sometimes the tank is also called as settling tank, settling basin or clarifier.

Principle of sedimentation :

It is noticed that large amount of suspended impurities have a specific gravity greater than that of water (i.e. 1). These impurities, however, remain in suspension due to turbulence in water. If this turbulence is brought down to zero (i.e. still water) or reduced to a considerable extent by reducing flow velocity, these impurities will settle down.

Hence, in short, reducing the velocity of water to cause the settlement of suspended solids by gravity is the principle of sedimentation.

Principle of sedimentation is applied for the removal of :

(i) Grit in grit chamber, (ii) destabilised floc in cariflocculators, (iii) particulate matter in primary and secondary settling basins.

Types of sedimentation :
1. Plain sedimentation.
2. Sedimentation with coagulation or chemically assisted sedimentation.

1. Plain sedimentation :

When suspended matter in water is separated by the action of gravitation and natural aggregation, the process is called plain sedimentation. Suspended particles of size 0.01 mm and more and having specific gravity greater than 1 are removed by plain sedimentation.

When the turbidity of raw water is greater than 400 mg/lit, plain sedimentation process is recommended.

Discrete particles : When a unigranular particle of spherical shape do not undergo any change in its size, shape and density during settling or rising in water, it is called as 'Discrete Particle'. These particles have little or no tendency to flocculate. They behave as individual particles and hence settle freely. Particle size is greater than 10^{-4} cm.

Theory of sedimentation : The settling of particles in water depend upon the following factors :

1. Velocity of flow of water.
2. Viscosity of water.
3. Size, shape and specific gravity of suspended particle.
4. Detention time.

It is assumed that discrete settling takes place in plain sedimentation as majority of particles are assumed to be discrete particles. When discrete particle is placed in still fluid, it will accelerate until the frictional resistance (drag force) of water equals the driving force acting on the particle. At this instant the discrete particle attains a uniform or terminal velocity and settles down with this constant velocity, often called as settling velocity.

Stoke's law : Settling velocity of a discrete particle depends upon specific gravity and diameter of the particle, gravitational acceleration (g) and kinematic viscosity of fluid (water in sedimentation treatment). Stoke's law relation is as follows :

Settling velocity, $V_s = \dfrac{g}{18} (s_s - 1) \dfrac{d^2}{\nu}$,

where, g = Gravitational acceleration,

s_s = Specific gravity of the particle,

ν = Kinematic viscosity of water in centistokes (dependent on temperature of water).

Stoke's law is applicable to all discrete particles ranging in size 10^{-5} cm to 10^{-1} cm. This is the requisite range of particles which is significant in water treatment.

Limitations of Stoke's law :

1. All particles, as assumed, may not be discrete.
2. Temperature of water may not be consistant.
3. The liquid (water) may not be at rest (quiescent).
4. The shape and size of the particles may not be truly spherical.
5. The law is valid only when Reynold's number $R_e < 1$.

Types of sedimentation tanks :

1. Fill and draw type (Batch – process).
2. Continuous flow type (developed by Hazen) – These tanks are popularly used.

I. Depending upon the shape, settling tanks may be

   (1) Square, (2) Rectangular and (3) Circular.

II. Depending upon direction of flow, settling tanks may be

   (1) Horizontal flow and (2) Vertical flow.

For water treatment, generally continuous horizontal flow type, either circular or rectangular, are commonly used.

1. Fill and draw type :

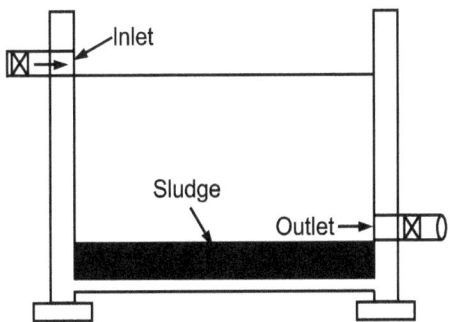

Fig. 6.11 : Fill and draw type tank

In this type, tank is filled by opening the inlet valve provided at the top of tank. Water is kept in stand still condition for a detention period of 24 hours. During the rest, suspended particles settle down at the bottom of the tank. The clear water is withdrawn by opening outlet valve after 24 hours. Settled matter (sludge) is removed and the tank is cleaned. The cleaning may take 6 to 12 hours. After cleaning, tank is filled again. Thus, one cycle of operation requires about 36 hours. Three or four such tanks may be required to provide constant supply. Fig. 6.11 shows section of the tank.

2. Continuous flow tank :

(a) Horizontal flow type : In this type, the direction of flow of water in the tank is essentially horizontal. Tanks may be (i) Rectangular, (ii) Circular tanks with radial flow or circumferential flow. They are shown in the following sketches.

The water continuously moves from inlet end to outlet end of the tank, with a small velocity. Due to reduction in velocity suspended solid particles settle down at the bottom of the tank, in the sludge pocket, from where sludge is periodically pumped out.

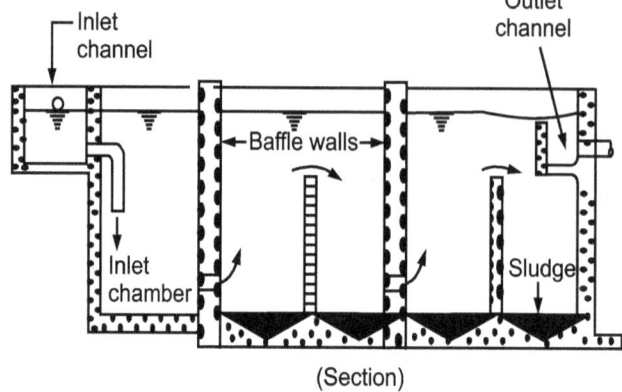

(a) 'Up and Down' baffle tank

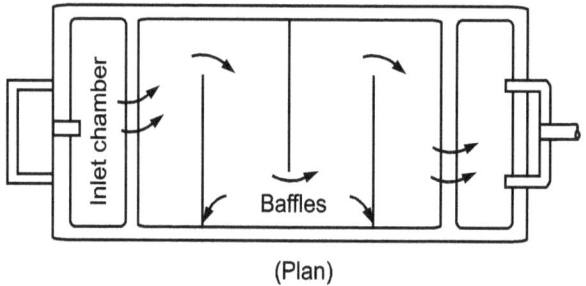

(b) 'Around the end' baffle tank

Fig. 6.12 : Rectangular tank with baffles

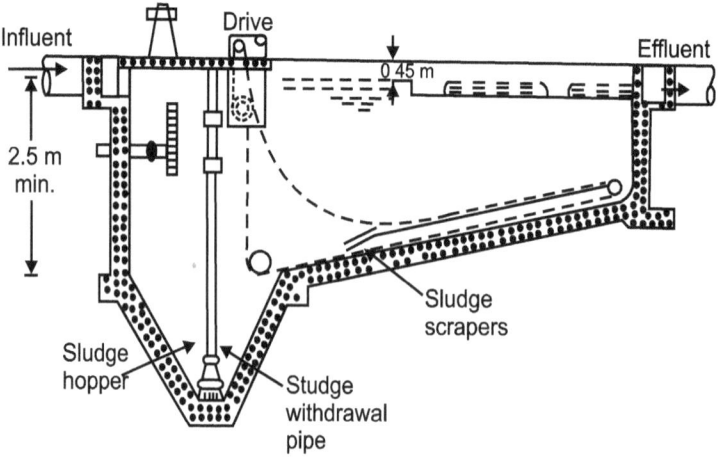

Fig. 6.13 : Rectangular tank with sloping bottom

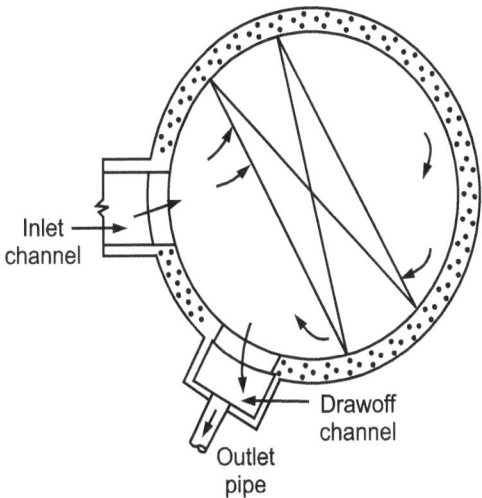

Fig. 6.14 : Circular tank with spiral flow

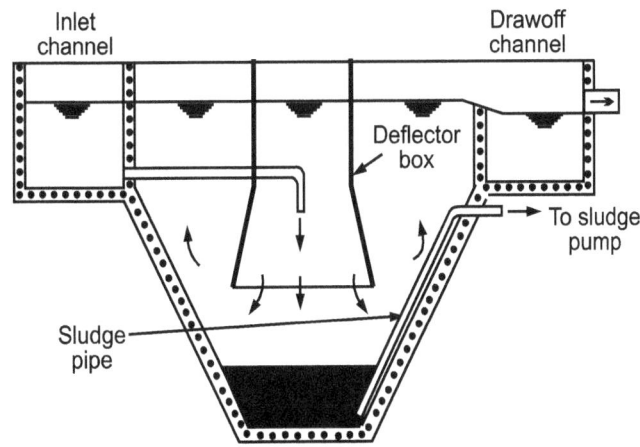

Fig. 6.15 : Hopper bottom tank with vertical flow

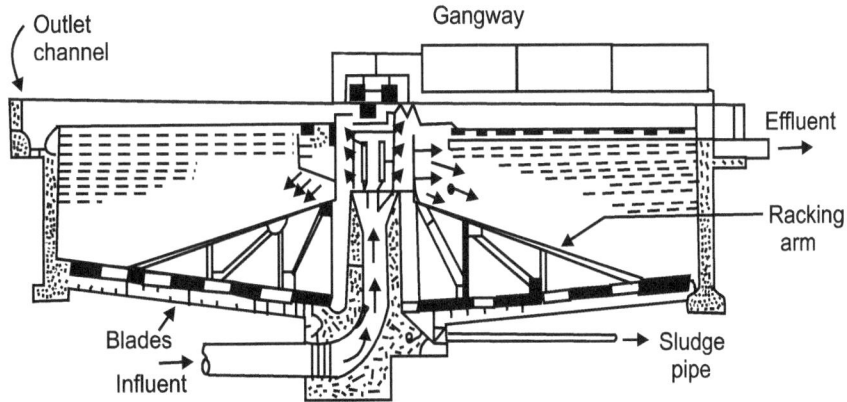

Fig. 6.16 : Circular settling tank (Dorr-clarifier)

(b) Vertical flow type : Generally, this type of tank has a hopper bottom. Water is admitted in the central portion of tank through centrally placed inlet pipe. It is deflected downwards by deflector box as shown in the sketch. Water travels vertically downwards. Suspended solids settle at the bottom of hopper. This deposited sludge is withdrawn by a sludge pump with the help of sludge pipe.

6.7.1 Design of Horizontal Flow Sedimentation Tank

1. **Assumptions :** The design is based on the following assumptions :

   (i) Within the settling zone, the suspended particles settle in the same way as they do in a quiescent tank.

   (ii) Flow is steady, uniform in the settling zone.

   (iii) The concentration of suspended particles of each size is uniform throughout the cross-section at right angles to the flow.

   (iv) Incoming flow is uniformly distributed over the cross-sectional area of the tank.

   (v) Particles reaching the sludge zone, are effectively removed.

2. **Design background :**

   (a) Detention time (t_o) : This is the theoretical time for which the water is detained in the settling tank. If V is the volume of the tank, Q is the discharge rate of water, then the detention time, $t_o = \dfrac{V}{Q} = \dfrac{LBH}{Q}$ (L, B and H are length, width and depth of tank). The detention time may vary from 4 to 8 hours depending upon type of suspended solids.

   (b) Flow through period (t_d) : It is the actual time of travel of flow from the inlet to the outlet of settling tank.

   Flow through period is always less than detention time due to short circuiting.

   (c) Displacement efficiency (η_d) : It is defined as the *ratio of 'flow through period' to the 'detention period'*. $\eta_d = \dfrac{t_d}{t_o}$. A well designed tank should have a flow through period (t_d) equal to at least 30% of the detention period (t_o). For plain sedimentation tank, η_d varies from (0.25 to 0.5).

   (d) Surface loading or overflow rate : The volume (quantity) of water passing per hour or per day per unit horizontal area is known as surface loading or overflow rate. Hence, surface loading $= \dfrac{Q}{A}$ lit/day/m².

   Also velocity of settling, $V_s = \dfrac{Q}{A}$.

Hence, surface loading rate and settling velocity are numerically equal, provided adjustment is made for units. If V_s is expressed in cm/sec., Q in litres per day, horizontal area A in square metres,

Then $V_s = \dfrac{Q}{A} = Q = \left(\dfrac{10^6}{10^3}\right) \times \left(\dfrac{1}{24 \times 60 \times 60}\right) \times A \left(\dfrac{1}{10000}\right) = \dfrac{Q}{864000\,A}$.

Hence surface loading, S.L. $= 864000 \times V_s$ lit/day/m².

Note : Settling velocity of 1 cm/sec. corresponds to surface loading of 864000 lit/day/m² or 36000 lit/hour/m².

(e) Weir loading : Clear water is withdrawn at the other end through some outlet arrangement. If it is in the form of weir, water falling over the weir is called as weir loading. It is expressed as the quantity of water discharged per hour or per day per unit length of weir. In general, weir loading should not be greater than 450 kilolitres/day/m.

For the purpose of designing the sedimentation tank, it is assumed that the tank consists of the following four zones as shown in the Fig. 6.17.

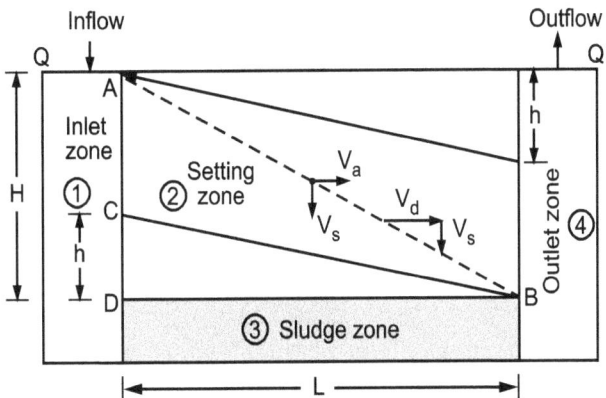

Fig. 6.17 (a) : Vertical cross-section of tank

(i) Inlet zone : It is the zone through which raw water enters in the sedimentation tank. Suspended particles get uniformly distributed all over the cross-section of the tank at right angles to the direction of flow.

(ii) Settling zone : In this zone, discrete particles settle down under influence of gravity. The velocity of flow is so low as to provide laminar flow. No turbulence is caused. Particles settle down without hindrance.

(iii) Sludge zone : Sediments settle at the bottom of the tank and form so called sludge zone.

(iv) Outlet zone : It is a zone where effluent water comes out of the sedimentation tank with residual turbidity. It is assumed that particles having less settling velocity, reach outlet zone and escape with the effluent water. [Clarified water with residual suspended particles is drawn out as effluent water.]

In the Fig. 6.17, let L and H be the length and depth of the settling zone. Let, B be the width of the tank and Q be the discharge.

The horizontal discharge velocity, $V_d = \dfrac{\text{Discharge}}{\text{Cross sectional area}} = \dfrac{Q}{H \times B}$ ... (6.1)

The time of horizontal flow, $t_o = \dfrac{\text{Length of tank}}{\text{Velocity}} = \dfrac{L}{V_d} = \dfrac{LBH}{Q}$

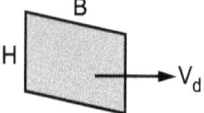

Fig. 6.17 (b)

Consider a particle entering the tank is having a settling velocity V_s. The time for falling through height $H = \dfrac{H}{V_s}$. For the particle to reach the bottom of the tank before water leaves the tank, the time of fall should be equal to time of horizontal flow.

∴ $\qquad t_o = \dfrac{LBH}{Q} = \dfrac{H}{V_s}$

∴ $\qquad V_s = \dfrac{Q}{LB} = \dfrac{Q}{A} = \dfrac{\text{Discharge}}{\text{Plan area}} = \text{Overflow rate}$ ... (6.2)

Fig. 6.17 (c)

∴ From equations (6.1) and (6.2),

$$\dfrac{V_d}{V_s} = \dfrac{Q/HB}{Q/LB} = \dfrac{L}{H} \qquad \text{... (6.3)}$$

∴ Detention time, $\quad t_o = \dfrac{L}{V_d} = \dfrac{H}{V_s}$ ... (6.4)

If a smaller particle having settling velocity $V'_s < \dfrac{Q}{A}$ enters the tank at point A, it will settle through only height, h during the detention time, t_o given by $\dfrac{h}{V'_s} = t_o = \dfrac{LBH}{Q}$.

∴ $\qquad h = \dfrac{LBH}{Q} \times V'_s = \dfrac{V'_s}{V_s} \times H$

This particle, therefore, will not settle to the bottom if it enters the tank above point C. The ratio of removal of this size particle to that of settling value V_s will be given by

$$x_r = \frac{h}{H} = \frac{V_s'}{V_s} = \frac{V_s'}{Q/A}$$

Hence, the efficiency of removal of particles of a given settling velocity is inversely proportional to the surface loading rate. Also removal efficiency of the tank is independent of the depth and is only related to floor area in such type of sedimentation.

Smaller particles will settle down, if the overflow rate is reduced. For a given discharge Q, the overflow rate can be reduced by increasing the plan (i.e. floor) area of the tank. In short, increase in the plan area (length × width of tank), will increase the efficiency of the tank.

3. Design criteria :

(i) Detention time 3 to 4 hours. Also $D.T. = \dfrac{\text{Volume of tank}}{\text{Discharge rate}} = \dfrac{V}{Q}$.

(ii) Velocity of flow (V_d) : As far as possible the velocity should not exceed 0.3 m/min. In most cases, the velocity of flow varies from 0.3 to 3 m/min.

(iii) By Stoke's law, velocity of settling (V_s) = $\dfrac{g}{18} (s_s - 1) \dfrac{d^2}{v}$,

where,
g = 981 cm/sec².
s_s = Specific gravity of suspended particle
d = Diameter of particle in cm.
v = Kinematic viscosity in cm²/sec.
(1 centistoke = 0.01 cm²/sec.)

Temperature in °C	0	5	10	15	20	25
v (centistokes)	1.79	1.52	1.31	1.15	1.01	0.9

(iv) Surface loading or overflow rate :

    (a) For rectangular tank

        S.L. = 15 – 30 m³/m²/day

    (b) For horizontal flow circular tank

        S.L. = 30 – 40 m³/m²/day

    (c) Vertical up flow clarifiers

        S.L. = 40 – 50 m³/m²/day

    (d) For settling velocity of 1 cm/sec.

        S.L. = 864 m³/m²/day

(v) **Weir loading :** As far as possible, weir loading should not be greater than 450 m³/m/day (Range 120 – 450 m³/m/day)

(vi) **Tank dimensions :**

(a) Capacity of the tank, $C = \dfrac{\text{Discharge rate}}{\text{Surface loading}} = \dfrac{Q}{S.L.}$

(b) For rectangular tank, $\dfrac{\text{Length}}{\text{Breadth}} = 3 \text{ to } 5 \begin{pmatrix} \text{limiting length} = 30 \text{ m} \\ \text{limiting width} = 12 \text{ m} \end{pmatrix}$

(c) The minimum water depth for rectangular and circular horizontal flow = 2.5% m.

(d) Depth of tank ranges from 2.5 – (3 – 4.5 normal) – 6 m.

(e) Sludge depth = 25% extra.

(f) Bottom floor slope – 1 in 100 with mechanical scrappers for sludge removal, for rectangular tank and 8% for circular tank.

(vii) Hydraulic efficiency for real tanks affected by short circuiting,

$$\eta = \dfrac{y}{y_o} = \dfrac{h}{H} = 1 - \left[1 + \dfrac{nV_s}{Q/A}\right]^{-1/n}$$

where, $n = 0$ for best performance

$n = \dfrac{1}{8}$ for very good performance

$n = \dfrac{1}{4}$ for good performance

$n = \dfrac{1}{2}$ for poor performance

$n = \dfrac{1}{1}$ for very poor performance

Note : Settling tank efficiency is reduced by the following currents :

1. Eddy currents induced by the inertia of incoming water.
2. Density currents caused due to cold and warm water flowing at a time.
3. Surface currents caused by wind in open tanks.
4. Vertical convection currents formed due to thermal gradient along the depth of the tank.

Inlet and outlet arrangements :

Inlet arrangement should distribute the water uniformly across the width and depth of the tank to prevent density currents. Also it should minimise large scale turbulence and cause radial or longitudinal flow to achieve high solid (Turbidity) removal efficiency. Generally, uniform velocity is achieved by inleting the water through baffle or dispersion wall having holes or slots. The diameter of the hole should be less than the thickness of diffuser wall. The velocity developed through the slot should be about 0.2 to 0.3 m/sec. Fig. 6.18 shows different types of inlet arrangements.

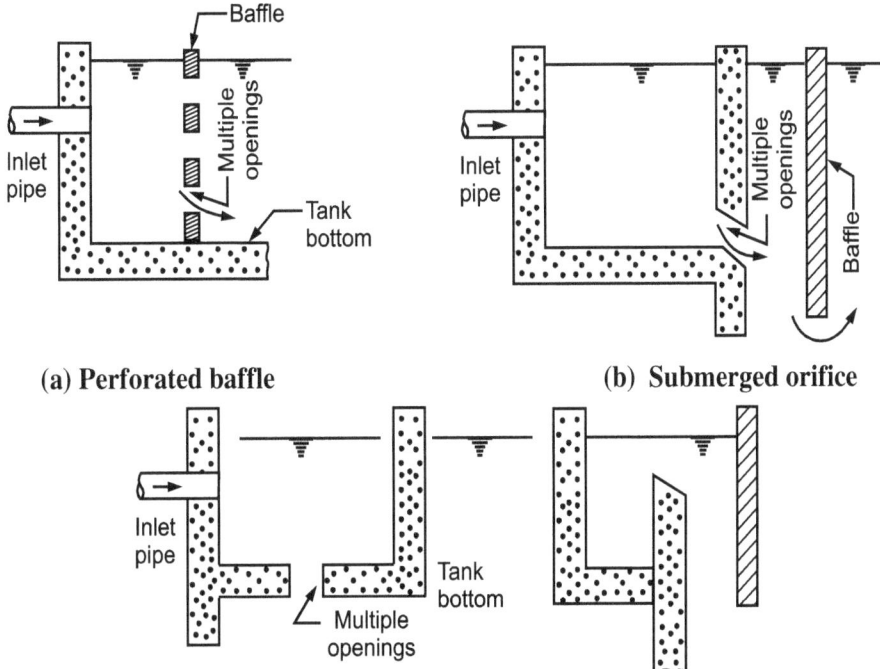

(a) Perforated baffle (b) Submerged orifice

(c) Influent channel with bottom opening (d) Overflow weir with baffle

Fig. 6.18 : Inlet arrangements

Outlet arrangements (see Fig. 6.19) : They consist of (a) weirs, notches or orifices, (b) effluent troughs or launder and (c) outlet pipe to withdraw effluent.

Weirs consist of V type notches, 50 mm depth, placed 150 to 300 mm centre to centre. Also a baffle is provided in front of the weir to arrest escaping of floating matter.

Normal weir loading may be upto 300 m^3/day/m length of weir. Maximum weir loading allowed is 450 m^3/day/m.

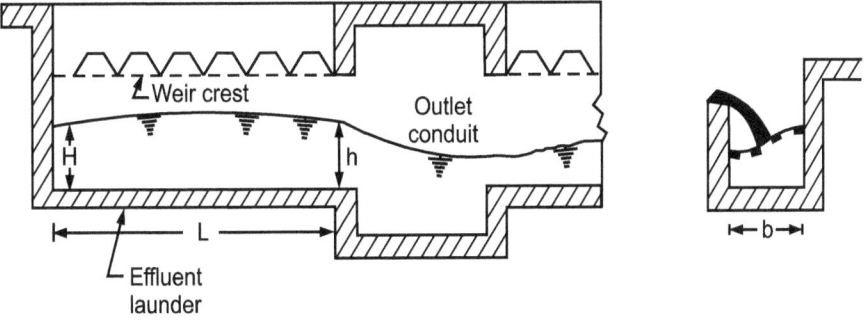

(a) Outlet with effluent launder

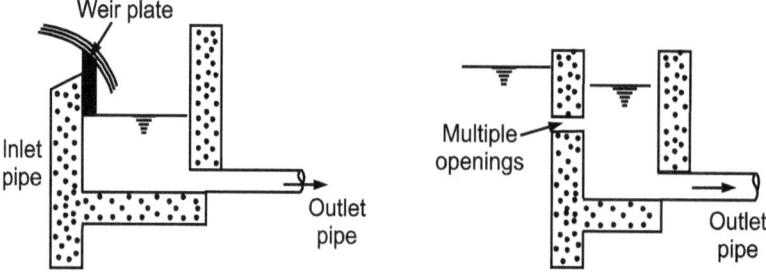

(b) Outlet with weir plate   (c) Outlet with multiple openings

Fig. 6.19 : Outlet arrangements

Sludge removal : The deposited suspended matter at the bottom of the tank is called as a sludge. It can be removed manually or mechanically. In manual removal, tank working is stopped and water drained out and bottom sludge removed by workers. This method is adopted only when the amount of sludge collected is small and sludge removal is required once in 2 to 4 months. But if the amount of sludge collected is large, mechanical method of sludge removal is adopted. Generally, travelling or rotating sludge scrapers are provided in continuous flow tank to divert the deposited sludge towards sludge pockets from where sludge is sucked out through a sludge pipe connected to sludge pump, as shown in the sketches of various tanks described earlier.

Example 6.2 : The maximum daily demand of water is 6 MLD. Design a plain sedimentation tank rectangular in shape, assuming the detention time of 4 hours and flow through velocity of 20 cm/minute. Also check up the flow rate. Draw the line sketch of the unit designed. **(1993)**

Solution : Data : Daily demand = 6 MLD, Detention time = 4 hours.

Flow through velocity = 20 cm/min.

1. Water to be treated per hour = $\dfrac{6 \times 10^6}{24}$ litres = 0.25×10^6 lit/hr.

2. Capacity of sedimentation tank = Hourly demand × D.T
   $= 0.25 \times 10^6 \times 4 = 10^6$ lit $= 1000$ m^3

3. Length of the tank = Flow velocity × D.T
   $= 0.2 \times 4 \times 60 = 48$ m

4. Assume width of the tank = 10 m

5. Depth of the tank = $\dfrac{\text{Capacity of the tank}}{\text{Length} \times \text{Width}} = \dfrac{1000}{48 \times 10} = 2.08$ m

   Assuming free board of 0.42 m, provide overall depth = 2.5 m

6. Tank dimension 48 m long × 10 m wide × 2.5 m deep.

7. Over flow rate = $\dfrac{\text{Discharge rate per hour}}{\text{Surface area}} = \dfrac{0.25 \times 10^6}{48 \times 10} = 520.83$ lit/m^2/hr.

Example 6.3 : Design a rectangular sedimentation tank using the following data :

(1) Population 1 lakh, (2) Overflow rate of 25 m/day, (3) Depth of tank = 3.2 m.

Solution : Data : Population = 10^5, Overflow rate = 25 m/day, Tank depth = 3.2 m.

Assume the rate of water supply to be 200 lit/hr/day

1. Daily demand = Rate of water supply × Population

$$= 200 \times 10^5 = 2 \times 10^7 \text{ lit/day} = \frac{2 \times 10^7}{24} = 833.33 \text{ m}^3/\text{hr}.$$

2. Overflow rate = $\frac{Q}{A}$ = 25 m/day = $\frac{25}{24}$ m/hr.

Here, $\frac{Q}{A} = \frac{25 \times 100}{24 \times 60 \times 60} = V_s = \frac{25}{24 \times 36} = 0.029$ cm/sec.

3. Detention time = $\frac{\text{Depth of tank}}{\text{Overflow rate}} = \frac{3.2}{25/24} = 3.072$ hrs.

4. Capacity of the tank = Hourly discharge × D.T.

$$= 833.33 \times 3.072 = 2560 \text{ m}^3$$

5. Surface area of the tank = $\frac{\text{Capacity}}{\text{Depth}} = \frac{2560}{3.2} = 800 \text{ m}^2$

Providing two units, surface area of one unit = 400 m².

6. Tank dimensions : Let length of tank = 4 × Width

∴ L = 4 B

Surface of the tank, A = L × B = 4 B × B = 4 B²

∴ 4 B² = 400

B² = 100 ∴ B = 10 m

L = 4 × B = 40 m

∴ Provide 2 units, each of size 40 m × 10 × 3.5 (assuming free board = 0.3 m).

Example 6.4 : Design horizontal flow type sedimentation tank of rectangular shape with the following data :

1. Diameter of the particle to be settled = 0.001 cm
2. Temperature of water = 10°C
3. Design discharge = 1 MLD
4. Specific gravity of silt and clay = 2.65
5. Kinematic viscosity = 1.3101 × 10^{-2} cm²/sec.

Solution : Data : Particle diameter = d = 0.001 cm, s_s = 2.65, t = 10°C

Discharge, Q = 1 MLD, v = 1.3101 × 10^{-2} cm²/sec.

1. Velocity of settling,

$$V_s = \frac{g}{18}(s_s - 1)\frac{d^2}{v} = \frac{981}{18}(2.65 - 1)\frac{(0.001)^2}{1.3101 \times 10^{-2}}$$

$$V_s = 6.8639 \times 10^{-3} \text{ cm/sec.}$$

2. Surface loading : Adopt surface loading of 864 m³/m²/day for V_s = 1 cm/sec.

∴ Surface loading for the velocity 6.8639 × 10^{-3}

$$= 864 \times 6.8639 \times 10^{-3}$$

$$= 5.9305 \text{ m}^3/\text{m}^2/\text{day}$$

3. Size and capacity of the tank :

$$Q = 1 \text{ MLD} = 10^3 \text{ m}^3/\text{day}$$

$$\text{Surface area} = \frac{\text{Daily demand}}{\text{Surface loading}} = \frac{10^3}{5.9305} = 168.620 \text{ m}^2$$

Adopt Length : Breadth = 2 : 1

$$A = 2B^2 = 168.62$$

Solving, B = 9.2 m and L = 18.4 m

Assume effective depth = 1.5 m and free board = 0.3 m

Tank dimensions 18.4 m long × 9.2 m wide × 1.8 m deep

∴ Capacity of the tank = 18.4 × 9.2 × 1.5

$$= 253.92 \text{ m}^3$$

4. Detention time = $\frac{\text{Capacity}}{\text{Discharge per hour}} = \frac{253.92}{10^3/24}$ = 6.09 hours ≈ 6.1 hours

5. Weir loading = $\frac{Q}{\text{Width}} = \frac{10^3}{9.2}$ = 108.7 m³/m/day.

Example 6.5 : Design a rectangular settling tank to treat 2 MLD of water. Assume detention time of 3 hours and flow through velocity of 7.5 cm/min. If the depth of the tank is 3 m, find the overflow rate and dimensions of the tank. **(1987)**

Solution : Data : Q = 2 MLD, Flow velocity = 7.5 cm/min., D.T. = 3 hrs., depth of the tank = 3 m.

1. Water to be treated = 2 MLD = $\frac{2 \times 10^3}{24}$ = 83.33 m³/hour.

2. Detention time = 3 hours.

3. Capacity or volume of settling tank = Hourly Q × D.T. = 83.33 × 3 = 250 m³.

4. Length of the tank, L = Flow velocity × D.T. = 0.075 × 3 × 60 = 13.5 m.

5. Width of the tank = $\dfrac{\text{Volume}}{L \times D}$ = $\dfrac{250}{13.5 \times 3}$ = 6.173 ≈ 6.2 m.

6. Tank dimensions = 13.5 m long × 6.2 m wide × 3.5 m deep.
   (Considering 0.5 m as free board)

7. Overflow rate = $\dfrac{\text{Daily demand}}{\text{Surface area}}$ = $\dfrac{2 \times 1000}{13.5 \times 6.2}$ = 23.89 m³/m²/day

Example 6.6 : Design a plain settling tank of rectangular shape to treat 2 MLD of water with 2 hours detention time. The overflow rate should be less than 50,000 lit/day/m². If water contains 600 mg/lit of suspended solids, 30% of which are settleable, calculate the volume of sludge for 40 days cleaning period.

Solution : Data : Q = 2 MLD = 2 × 10⁶ lit/day, D.T. = 2 hrs. S.L. ≯ 50000 lit/day/m².

1. Volume of the tank = Discharge per hour × D.T. = $\dfrac{2 \times 10^6}{24} \times \dfrac{2}{1000}$ = 166.66 m³.

   Provide 2 units, each of capacity = 83.33 m³.

2. Assume depth of each tank = 3 m.

   Surface area of each tank = $\dfrac{\text{Volume}}{\text{Depth}}$ = $\dfrac{83.33}{3}$ = 27.775 m².

   Assume L : B = 3 : 1 ∴ A = 3 B² = 27.775, solving B = 3.04 ≈ 3 m.

   ∴ Length = 3 × 3 = 9 m

3. Check for surface loading, S.L. = $\dfrac{\text{Discharge per tank}}{\text{Surface area}}$ = $\dfrac{1000 \times 1000}{27.775}$

   = 36003.6 lit/day/m² < 50,000 lit/day/m²

   Hence. OK.

4. Sludge volume / tank

(a) S.S. = 600 mg/lit

   ∴ Total S.S. per tank = (600 mg/lit) × (10⁶ lit/day) = 600 × 10⁶ mg/day.

(b) Settleable S.S. = 30% of T.S. = 0.30 × 6 × 10⁸ mg/day = 18 × 10⁷ mg/day.

(c) Volume of sludge deposited in 40 days per tank

   = 40 × 18 × 10⁷ mg = $\dfrac{40 \times 18 \times 10^7}{1000 \times 1000}$ kg

   = 7200 kg

(d) Total sludge for 2 tanks = 2 × 7200 = 14,400 kg

Example 6.7 : In a continuous flow sedimentation tank 3.5 deep and 75 m long, what flow velocity of water would you recommend for effective removal of 0.025 mm particles at 25°C. The specific gravity of particles is 2.65 and kinematic viscosity for water may be taken as 0.01 cm²/sec.

Solution : Data : $s_s = 2.65$, $d = 0.025$ mm $= 0.0025$ cm, $v = 0.01$ cm²/sec.

1. Applying Stoke's law,

$$\text{Settling velocity, } V_s = \frac{g}{18} (s_s - 1) \frac{d^2}{v}$$

$$V_s = \frac{981}{18} \times \frac{(2.65 - 1) \times (0.0025)^2}{0.01} = 0.0562 \text{ cm/sec.}$$

2. Now using relation $\dfrac{\text{Flow velocity}}{\text{Settling velocity}} = \dfrac{\text{Length of tank}}{\text{Depth of water}}$

$$\therefore \quad \frac{V}{V_s} = \frac{L}{h}$$

where, $V_s = 0.0562$, $L = 75$ m, $h = 3.5 - 0.5$ (free board) $= 3.0$ m.

$$V = 0.0562 \times \frac{75}{3} = 0.0562 \times 25 = 1.405 \text{ cm/sec.}$$

Hence, for effective removal of particles of the given size, the flow velocity in the sedimentation tank should not be more than 1.405 cm/sec.

Example 6.8 : Deign a rectangular plain sedimentation tank for the following data. The tank is expected to remove discrete and non-flocculent particles.

(i) Desired average outflow from the sedimentation tank = 275 m³/hr.

(ii) Water lost in desludging = 2%.

(iii) Minimum size of the particle to be removed = 0.02 mm.

(iv) Expected removal efficiency of minimum size particles = 70%.

(v) Specific gravity = 2.65.

(vi) Assumed performance of settling tank = good (h = 1/4).

(vii) Kinematic viscosity at 20°C = 1.01×10^{-6} m²/sec.

(viii) L : B = 4 : 1.

(ix) Detention time = 3.5 hrs.

Determine of V_s and R_e, tank dimensions and check against resuspension of deposited particles is excpected in the design.

(May 2008)

Solution : (1) Design average flow :

$$\text{Average discharge} = 275 \text{ m}^3/\text{hr.}$$

$$\text{Design average flow} = \frac{275}{(100-2)} \times 100 = 280.61 \text{ m}^3/\text{hr.}$$

(2) Velocity of settling :
$$V_s = \frac{g}{18}(S_s - 1)\frac{d^2}{\upsilon}$$

$$= \frac{9.81}{18}(2.65 - 1) \times \frac{(0.02 \times 10^{-3})^2}{1.01 \times 10^{-6}}$$

$$= 0.356 \times 10^{-3} \text{ m/sec.}$$

$$\therefore \quad R_e = V_s \cdot \frac{d}{\upsilon}$$

$$= \frac{0.356 \times 10^{-3} \times (0.02 \times 10^{-3})}{1.01 \times 10^{-6}}$$

$$= 7.04 \times 10^{-3} < 1,$$

therefore, Stocke's law is applicable.

(3) Determination of surface overflow rate :

For 100% removal $V_s = V_0$

$$\therefore \quad V_0 = 0.356 \times 10^{-3} \text{ m/s} = 0.356 \times 10^{-3} \times 86400$$

$$= 30.76 \text{ m}^3/\text{d/m}^2$$

For practical removal efficiency, η of 70%,

$$\frac{y}{V_0} = 1 - [1 + n(V_0/(Q/A))]^{-1/n} = 0.7$$

$$= 1 - \left[1 + \frac{1}{4}(30.76/(Q/A))\right]^{-1/4} = 0.7$$

$$\therefore \quad (Q/A) = 21.9 \text{ m}^3/\text{d/m}^2$$

(Acceptable because it is between 15 to 30 m³/d/m².

(4) Calculations of tank dimensions :

$$SA = Q/(Q/A) = 30.76 \text{ m}^2$$

Now, $\quad L : B = 4 : 1$

Solving, $\quad B = 8.8 \text{ m}, \ L = 35.2 \text{ m}$

Detention time = 3.5 hrs.

∴ Depth of water $= \dfrac{Q \times t}{A}$

$= \dfrac{280.61 \times 3.5}{(8.8 \times 35.2)} = 3.17$ m

(5) Critical velocity, $V_c = \sqrt{\dfrac{8k}{f}\, g\, (S_s - 1)}$

Assume, $k = 0.04,\ f = 0.03$

∴ $V_c = \sqrt{\dfrac{8 \times 0.04}{0.03} \times 9.81 \times (2.65 - 1)}$

∴ $V_c = 5.88 \times 10^{-2}$ m/sec.

Now, $V_h = \dfrac{Q}{B \cdot L}$

$= \dfrac{280.61}{8.8 \times 35.2 \times 3600} = 2.51 \times 10^{-4}$ m/sec.

$V_c < V_h$, therefore Acceptable

6.8 NECESSITY OF CHEMICAL COAGULATION

Water contains wide variety of suspended particles like clay, silt, very fine silt, algae, bacteria and other organic matter. These particles may have size ranging from 10^{-2} to 10^{-7} cm. Impurity particles having size greater than 10^{-4} cm are removed in plain settling tanks. Solids present in the form of impurities are broadly classified on the basis of their size as given in table 6.1.

Table 6.1 : Classification of solids

Class of solids	Size in mμ (10^{-9} m)
1. Coarse solids	Greater than 1000
2. Fine solids	100 – 1000
3. Colloidal solids	1 – 100
4. Molecular dispersions	Less than 1

Many of the impurities are too small to be settled out by gravitation in settling tanks. Hence, for their effective settling, aggregation of these small particles into large and more readily settleable solids is necessary. This is done by using some chemicals which are called as coagulants.

Coagulation : The term coagulation is derived from the Latin word *'Coagulare'*, meaning *to drive together*. Colloidal particles carry electrical charges on them and as such they are in continuous motion and never settle down under gravity in a reasonable period. Coagulation is a chemical process in which these charged colloidal particles are neutralized (destabilised).

Definition : The process of mixing certain chemicals to water to neutralise the electrical charges and to form an insoluble, gelatinous flocculent precipitate for absorbing and entraining suspended and colloidal particles of impurities is called *coagulation*.

Theory of coagulation :

Diffused double layer theory : It states that the stability of colloidal particles depends upon the electric charge that they carry (possess). The primary charge of the colloidal particle may be due charged groups within the particle surface or due to adsorption of a layer of ions from the surrounding medium. This primary charge is counter balanced by ions of opposite charge in water phase. Electrical double layer is formed at the interface between the water and solid as seen in the Fig. 6.20.

The double layer consists of

(1) The charged colloidal particles.

(2) An equivalent excess of oppositely charged counter ions, which accumulate in the water near the surface of particle.

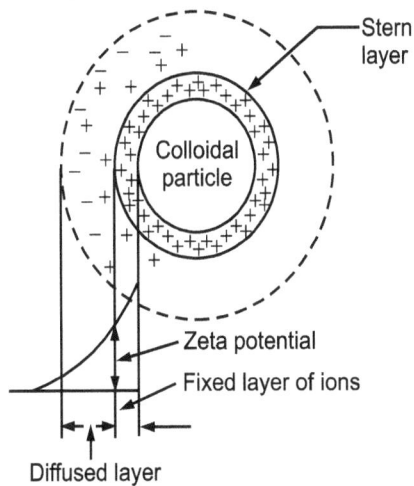

Fig. 6.20 : Diffused double layer theory

The counter ions are attracted electrostatically to the particle surface and cause high concentration at the particle surface. The concentration decreases as the distance increases from solid water surface. This decrease or diffusion of counter ions may be due to agitation and replacement by other ions. When water contains a high concentration of counter ions, the diffused layer is compacted. This explanation of stability of colloidal particles is called as *diffused double layer theory*.

Zeta potential : A fixed covering of positive ions is formed around the negatively charged particle by electrostatic attraction. This ring of compacted positive ions is called as 'stern layer.' It is surrounded by a movable diffused layer of positive ions. The concentration of positive ions in the diffused zone decreases away from the particle. Zeta potential is the magnitude of the charge at the surface of shear.

Repulsive and attractive potentials : When two similar charged colloidal particles face each other, repulsive force sets up, retraining them from aggregation (coming together). This is known as *repulsive potential energy, V_R*. Simultaneously, certain attractive potential also exists when colloidal particles come close to each other. These attractive forces are called as Van-der-Waal's forces of attraction and attractive potential energy is denoted by V_A. The net interaction energy $(V_R - V_A)$ is an obstacle for the aggregation of colloidal particles. $(V_R - V_A)$ is also referred to as an *Energy barrier*. Hence, to coagulate the colloidal particles, it is necessary to induce adequate kinetic energy by adding chemical coagulants to overcome this energy barrier.

List of impurities requiring coagulation :
1. Finely divided mineral matter, including clay and other colloidal 'sols'.
2. Organic colouring matter, either in solution or in colloidal form.
3. Miscellaneous fragments of animals and vegetable matter.
4. A complex mixture of colloidal and dissolved organic compounds derived from sewage and industrial effluents.
5. Phytoplankton, bacteria and viruses.

Factors affecting coagulation :
(a) Type of coagulant
(b) Dose of coagulant
(c) Time and method of mixing the coagulant.
(d) Character of water :
    (i) pH of water
    (ii) Temperature of water
    (iii) Nature and quantity of suspended matter.

Common coagulants :
1. Alum or aluminium sulphate.
2. Chlorinated copperas.
3. Magnesium carbonate and lime.
4. Ferrous sulphate and lime.
5. Sodium aluminate.
6. Polyelectrolytes.

1. **Alum or Aluminium sulphate :** This is easily available and widely used in water works. Its chemical composition is $Al_2(SO_4)_3 \cdot 18\ H_2O$. It is effective in the pH range of 6.5 to 8.5. The alum produces good floc in the alkaline range. Many waters have bicarbonate alkalinity naturally in them. When alum is added, floc of $Al(OH)_3$ is formed. This floc attracts colloidal suspended matter, grow in size and finally settle down. Following is the chemical equation :

$$Al_2(SO_4)_3 \cdot 18\ H_2O + 3\ Ca(HCO_3)_2 \rightleftharpoons 2\ Al(OH)_3 + 3\ CaSO_4 + 18\ H_2O + 6\ CO_2$$

Calcium sulphate causes permanent hardness, while CO_2 formed causes corrosion.

If natural alkalinity is insufficient or absent, lime (33% of Alum) in the form of $Ca(OH)_2$ (also called as hydrated lime) is added along with alum. Following reaction takes place :

$$Al_2(SO_4)_3 \cdot 18\ H_2O + 3\ Ca(OH)_2 \rightleftharpoons 2Al(OH)_3 + 3\ CaSO_4 + 18\ H_2O$$

Sometimes instead of lime, soda ash i.e. sodium carbonate is added to form alkalinity. Following is the reaction :

$$Al_2(SO_4)_3 \cdot 18\ H_2O + 3\ Na_2CO_3 \rightleftharpoons 2Al(OH)_3 + 3\ Na_2SO_4 + 18\ H_2O + 3\ CO_2$$

Soda ash does not cause hardness, but it is costly and hence less used.

Alum produces clear water and also reduces taste and colour of raw water.

2. **Chlorinated copperas :** Hydrated ferrous sulphate ($FeSO_4 \cdot 7\ H_2O$) is called as copperas. When chlorine is added to a solution of copperas, two react chemically to form ferric sulphate and ferric chloride. The chemical equation is :

$$6\ FeSO_4 \cdot 7\ H_2O + 3\ Cl_2 \longrightarrow 2\ Fe_2(SO_4)_3 + 2\ FeCl_3 + 42\ H_2O$$

The resultant combination of ferric sulphate and ferric chloride is known as chlorinated copperas. Both the constituents of chlorinated copperas are effective coagulants along with lime.

$$Fe_2(SO_4)_3 + 3\ Ca(OH)_2 \longrightarrow 3\ CaSO_4 + 2\ Fe(OH)_3$$

$$2\ FeCl_3 + 3\ Ca(OH)_2 \longrightarrow 3\ CaCl_2 + 2\ Fe(OH)_3$$

The ferric hydroxide forms the floc and helps settling.

It is effective in removing colour also. Ferric sulphate is quite effective in pH range of 4 to 7 and above 9. Ferric chloride is quite effective in pH range of 3.5 to 6.5 and above 8.5. At higher pH, it removes manganese.

3. **Magnesium carbonate and lime :** When these two compounds are dissolved in water, magnesium hydroxide and calcium carbonate are formed as under :

$$MgCO_3 + Ca(OH)_2 \rightleftharpoons Mg(OH)_2 + CaCO_3$$

Both $Mg(OH)_2$ and $CaCO_3$ result in the formation of sludge. It removes organic colour, iron and manganese. It is not commonly used.

4. **Ferrous sulphate and lime :** Ferrous sulphate (also called copperas) can react with natural calcium bicarbonate alkalinity. To speed up the reaction lime is used along with copperas. Following is the chemical reaction :

$$FeSO_4 \cdot 7\,H_2O + Ca(OH)_2 \rightleftharpoons Fe(OH)_2 + CaSO_4 + 7\,H_2O$$

The ferrous hydroxide, thus formed, soon gets oxidised due to dissolved oxygen in water and $Fe(OH)_3$, ferric hydroxide is formed as follows :

$$4\,Fe(OH)_2 + O_2 + 2\,H_2O = 4\,Fe(OH)_3$$

The ferric hydroxide so formed is a good gelatinous floc, which is heavier than the floc formed by alum. It is effective in pH range of 8.5 and above.

5. **Sodium aluminate ($Na_2Al_2O_4$) :** It is alkaline and is costly and is sometimes used. When added and mixed with water, floc of precipitate of aluminate of calcium or magnesium is formed. This coagulant removes temporary and permanent hardness and is effective in pH range of 6 to 8.50 naturally available in water. The reactions are as follows :

$$Na_2Al_2O_4 + Ca(HCO_3)_2 \rightleftharpoons CaAl_2O_4 + Na_2CO_3 + CO_2 + H_2O$$

$$Na_2Al_2O_4 + CaCl_2 \rightleftharpoons CaAl_2O_4 + 2\,NaCl$$

$$Na_2Al_2O_4 + CaSO_4 \rightleftharpoons CaAl_2O_4 + Na_2SO_4$$

6. **Polyelectrolytes :** These are water soluble polymers and have high molecular weight. Depending upon the change they carry, they are classed as anionic, cationic, and non-ionic. Cationic type can be used independently as effective coagulants. Cationic types are available under trade names like Floccal N, Mogul 980, Magnifloc.

Coagulant aids : These are chemical substances which are used to increase or hasten the coagulation process. They may be natural or man-made. Natural coagulant aids are Bentonite and other clays, which are commonly used. Acids and alkalies are added to water to adjust the pH for optimum coagulation. When activated silica is added to water, it produces a stable solution carrying negative charge. The activated silica is nothing but a sodium silicate activated with sulphuric acid, aluminium sulphate, carbon dioxide or chlorine. It reacts with positively charged metal hydroxides like $Al(OH)_3$ and produces tough and dense floc. Natural polyelectrolytes like 'nirmali seeds' also act as coagulant aid. Anionic and non-ionic polyelectrolytes are used as coagulant aids along with alum.

Example 6.9 : Acidity introduced by alum dose of 80 mg/lit is to be neutralised using lime as CaO. Commercial CaO available is of 85% purity. Work out the quantity of the commercial CaO required in kg/day, if the raw water to be treated is 5 MLD.

Solution : Data : Alum dose = 80 mg/lit

Purity of CaO = 85%

Volume of raw water = 5 MLD

Now lime in the form of CaO is added to neutralise acidity caused by alum. Alum reacts with water as per following equation :

$$Al_2(SO_4)_3 \cdot 18\,H_2O + 6\,H_2O \rightleftharpoons 2\,Al(OH)_3 + 3\,H_2SO_4 + 18\,H_2O$$

The acidity is caused by 3 H_2SO_4. This is neutralised by adding CaO.

∴ $\quad 3\,H_2SO_4 + 3\,CaO \rightleftharpoons 3\,CaSO_4 + 3\,H_2O$

∴ Molecular weight of alum = $2(26.97) + 3[32.066 + 4 \times 16] + 18[2 \times 1.008 + 16]$

$$= 666$$

Molecular weight of 3 CaO = $3[40 + 16] = 168$

∴ $\quad$ % age CaO to alum = $\dfrac{168}{666} = 25\%$

∴ CaO powder required to be added = 25% of alum

Water to be treated = 5 M*l*/d

Alum dose = 80 mg/lit = 80 kg/M*l*/day

∴ Alum quantity required for 5 M*l*/d = 5×80 kg/day = 400 kg/day

∴ 100% pure CaO required = 25% of alum

$$= \dfrac{25}{100} \times 400 = 100 \text{ kg/day}$$

But commercial lime available is 85% pure.

∴ $\quad$ Quantity of 85% purity CaO = $\dfrac{100}{0.85} = 117.65$ kg/day

Example 6.10 : Alum dose of 20 mg/lit is applied to treat 15 MLD of water. Find (a) quantity of alum required per day and (b) amount of CO_2 released.

Solution : (a) Weight of alum required per day = $\dfrac{20 \times 15 \times 10^6}{10^6} = 300$ kg.

(b) Chemical reaction involved :

$$Al_2(SO_4)_3 \cdot 18\,H_2O + 3\,Ca(HCO_3)_2 \rightleftharpoons 2\,Al(OH)_3 + 3\,CaSO_4 + 18\,H_2O + 6\,CO_2$$

Molecular weight of alum = $2(26.97) + (3 \times 32.066) + 16(4 \times 3 + 18) + 36 \times 1.008$

$$= 666.426 = 666$$

Molecular weight of CO_2 = $(1 \times 12.01) + 2 \times 16 = 44.01 = 44$ say

∴ $6 CO_2 = 44 \times 6 = 264$

∴ 666 mg of alum releases 264 mg of CO_2

∴ 300 kg of alum will release $\dfrac{264}{666} \times 300 = 118.9$ kg of CO_2

∴ Amount of CO_2 released per day = 118.9 kg

Example 6.11 : Calculate the quantity of lime and soda for cold softening of 2,50,000 litres of raw water to be supplied everyday, for which the following chemical composition has been found out.

$$\text{Dissolved } CO_2 = 39.6 \text{ mg/lit}$$
$$Ca^{++} = 44 \text{ mg/lit}$$
$$Mg^{++} = 18 \text{ mg/lit}$$
$$\text{Alkalinity, } HCO_3^- = 122 \text{ mg/lit}$$

(May 2008) (8 Marks)

Solution :

Sr. No.	Constituent	mg/l	Equivalent mass	m·eq./l
1.	CO_2	39.6	22	1.8
2.	Ca^{++}	44	20	2.2
3.	Mg^{++}	18	12	1.5
4.	HCO_3^-	122	61	2

Slacked lime required = (m.eq./l of CO_2 + m.eq./l of HCO_3^-
 + m.eq. of Mg^{++}) × eq. wt. of $Ca(OH)_2$
 = $(1.8 + 2 + 1.5) \times 37 = 196.1$ mg/l

Total for 2,50,000 = 49 kg/day

Na_2CO_3 = (m.eq./l of Ca^{++} + m.eq./l of Mg^{++}
 − m.eq./l of HCO_3) × equivalent weight of Na_2CO_3
 = $(2.2 + 1.5 − 2) \times 50$
 = 90.1 mg/l

∴ Na_2CO_3 required = $\dfrac{90.1 \times 250000}{10^6} = 22.52$ kg/day

6.9 COAGULATION PROCESS

Coagulation is carried out by the following processes :

(i) Feeding,

(ii) Mixing,

(iii) Flocculation and

(iv) Clarification or sedimentation.

(i) Feeding : There are two methods of feeding coagulants to water :

(a) Dry feeding,

(b) Wet feeding.

(a) Dry feeding : Two common devices, which are used in dry feeding, consist of (i) Toothed wheel device and (ii) Helical screw device. Each unit consists of conical hopper tanks in which the coagulant in powdered form is placed, and is allowed to fall in the mixing basins. Agitating plates, to prevent the arching of the powdered chemical, are provided inside the tanks. The dose of the coagulant is regulated by the speed of toothed wheel or helical screw mechanism. The mechanism in turn is connected to the venturi device in the raw water pipe or mixing basin.

Both devices are shown in the Fig. 6.21.

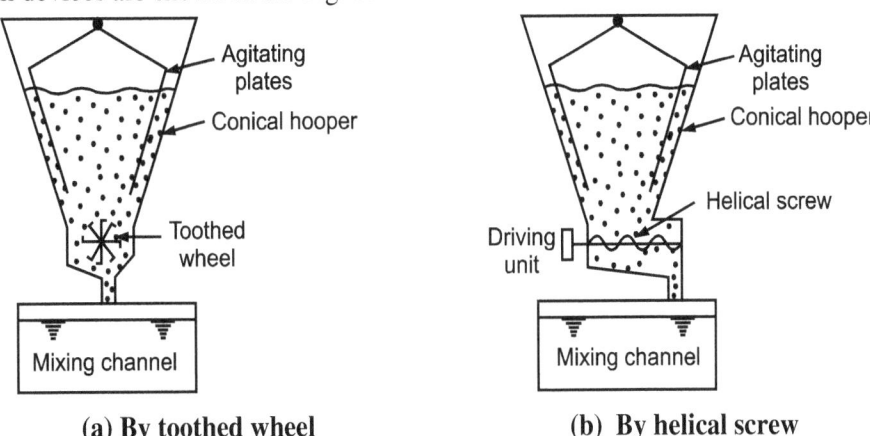

(a) By toothed wheel (b) By helical screw

Fig. 6.21 : Methods of dry feeding

(b) Wet feeding : In wet feeding system, the solution of the coagulant of the required strength is made and stored in a tank. This solution of coagulant is fed to the mixing channel through a mechanism in the required dose in proportion to the flow of water.

In one type of mechanism, conical plug arrangement is provided to control the addition of coagulant in proportion to water flow.

In another type, there is adjustable weir and float device. The adjustable weir is in the form of a sliding cylinder with rectangular holes on its surface. The raw water channel and the float channel are interconnected to control the dose automatically. Both these devices are shown in Fig. 6.22.

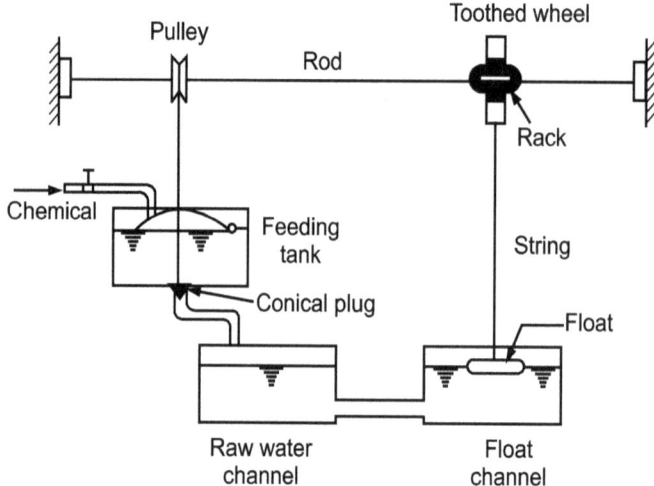

(a) Wet feeding by conical plug

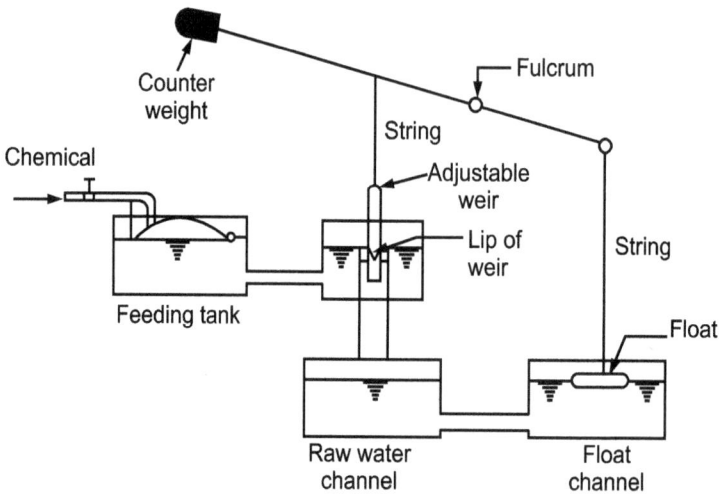

(b) Wet feeding by adjustable weir

Fig. 6.22 : Methods of wet mixing

(ii) **Mixing :** In order to cause the complete dispersion of the added coagulant into the entire mass of water, mixing devices are required. The violent agitation of water can be achieved by using mixing devices like compressed air, centrifugal pumps and mixing basins.

(a) **Compressed air device :** In this, raw water mixed with the proper dose of coagulant is agitated vigorously by passing compressed air from bottom surface of mixing basin.

(b) **Centrifugal pump :** Sometimes centrifugal pump is installed to raise the water to the sedimentation tanks. The proper dose of the coagulant can therefore be added to the suction pipe of the pump. There will be efficient dispersion of coagulant in water while passing through the impeller of pump.

(c) Mixing channel with flume : In this method, there is a narrow channel with vertical baffles. Baffle plates are placed in the channel inclined to the direction of flow. The mixing channel width is narrowed to form the flume. Such arrangement causes turbulence and mix the coagulant thoroughly. (See Fig. 6.23).

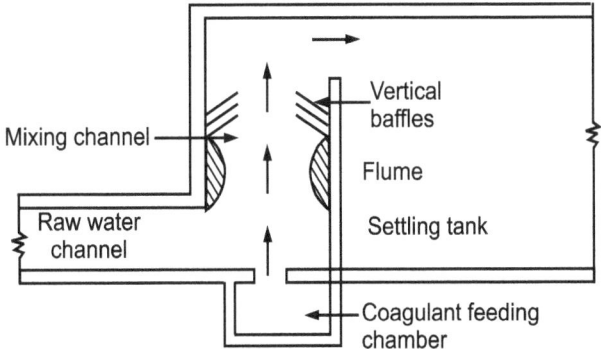

Fig. 6.23 : Mixing channel

(d) Mixing basin with baffle walls : The mixing basin is provided with baffle walls to cause turbulence to enable thorough mixing. Based upon the direction of flow, there are two types. In one type, the water mixed with the coagulant flows horizontally around the ends of the baffle walls as shown in the Fig. 6.24 (a) causing thorough mixing.

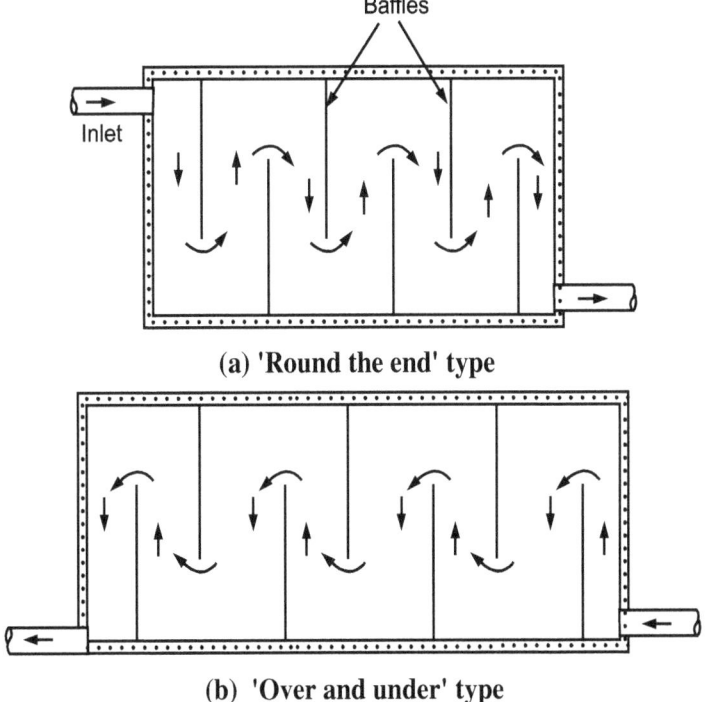

Fig. 6.24 : Mixing basins with baffle walls

In other type, the water is forced to flow up and down by means of hanging baffle walls as shown in Fig. 6.24 (b).

Drawbacks:

1. Mixing basin with baffle walls require more quantity of coagulants.
2. They cause greater loss of head (about 3.2 times velocity head in the channel).
3. They are less efficient compared to mechanical type mixers.
4. They are not suitable on large capacity water plants.

(e) Mixing basin with mechanical devices : This is the best type of mixing device and is used in modern and large water treatment plants. It consists of rectangular or cylindrical tank. The paddle or impeller is fixed to shaft and is driven by electrical drive unit at high rotating speed.

The coagulant is added at the tip of the rotating paddle. The water is admitted from inlet pipe and is deflected towards moving paddle to cause intimate mixing. The flash mixed water goes to flocculator through outlet pipe. The speed of paddle is between 100 – 200 rpm. The detention time is 30 to 60 seconds. Ratio of height of tank to diameter (or side) is 1 : 1 or 3 : 1. The value of mean velocity gradient G is kept 300 sec^{-1} or more. The ratio of impeller diameter to tank diameter is 0.2 to 0.4.

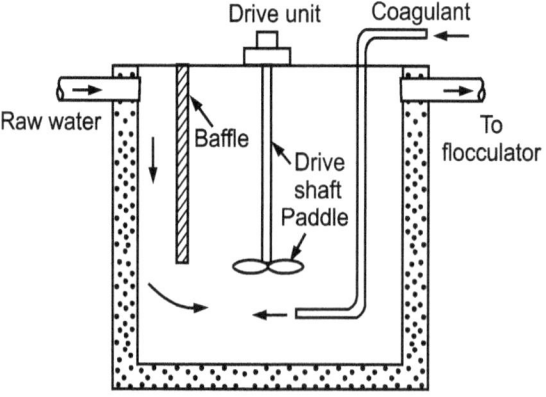

Fig. 6.25

(iii) Flocculation : This term is derived from the Latin word *flocculare*. The meaning of the word is to 'form a floc'. Hence, flocculation is stimulation by mechanical means to agglomerate destabilised particles into compact, fast setteable particle (or flocs). Flocculation is a gentle agitation causing velocity gradient in the coagulated water and forcing destabilised particles come together to become large and readily settlable floc.

This process is carried out in a basin or tank and it is known as flocculation basin, or flocculation tank. In this tank, slow mixing is done by revolving paddles, during which the growth of floc takes place. Many patented devices are available. Most famous is Dorrocoflocculator designed by Dorr Oliver and Co, U.S.A. A typical flocculator fitted with slow moving paddles is shown in Fig. 6.26.

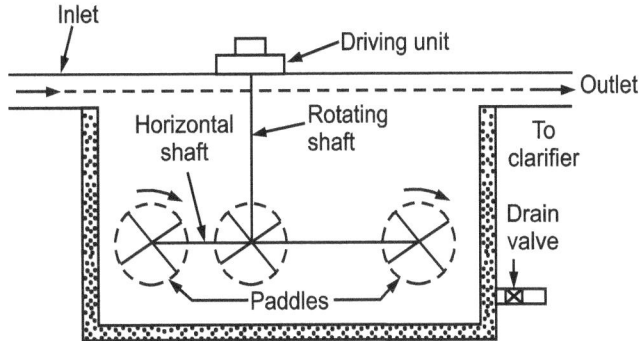

Fig. 6.26 : Flocculator fitted with paddles

(iv) Clarification (Sedimentation) : After flocculation, water is admitted into basins called clarifiers or settling basins. Water is detained in such tanks for a detention period of 2 to 3 hours. During this period, floc which was generated under flocculation, settles down in the form of sludge. The clear water is taken out through outlet arrangements and generally admitted to filtration tanks for further purification. The overflow rate of 1000 to 1200 lit/m²/hour is kept for settling. Sludge deposited in clarifiers is continuously scraped by mechanical means driven on electric power.

6.9.1 Clariflocculator

This is a combination of various units like flash mixer, flocculator and sedimentation (i.e. clarifier). Hence, it is popularly called as clariflocculator. Such a combined unit is designed by Dorr Co and is shown in Fig. 6.27. From inlet side, raw water is admitted in the flash mixer component and chemical feed pipe supplies required dose of coagulant and intimate mixing is done.

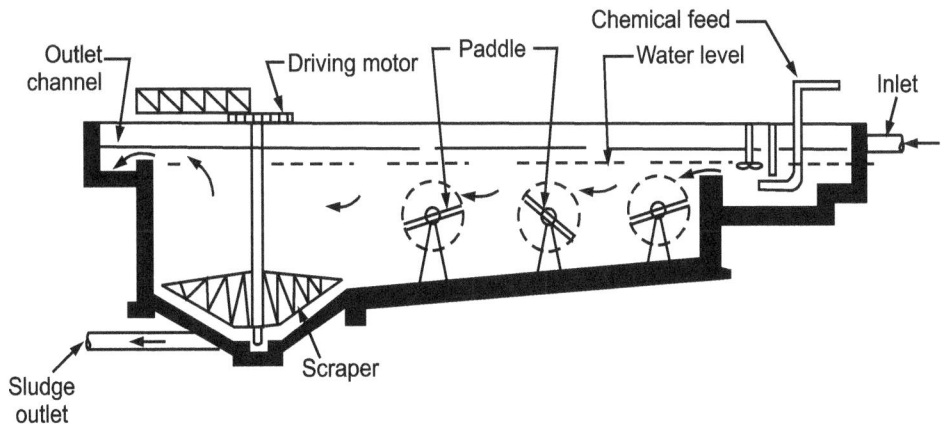

Fig. 6.27 : Dorr Co clariflocculator

Water then enters next compartment or zone known as flocculating zone, where water is slowly dispersed by rotating paddles to form stable floc and impurities present in water get entrapped in the floc.

Water containing floc moves further to sedimentation zone where sedimentation (i.e. clarification) of floc takes place at the bottom which is called as sludge. By slowly rotating mechanical scraper, the sludge is diverted in the sludge pocket from where it is removed by pumping intermittently.

Circular clariflocculators are also installed on many water works.

Concept of mean velocity gradient (G) :

It is already seen that the flocculation is controlled motion of water assisting formation of floc. The rate of flocculation depends upon factors like turbidity, type of coagulant and its dose and *the mean velocity gradient 'G'*.

Definition : The mean velocity gradient (G) is defined as the *rate of change of velocity per unit distance normal to a section i.e. metres per second per m*. Hence, a dimension of $\frac{1}{T}$ results. Therefore, 'G' is always expressed as sec^{-1}.

The value of 'G' is found out by the relation $G = \sqrt{\dfrac{P}{\mu V}}$,

where, P = Power dissipated measured in watts
  μ = Absolute viscosity in N-s/m^2
  V = Volume to which power P is applied measured in m^3 and G in sec^{-1}.

Relation of G and t :

When the water flows through the tank of volume V at the rate Q, then the displacement time $t = \dfrac{V}{Q}$. If the product of velocity gradient, G and this displacement time, t is taken, a dimensionless relation results.

$$\therefore \quad G \times t = \sqrt{\dfrac{P}{\mu V}} \times \dfrac{V}{Q} = \sqrt{\dfrac{PV}{\mu Q}}$$

In the above relation, $\sqrt{\dfrac{PV}{\mu}}$ is called as power induced flow, while Q is displacement flow. Hence, the product G × t is the ratio of power induced flow to displacement flow. The total number of particle collisions is proportional to G × t. Hence, G × t becomes a useful design parameter in flocculation.

Mechanical flocculation :

Mechanical flocculator consists of rotating paddles with horizontal or vertical shafts. The paddles are usually driven by a motor. The power required to overcome the drag of a single rotating blade is the product of drag force (F_D) and relative velocity (V_r) of impeller and surrounding liquid. Also $V_r = (1 - k) V_p$, where k = ratio of velocity of water to paddle velocity (V_p).

Power per unit volume = $P = F_D \times V_r$

F_D = Drag force = $C_D \times F_I$

where, C_D = Coefficient of drag

F_I = Impeller force

But $F_I = \rho \dfrac{A_p V_r^2}{2}$

where, A_p = Area of paddles

$\therefore \quad P = \rho \dfrac{A_p V_r^2}{2} \times C_D \times V_r = \dfrac{1}{2} C_D \times \rho \times A_p \times V_r^3$

$\therefore \quad P = \dfrac{1}{2} C_D \rho A_p V_r^3$

Now relative velocity, $V_r = V_p - V_w$

= Velocity of tip of paddles – Velocity of adjacent water

$\therefore \quad P = \dfrac{1}{2} C_D \rho A_p (V_p - V_w)^3$

$\therefore$ Velocity gradient = $G = \sqrt{\dfrac{P}{\mu V}} = \sqrt{\left[\dfrac{\frac{1}{2} C_D \rho A_p (V_p - V_w)^3}{\mu V}\right]}$

$G = \sqrt{\dfrac{\frac{1}{2} C_D A_p (V_p - V_w)^3}{\nu V}}$

($\because \mu = \nu \times \rho$ i.e. Absolute viscosity = Kinematic viscosity $\times \rho$)

$\therefore \quad G = \sqrt{\dfrac{C_D A_p V_r^3}{2\nu V}}$

6.9.2 Design Criteria for Flocculation Basin using Rotating Paddles

1. Depth of basin = 3 m to 4.5 m
2. Detention time (Flocculation period) = 20 to 60 minutes.
3. For rectangular type, $\dfrac{\text{Length}}{\text{Width}}$ = 2 to 3.
4. Total paddle area = 15 to 20% of vertical cross-section of basin.

5. Distance between paddle edge and bottom or side of basin = 15 to 30 cm.
6. The peripheral velocity (V_p) of paddles = 0.2 to 0.6 m/s (average = 0.35)
7. Horizontal velocity of flow = 1.5 to 2.0 cm/sec.
8. Velocity differential between paddle and water = 75% of paddle velocity.
9. G = Velocity gradient = 10 to 75 sec^{-1}.
10. Power consumption = 18 to 36 kW/Mld ($P = G^2 \cdot V \cdot \mu$)
11. C_D = Coefficient of drag = 1.8 for flat paddles with flat plates.
12. Product G × t should be between 10^4 to 10^5.
13. Relative velocity $V_r = V_p - kV_p = V_p(k-1)$, where, k = 0.25.

Example 6.12 : Design a circular flocculator for a design discharge of 3.75 Mld with mechanical paddle and detention period of 30 minutes.

Solution : (1) Required capacity of tank = Discharge × D.T. = $\dfrac{3.75 \times 10^3}{24 \times 60} \times 30 = 78.13$ m^3

2. Assume depth of tank = 3 m
3. Base area of basin = $\dfrac{78.13}{3}$ = 26 m^2

If 'D' is diameter of basin, $A = \dfrac{\pi D^2}{4} = 26$, solving D = 5.75 m

4. Design of rotating paddles :

Area of paddles = 20% of vertical cross-section

Vertical c/s area of paddles = $\dfrac{20}{100} \times 5.75 \times 3 = 3.45$ m^2

Assuming 4 paddles and B is the width of paddle and 2.4 m the depth of paddle (3 m depth – 0.3 clearance from top and bottom)

∴ 4 × 2.4 × B = 3.45, solving B = 0.36 m = 36 cm

∴ Provide 4 rotating arms, each arm having two paddles.

Each paddle dimension is 240 cm × 18 cm × 5 cm (thickness).

Example 6.13 : Design a mechanical flocculator to treat water for a population of one lakh, water being supplied at the rate of 150 litres per capita per day. The temperature of water is 30°C, detention time is 30 minutes and paddle speed is 3 r.p.m.

Solution : 1. Rate of flow per sec. = $Q = \dfrac{150 \times 10^5}{24 \times 3600 \times 1000} = 0.174$ m^3/sec.

2. Volume of tank = Detention time × Q = 30 × 60 × 0.174 = 313.2 m^3.

3. Assuming depth of basin = 3 m, surface area = $\dfrac{313.2}{3}$ = 104.4 m^2.

4. Assuming horizontal velocity of flow of 1 m/min,

   Length of basin = Detention time × Velocity = 30 × 1 = 30 m.

   Width of basin = $\dfrac{104.4}{30}$ = 3.48 m say 3.6 m.

∴ Provide flocculator basin of size 30 m (long) × 3.6 m (wide) × 3 m (deep) giving volume of 324 m³.

5. Assume c/c distance between shafts and paddles = 3 m

   ∴ Number of shafts = $\dfrac{\text{Length of basin}}{3} - 1 = \dfrac{30}{3} - 1 = 9$.

6. Vertical c/s area of basin = Width × Depth = 3.6 × 3 = 10.8 m²

   Assume paddle area = 45% of c/s area = $\dfrac{45}{100}$ × 10.8 = 4.86 m²

   Assume 2 planks of 3 m height for each shaft.

   Total length of plank = 2 × 3 × 9 (shafts) = 54 m

   ∴ Width of each plank = $\dfrac{\text{c/s area}}{\text{Length}} = \dfrac{4.86}{54}$ = 0.09 m = 9 cm

   ∴ $\dfrac{L}{B}$ of plank = $\dfrac{300 \text{ cm}}{9 \text{ cm}}$ = 33 > 20.

7. C_D = 1.8 for flat plank, kinematic viscosity 30° C = 0.8039 × 10⁻² cm²/sec.

   = 0.8039 × 10⁻⁶ m²/sec.

8. Paddle velocity, $V_p = \dfrac{\pi D N}{60} = \dfrac{3.14 \times 3 \times 3}{60}$ = 0.471 m/sec.

   (D = Diameter of circular path of paddle plank)

   Assuming velocity differential = 75% of paddle velocity

   ∴ V_r = 0.75 × 0.471 = 0.353 m/sec.

9. Velocity gradient, $G = \sqrt{\dfrac{C_D A_p V_r^3}{2 \nu V}}$

   $= \sqrt{\dfrac{1.8 \times 4.86 \times (0.353)^3}{2 \times 0.8039 \times 10^{-6} \times 313.2}}$

   = 27.64 sec⁻¹ (∵ G should be between 10 to 75)

10. Product, $G \times t$ = 27.64 × 30 × 60

    = 4.98 × 10⁴

This value is between 10⁴ to 10⁵, hence OK.

Example 6.14 : Design a clariflocculator for treating 5 M/D water with the help of following data : (1) Surface loading of 1000 lit/hr/m². (2) Detention period of 3 hours. (3) Tank is circular with flocculator in the centre and clarifier surrounding it. (4) Detention time for flocculation = 20 minutes.

Solution : Let, D_1 is the diameter of clariflocculator and D_2 is the diameter of flocculator.

1. **Flocculator design :** Detention time 20 min.

$$Q = \text{Discharge/min.} = \frac{5 \times 10^6}{24 \times 60 \times 10^3} = 3.472 \text{ m}^3/\text{min}$$

∴ Volume of flocculator chamber = $Q \times D.T.$ = $3.472 \times 20 = 69.44$ m³

Assume depth of flocculation zone = 3 m

Surface area of tank = $\dfrac{\text{Volume}}{\text{Depth}} = \dfrac{69.44}{3} = 23.15$ m²

∴ $\dfrac{\pi D_2^2}{4} = 23.15$, solving $D_2 = 5.43$ say 6 m.

∴ Provide central chamber for flocculator of diameter 6 m.

2. **Clariflocculator design :**

$Q = 3.472$ m³/min. Detention time = 3 hrs.

∴ Volume = $Q \times D.T.$ = $3.472 \times 3 \times 60 = 625$ m³.

Since surface loading is 1000 lit/hr/m².

$$\text{Area of tank} = \frac{\text{Discharge/hour}}{\text{Surface loading}}$$

∴ $\text{Area} = \dfrac{3.472 \times 60}{1000 \times 10^{-3}} = 208.32 = 210$ m² (say)

∴ Clarifier surface area (ring form) = $\dfrac{\pi}{4} (D_1^2 - D_2^2) = 210$

∴ $D_1^2 - D_2^2 = \dfrac{210 \times 4}{\pi}$

$D_1^2 = \dfrac{210 \times 4}{\pi} + D_2^2$

$D_1^2 = 267.516 + 36 = 303.52$ ∴ $D_1 = 17.42 \approx 17.5$ m

Depth = $\dfrac{\text{Volume}}{\text{Area}} = \dfrac{625}{210} = 2.97$ m = 3 m.

Add 0.5 m for sludge and 0.5 m for free board. ∴ Overall depth = 4 m.

Example 6.15 : A water treatment plant treats 250 m³/hr. of water. Work out the following with respect to flocculator :

(i) Dimensions of flocculator unit.

(ii) Power input by paddles to water.

(iii) Size and number of paddles.

Assume water temperature = 25°C and $\mu = 0.89 \times 10^{-3}$ N.s/m².

Solution :

(i) **Dimensions of flocculator unit :**

Assume an average G value of 30 s⁻¹ and $Gt = 4 \times 10^4$

∴ $\quad Gt = 4 \times 10^4$

∴ $\quad t = \dfrac{4 \times 10^4}{30} \times \dfrac{1}{60} = 22.22$ min.

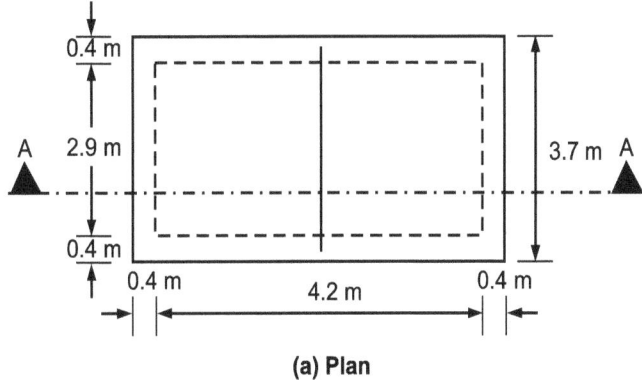

(a) Plan

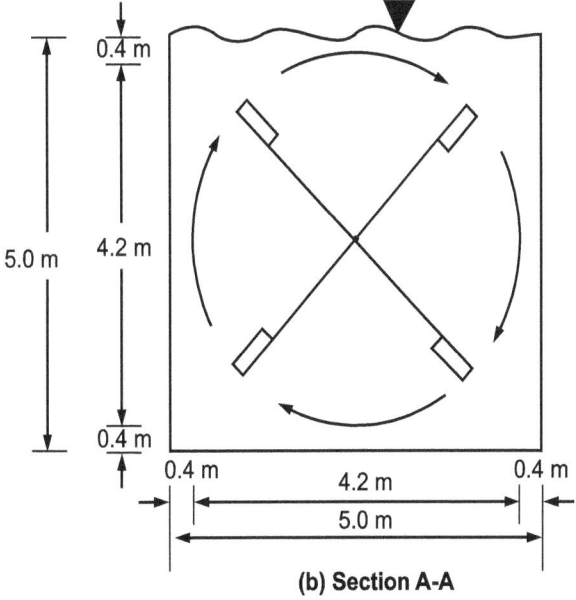

(b) Section A-A

Fig. 6.28

Volume of the tank,

$$V = Qt$$

Now, $Q = 250 \text{ m}^3/\text{hr}$

$$= 250 \times \frac{1}{60} = 4.166 \text{ m}^3/\text{min}.$$

$\therefore \quad V = 4.166 \times 22.22 = 92.58 \text{ m}^3$

Assuming depth and length of 5 m,

$$\text{Area of tank} = \frac{92.58}{5} = 18.52 \text{ m}^2$$

$$\text{Width of tank} = \frac{\text{Area of tank}}{\text{Length of tank}}$$

$$= \frac{18.52}{5}$$

$$= 3.7 \text{ m}$$

(ii) Power :

$$P = G^2 V \mu$$

$$= (30)^2 \times 92.58 \times 0.89 \times 10^{-3}$$

$$= 74.16 \text{ W}$$

$$= 0.074 \text{ kW}$$

(iii) Size and number of paddles : Each paddle wheel has four boards 2.9 m long and w wide. Number of paddle wheel is one (As only one compartment is provided and only 3.7 m width).

Now, calculate w from power input and paddle velocity.

$$P = \frac{C_D A_p \rho v_r^3}{2}$$

Assume, $v_r^3 = 0.67 \text{ m/sec.} \times 0.75 = 0.5 \text{ m/sec.}$ and $C_D = 1.8$

A_p = Length of boards × w × Number of boards

$A_p = 2.9 \times w \times 4 = 11.6 \text{ w}$ (∵ 4 boards per paddle)

$$P = 74.16 = \frac{1.8 \times 11.6 \text{ w} \times 1000 \times (0.5)^3}{2}$$

$\therefore \quad w = 0.06 \text{ m}$

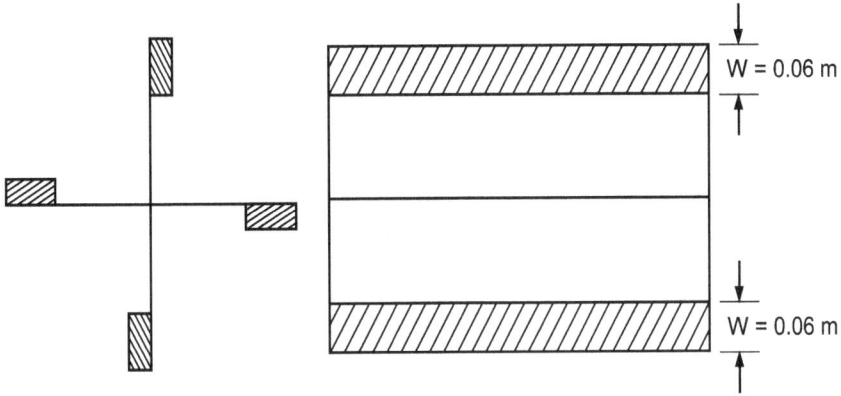

Fig. 6.29 : Paddle configuration

Example 6.16 : A water treatment plant treats 250 m³/hr. of water. Work out the following with respect to flocculator.

(i) Dimensions of flocculator unit.

(ii) Power input by paddles to water.

(iii) Size and number of paddles.

Assume water temperature = 25°C and absolute viscosity = 0.89×10^{-3} N.s/m². Detention time = 30 minutes.

Given that velocity of water in inlet pipe = 1.2 m/sec. Drag coefficient C_D = 1.8, G = 40 sec⁻¹, velocity at tip of paddle = 0.5 m/sec.

Velocity of water at paddle tip = 25% of velocity at tip of paddle.

Solution :

(i) Dimensions of the flocculator tank :

Volume of the tank, V = Qt,

$$V = \left(250 \times \frac{1}{60}\right) \times 30 = 125 \text{ m}^3$$

Assuming depth and length of 5 m,

$$\text{Area of tank} = \frac{125}{5} = 25 \text{ m}^2$$

∴ Width of tank = $\frac{\text{Area of tank}}{\text{Length of tank}}$

$$= \frac{25}{5} = 5 \text{ m}$$

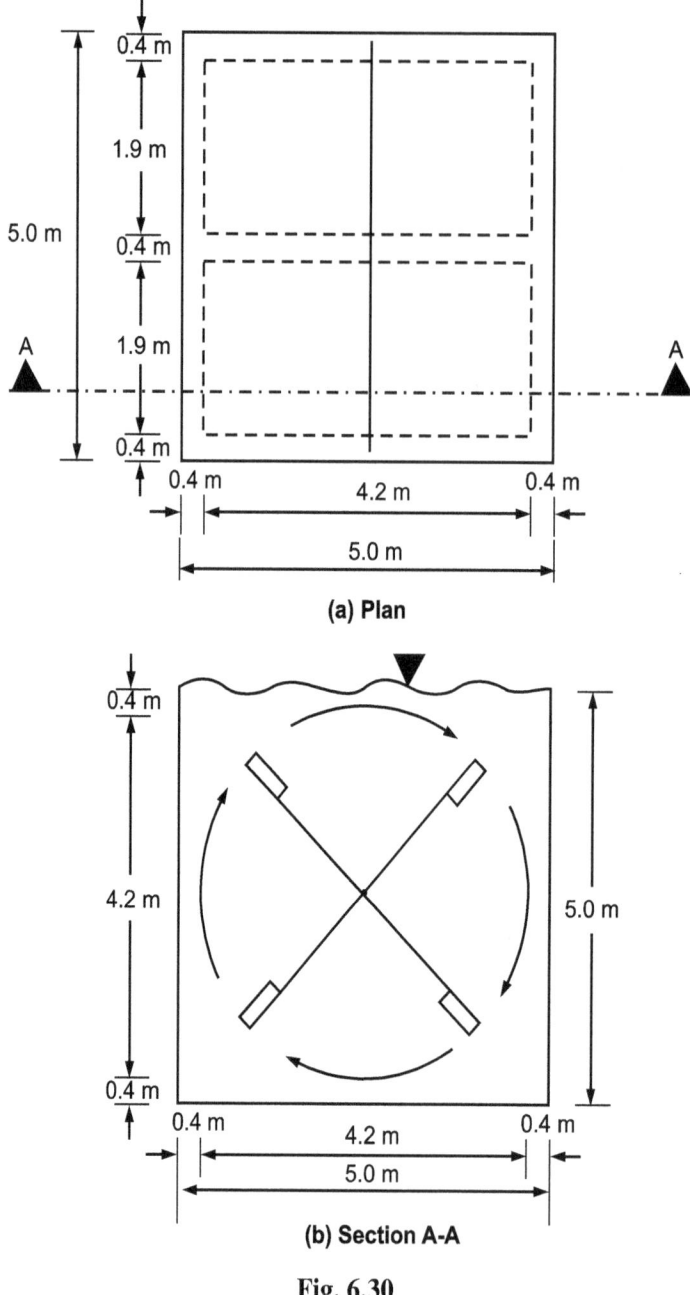

Fig. 6.30

(ii) Power : $P = G^2 \cdot V \mu = (40)^2 \times 125 \times 0.89 \times 10^{-3}$

$= 178 \text{ W} = 0.178 \text{ kW}$

(iii) Size and number of paddles : Each paddle wheel has four boards 1.9 m long and w wide – two paddle wheels per compartment.

Now, calculate w from power input and paddle velocity.

$$P = \frac{C_D A_p \rho v_p^3}{2}$$

A_p = Length of boards × w × Number of boards

2 paddles at 4 boards per paddle = 8 boards

$$A_p = 1.9 \times w \times 8$$
$$= 15.2 \, w$$
$$P = 178 = \frac{1.8 \times 15.2 \, w \times 1000 \times (0.5)^3}{2}$$

∴ w = 0.1 m

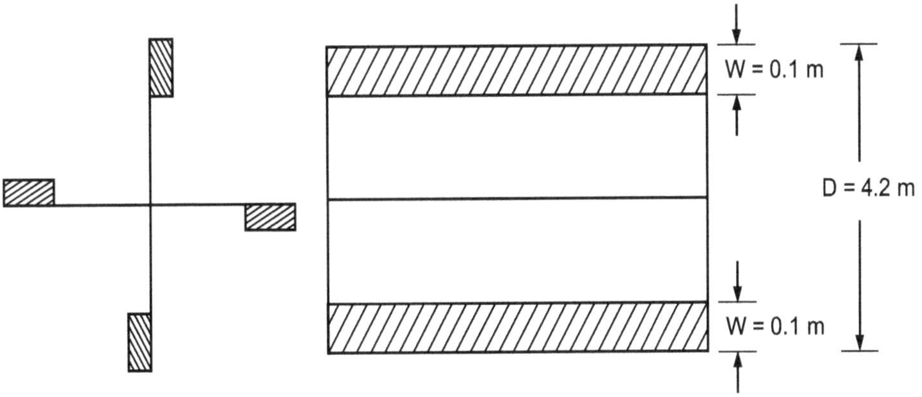

Fig. 6.31 : Paddle configuration

Example 6.17 : Design a mechanical flocculator to treat water for a population of one lakh, water being supplied at the rate of 150 lit. per capita per day. Detention time is 30 minutes and paddle speed is 3 rpm.

Assume C_D = 1.8 for flat plank, Kinematic viscosity = 0.83039×10^{-6} m/sec.

Solution :

$$\mu = \text{Kinematic viscosity} \times \rho$$
$$= 0.83039 \times 10^{-6} \times 1000$$
$$= 0.83 \times 10^{-3} \, N\text{-}s/m^2$$

Flow rate, Q = Population × Rate of water per capita per day
$$= 1,00,000 \times 150$$
$$= 150 \times 10^5 \, lit/day$$
$$= \frac{150 \times 10^5}{10^3} \times \frac{1}{24 \times 60}$$
$$= 10.42 \, m^3/min.$$

(i) Dimensions of flocculator unit :

$$V = Q \times t$$
$$= 10.42 \times 30 = 312.5 \text{ m}^3$$

Assume depth is 5 m and length is 10 m.

$$\therefore \quad \text{Area of tank} = \frac{312.5}{5} = 62.5 \text{ m}^2$$

$$\therefore \quad \text{Width of tank} = \frac{62.5}{10} = 6.25 \text{ m}$$

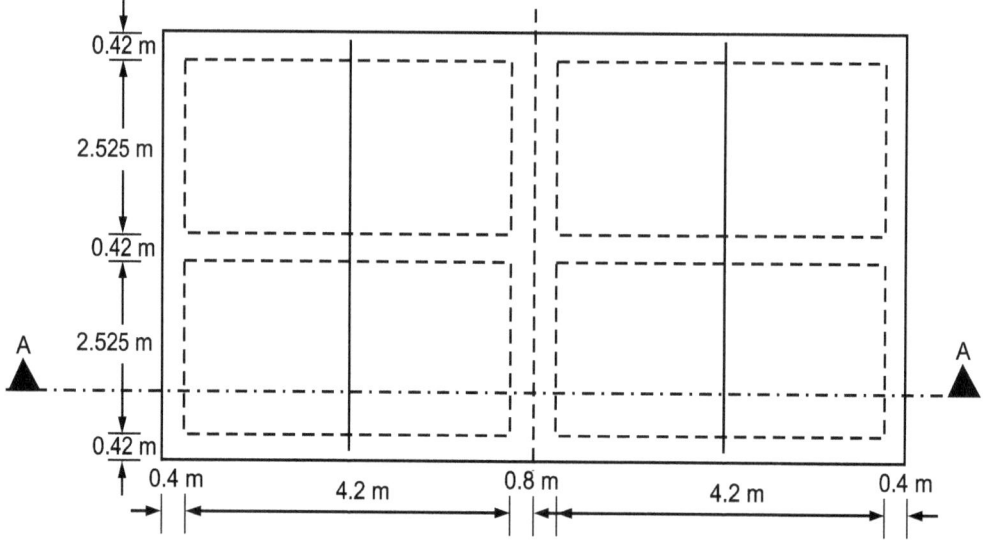

(a) Plan

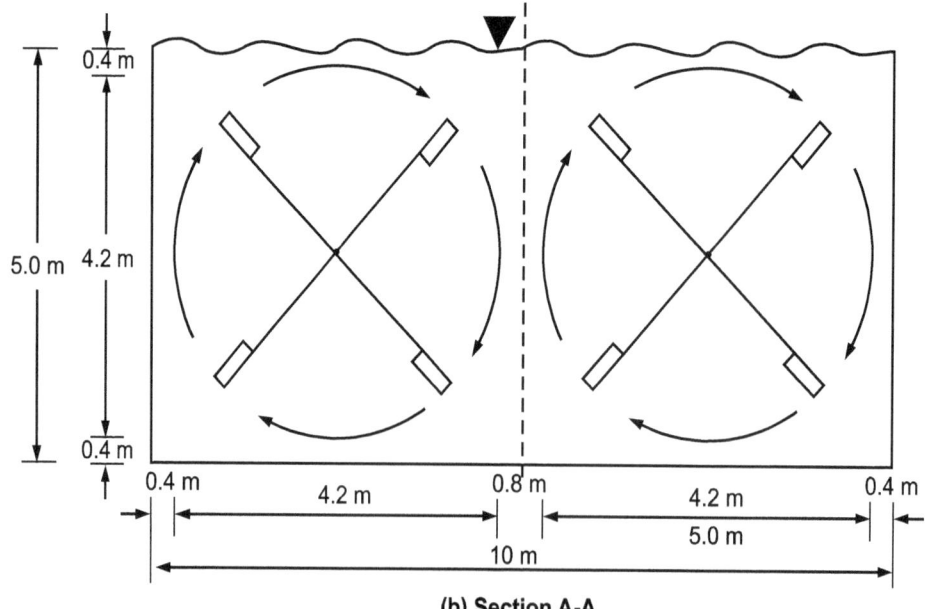

(b) Section A-A

Fig. 6.32

Note : For equal distribution of velocity gradients, the end area of each compartment should be square. Here we use two compartments, so depth equals $\frac{1}{2}$ length.

(ii) Power requirements : Assume G values tapered as follows :

First compartment, $\quad G = 40 \text{ sec}^{-1}$

Second compartment, $\quad G = 30 \text{ sec}^{-1}$

Calculate the power requirements for 1 and 2.

$$P = G^2 V \mu$$

$$V = \frac{312.5}{2} = 156.25 \text{ m}^3$$

$$P_1 = (40)^2 \times 156.25 \times 0.83 \times 10^{-3}$$

$$= 207.5 \text{ W} = 0.21 \text{ kW}$$

$$P_2 = (30)^2 \times 156.25 \times 0.83 \times 10^{-3}$$

$$= 116.72 \text{ W} = 0.117 \text{ kW}$$

Calculate w from power input and paddle velocity : Each paddle wheel has four boards 2.525 m long and w wide, two paddle wheels per compartment.

$$\text{Power, } P = \frac{C_D \cdot A_p \rho \cdot v_p^3}{2}$$

Paddle speed, $\omega = 3$ rpm (given)

$$v_r = \pi D \times \omega$$

$$= \pi \times 4.2 \times 3 \times \frac{1}{60}$$

$$= 0.66 \text{ m/sec.}$$

Consider, $\quad v_r = 0.66 \times 0.75 = 0.5 \text{ m/sec.}$

$$A_p = \text{Length of boards} \times \text{Number of boards}$$

2 paddles at 4 boards per paddle = 8 boards

$\therefore \quad 8 \times 2.525 \times w = 20.2 \text{ w} = A_p$

$$P_1 = 207.5 = \frac{[1.8 \times 20.2 \text{ w} \times 1000 \times (0.5)^3]}{2}$$

$\therefore \quad w = 0.09 \text{ m}$

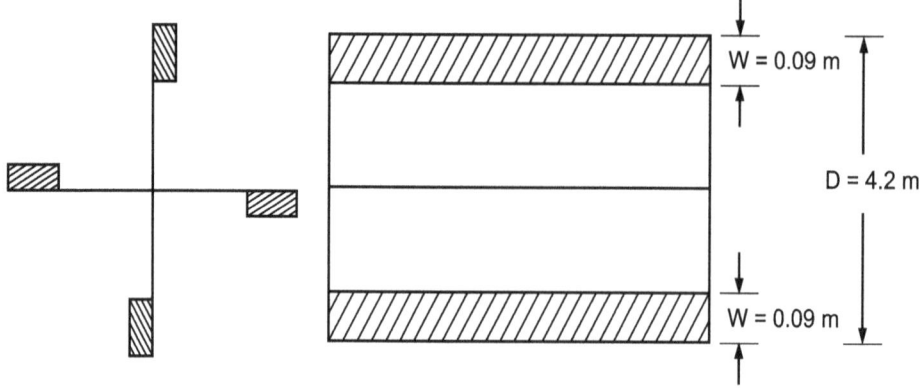

Fig. 6.33 : Paddle configuration

EXERCISE

1. What do you mean by treatment of water ? State the objects of treatment of water. **(May 2007, Dec. 2010)**
2. Explain the purpose of aeration. What are its limitations ? **(May 2000, 2006, 2008; Nov. 2000, Dec. 2006, 2010)**
3. Explain various methods of aeration.
4. State the various impurities that are removed by screening and aeration.
5. Draw a layout plan for a typical water treatment plant.
6. What are bar screens ?
7. Draw a sketch and explain the process of plain sedimentation tank in Hopper tank. What particle sizes are removed in this tank ?
8. What do you mean by discrete particle and how does it differ from colloidal particle ? **(May 2007, 2008)**
9. What is Stoke's law ? What are its limitations ? **(Nov. 2000)**
10. Describe briefly horizontal flow settling basins. **(Dec. 2006, 2009; May 2007, 2009)**
11. What do you mean by surface loading and weir loading ?
12. List the design criteria for plain sedimentation tank.
13. Explain with sketches inlet and outlet arrangement for sedimentation basin. **(May 2008)**
14. A plain sedimentation tank 1.5 m deep, settles silt with a velocity of 1.6×10^{-2} cm/sec. Work out
    (i) Surface loading if detention time is 2.25 hrs.
    (ii) Practical efficiency of unit
    (iii) The weir loading if L = 2B and B = 6.5
    (**Ans.** (i) S.L. = 600 lit/hr/m², (ii) E = 56.4%, (iii) W.L. = 202.8 m³/m/day)

15. For a rectangular flocculator of 40 m³ capacity with effective cross-section of 2 m (wide) × 3 m (deep), find out :
    (i) Power output for paddles rotating at 7 rpm
    (ii) Velocity gradient G
    (iii) G × t if the detention time is 45 minutes and absolute viscosity is 1.3×10^{-4}.
    (**Ans.** (i) P = 7.28 W, (ii) G = 37.4 sec⁻¹, (iii) 1.01×10^5)

16. Explain theory of coagulation. Give equations of coagulation by alum.
    (Nov. 2000, 2001, May 2006, Dec. 2006, May 2009)

17. Why flash mixing and slow mixing is necessary ? **(May 2007)**

18. Design a rectangular settling tank to treat 2 MLD of water. Adopt detention time of 3 hours and flow through velocity of 7.5 cm/min. If the depth of tank is 3 m, find overflow rate and dimensions of the tank.
    (**Ans.** 995 m³/m²/hr., size – 13.5 × 6.2 × 3.5 m)

19. Explain diffused double layer theory.

20. Enlist different coagulants used. Why alum is universally used ?

21. Write a note on coagulant aids.

22. Explain the terms and give their units :
    (i) Detention period
    (ii) Overflow rate **(Dec. 2006, 2007, 2008, May 2009)**
    (iii) Weir loading **(Dec. 2006, 2008, May 2009)**
    (iv) Flow through velocity **(Dec. 2006, 2007)**
    (v) Displacement velocity
    (vi) Detention time **(Dec. 2007)**
    (vii) Mean velocity gradient. **(Dec. 2007)**

23. State the characteristics of raw water for which you would recommend :
    (i) Provision of plain sedimentation
    (ii) By-passing plain sedimentation.
    Also describe the character of suspended particles for which Stoke's law is applicable.

24. Prove that theoretically, the surface loading (Q/A) and not the depth is a measure of effective removal of particles in a sedimentation tank.
    (May 2000, 2006, 2008, 2009; Dec. 2006, 2009, 2010)

25. Explain how alum reacts with water by giving equation. **(May 2000)**

26. Give reasons for the following :
    (i) The rectangular sedimentation tanks are preferred to the square sedimentation tank. **(Nov. 2000)**

27. On what factors the dose of coagulants depends ? How the optimum coagulant dose is determined ? **(Nov. 2001, Dec. 2006, May 2007)**

28. What is the purpose of aeration of water ? Explain with a neat sketch cascade type of aerator. **(May 2004, Dec. 2008, May 2009, Dec. 2009)**

29. Define mean velocity gradient. How it is calculated in the design of clariflocculator ? **(May 2006)**

30. Draw a flow diagram of river water treatment process. **(Dec. 2006, 2009)**

31. Explain any two methods of aeration. **(May 2007)**

32. Explain in detail, the working of a circular clariflocculator. Draw the typical cross-section of a circular clariflocculator, showing various components. **(May 2008)**

33. Explain factors affecting coagulation. **(May 2010)**

34. Draw a flow diagram of river water treatment process for a city. Explain the purpose of any two units used for water treatment. **(Dec. 2010)**

CHAPTER SEVEN

FILTRATION

7.1 INTRODUCTION AND OBJECTS OF FILTRATION

Filtration is a process of removing particulate and bacterial impurities which could not be removed in earlier processes, from water by passing it through a porous medium. It is an important stage in the purification of water.

Objects of filtration :

1. To remove suspended, colloidal and other impurities which impart turbidity to water and untrapped by previous processes.
2. To reduce bacterial load by about 90%.
3. To produce sparkling and aesthetically attractive water.
4. To reduce odour and colour imparted by fine colouring matter, by arresting them in filter media.
5. To alter the chemical characteristics of water.

7.2 CLASSIFICATION OF FILTERS

(A) Based on rate of filtration :

1. Gravity filters : (a) Slow sand filters and
    (b) Rapid sand filters
2. Pressure filters

(B) Based on material of filter media :

(a) Sand filters (natural silica sand),

(b) Anthracite filters (crushed grains of anthracite coal),

(c) Metal fabric filters or Microstainers (stainless steel fabrics) and

(d) Diatomaceous earth filters (a type of earth).

(C) Based on depth of filter media :

(a) Deep granular filters – dual media and multimedia granular activated carbon and

(b) Precoat filters - diatomaceous earth and powdered activated carbon.

7.3 MECHANISMS OF FILTRATION

Theory of filtration basically involves :

(a) Transport mechanism and (b) Attachment mechanism.

(a) Transport mechanism brings small particles from the solution to the surfaces of media. In this, actions like diffusion, interception, gravitational settling and hydrodynamic actions take place.

(b) Attachment mechanism assumes the adhering or retaining of particles over the grains of filter media. This is occurring due to (i) electrostatic interactions, (ii) specific adsorption or chemical bridging. This mechanism depends upon the type and dose of coagulants applied, chemical characteristics of water and properties of the filter media.

Based upon these mechanisms, the following actions are assumed to take place.

1. **Mechanical straining :** Voids are present in the filter media like sand. These voids act like sieves or strainers. When the water is applied on filter media, suspended impurities (usually larger than voids of filter media) are retained while the water passes through. Major impurities are retained in the upper part of the filter media. It is assumed that these earlier impurities caught function as a mat and help in straining impurities.

2. **Electrolytic action and sedimentation :** The clarified water contains the residual alum floc. This floc forms a thin coating on the surface of sand grain which is positively charged. The colloidal particles are negatively charged. When these opposite charged particles of sand and impurities come in contact with each other, they neutralize and get deposited in voids of sand, each void functioning as tiny sedimentation basin. Due to such action, bacteria and viruses are also removed.

3. **Attachment :** When water containing colloidal particles flows through sand, it follows a curved path and a centrifugal force acts on the particles in suspension and are drawn on the surface of the sand grain and get attached to the sand grains. Due to this action, impurities are reduced.

4. **Biological metabolism :** The surface of sand layer gets coated with a zoogleal film. The film contains colonies of living organisms. They feed on the organic impurities and convert them into harmless compounds by complex biological reactions. The impurities form a layer on the top in which the bacteria thrive and further absorb impurities.

7.4 FILTER MATERIALS

(a) Sand, (b) Anthracite, (c) Garnet sand or ilmenite, (d) Locally available materials and (e) Gravel.

7.4.1 Sand

It is the widely used material and is cheap. It should satisfy the following specifications :

1. It should be free from silt, clay, loam, suspended impurities and other organic matter.
2. It should be uniform in nature and size.

3. It should be hard and resistant. Wearing loss shall not exceed 3%.
4. When the sand is soaked in 10% HCl for 24 hours, loss of weight should not exceed 5%.
5. Its specific gravity shall be between 2.55 to 2.65.
6. Effective size shall be (a) 0.2 to 0.3 mm for slow sand filter, (b) 0.45 to 0.7 mm for rapid sand filter.
7. The uniformity coefficient shall be (a) 3 to 5 mm for slow sand filter, (b) 1.3 to 1.75 mm for rapid sand filter.

7.4.2 Anthracite

It is more costly than sand. But it is lighter than sand. Crushed anthracite alone, or jointly mixed with sand may be used as filter media.

7.4.3 Garnet Sand

It is heavier than normal sand (specific gravity = 4.2) and its use is recommended in mixed - media filter only.

7.4.4 Local Available Materials

Like shreded coconut husks, burnt rice husks, crushed glass, slag and metallic ores can be used as filter media.

7.4.5 Gravel

The gravel, if provided, supports the sand and permits the filtered water to pass freely to the under-drains and also allows wash water to move uniformly upwards.

Gravel should be hard, durable, rounded, free from flat, thin or long pieces, and impurities. The density of gravel should be about 1600 kg/m^3.

7.5 DEFINITIONS

1. **Effective size :** The effective size of sand is the sieve size in mm through which 10% of sand by weight passes. It is also called as effective diameter D_{10}.

2. **Uniformity coefficient :** This is the ratio of sieve size through which 60% of the sand passes to the effective size of sand.

For example, if the effective size of the sand is 0.30 mm and the size of sieve through which 60% of sand passes is 0.50 mm, then the uniformity coefficient is $\frac{0.50}{0.30}$ = 1.67.

7.6 SLOW SAND FILTER

Slow sand filters were first introduced in England in the year 1829. They were widely used till the rapid gravity sand filters were invented. These are becoming obsolete now-a-days. Due to smaller filtration rate, they require large areas and large quantities of filtering materials. Hence, they become costly and uneconomical, especially for treating water on large scale.

7.6.1 Essential Parts or Components

(1) Enclosure tank, (2) Under-drainage system, (3) Base material, (4) Filter media of sand, (5) Appurtenances. Fig. 7.1 shows the cross-section and plan of the filter.

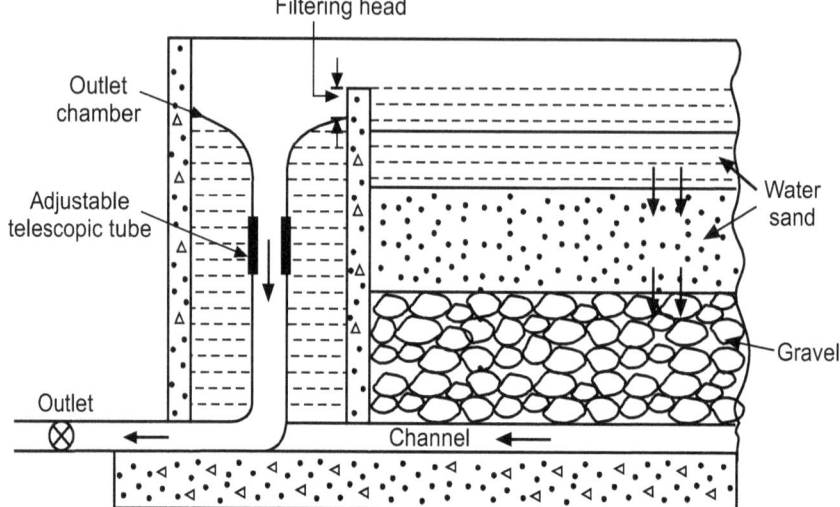

(a) Slow sand filter showing filtering head

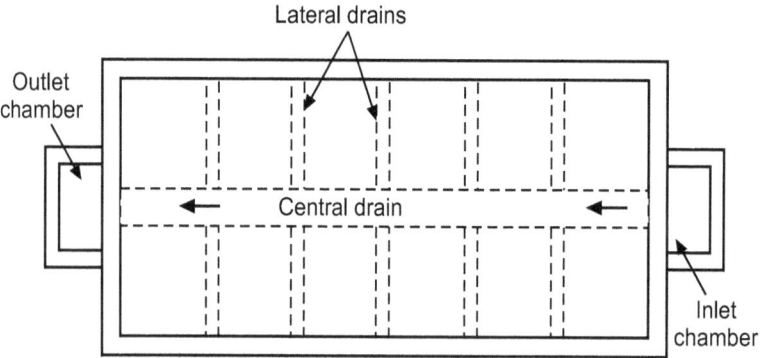

(b) Plan of under-drainage system for slow sand filter

Fig. 7.1

1. **Enclosure tank :** It is constructed in stone or brick masonry and is made water-tight, by applying water proof material to all inside surfaces and floor. A bed slope of 1 : 100 to 1 : 200 is given towards the central drain. The depth of tank is 2.5 to 3.5 m. The surface area of filter varies from 50 – 2000 m^2 or even more, depending upon amount of water to be treated.

2. **Under-drainage system :** It consists of lateral drains joining central drain which carries filtered water to outlet chamber. The lateral drains are placed at 2.5 to 3.5 m apart. The lateral drains may be open jointed pipes or porous patented drain devices, having 7.5 to 10 cm diameter. Sometimes they are made of open jointed tiles.

3. **Base material :** Base material is gravel and is placed on the top of under-drainage system. Its depth varies from 30 cm to 75 cm. It is well graded and laid in layers of 15 cm.

Topmost layer is of small size gravel and bottom layer is of larger size gravel. There are generally four layers as given below -

Layer	Size of gravel
First layer (bottom)	40 to 65 mm
Second layer	20 to 40 mm
Third layer	6 to 20 mm
Fourth layer (topmost)	3 to 6 mm

The filter media is supported by this base material.

4. Filter media of sand : It consists of sand layer and is placed above gravel base. The depth of filter media sand varies from 75 to 90 cm. The effective size of sand may vary from 0.2 to 0.35, the common value being 0.3. Uniformity coefficient varies from 2 to 3, the common value being 2.5. The upper 15 cm layer consists of finer sand than the rest which is of uniform grain size. Finer sand produces pure water as more impurities and bacteria will be trapped. Finer the sand, smaller is the filtration rate.

5. Filter appurtenances : These are installed to regulate the flow and to operate and maintain the filter system efficiently. They are for (i) measuring loss of head through filter, (ii) controlling depth of water above filter media, (iii) controlling constant rate of flow through filter. The Fig. 7.1 shows an adjustable telescopic tube for keeping constant discharge.

7.6.2 Working of Filter

Effluent water from plain sedimentation tank is admitted to filter tank through the inlet chamber. The depth of water applied over the filter media is generally equal to the thickness of filter sand. The water passes through sand bed and gravel base and enters under-drainage system.

It is assumed that both straining and microbiological actions are taking place during filtration.

Filter head is the difference of water level in the filter tank and outlet chamber. The maximum or limiting filter head value is about 0.7 to 1.2 m, or 70 to 80% of the thickness of filter media. When the filtration head reaches this maximum permissible value, its working is stopped and cleaning is taken up.

7.6.3 Cleaning of Filter

When the filter head reaches 1.3 m, the water in the tank is first drained out. The top 2 to 3 cm of sand layer is scrapped and removed. Before putting the filter into operation, the water is allowed to enter from below till the complete sand bed is fully covered by water. This is done to avoid entrapping of air in the sand. Now slowly the inlet valve is opened to avoid disloging of sand, till the normal water level is reached. The filter is allowed to stand for next 12 hours. Then filtrate is allowed to go to wash water drain slowly at the rate 20% of normal filtration rate for next 12 to 15 hours. During this period, the biological film gets formed. After this the filtered water is collected and passed on to filtered water reservoir, only taking care to keep the filtration rate of 33% of the normal rate. This condition is maintained for another 3 days. Thereafter the slow sand filter is allowed to run at its normal rate.

The time interval between two successive cleanings mainly depends upon nature of impurities in applied water. Cleaning interval may vary from 30 to 90 days.

When such cleaning is done several times, the thickness of filter sand gets reduced. A new layer of 15 cm thick is then added to the filter. In case fresh sand is not easily available, previously scrapped sand should be washed and used again.

7.6.4 Rate of Filtration

Under normal working the slow sand filter gives 0.10 to 0.15 $m^3/hr/m^2$ of surface area of filter.

7.6.5 Efficiency of Slow Sand Filter

1. Bacterial removal efficiency - 98 to 99.9%.
2. Less efficient in removing colour and taste - 20 to 25% only.
3. Turbidity removal efficiency is also low.

Turbidity upto 50 mg/l only can be removed. Slow sand filters are not suitable for sedimented waters having turbidity more than 50 to 60 mg/l.

4. They are effective in removing 'earthy' odours and tastes caused by growth of algae.

7.6.6 Guidelines for Design of Slow Sand Filters

The Manual on Water Supply and Treatment prepared by Central Public Health and Environmental Engineering Organisation (MUD) gives the following guidelines (Table 7.1).

Table 7.1 : Guidelines for design of slow sand filters

	Description	Recommended design value
1.	Design period	10 years
2.	Number of filter beds :	
	(i) Minimum	2
	(ii) Areas upto 20 m^2	2
	(iii) A = 20 to 249 m^2	3
	(iv) A = 250 to 649 m^2	4
	(v) A = 650 to 1200 m^2	5
	(vi) A = 1201 to 2000 m^2	6
3.	Depth of supernatant water	1.0 m
4.	Filtration rate	
	(i) Normal operation	0.1 m/hour
	(ii) Maximum overload rate	0.2 m/hour
5.	Free board	0.2 m
6.	Depth of filter sand	
	(i) Initial	1.0 m
	(ii) Final (min.)	0.4 m
7.	Sand specifications	
	(i) Effective size	0.2 to 0.3 mm
	(ii) Uniformity coefficient	5

… Contd.

8. Gravel (3 – 4 layers) depth	0.3 m
9. Under drains (made of bricks or perforated pipes)	0.2 m
10. Depth of filter box	2.7 m
11. Effluent weir level above sand bed	20 to 30 mm
12. Standards of performance	
(i) Turbidity of filtrate	1 NTU or less
(ii) Colour of filtrate	3 or less on the cobalt scale
(iii) Filter runs	When the raw water turbidity does not exceed 30 NTU, the filter runs should normally be not less than 6 to 8 weeks, with the filter head not exceeding 0.6 m.
(iv) Initial head loss	Should not exceed 5 cm; a higher head loss will indicate that the entire sand bed needs over-hauling.

7.7 RAPID SAND FILTER OR MECHANICAL SAND FILTER

These filters were developed, about 90 years ago, in America. These filters are smaller in size and use coarser sand media. The rate of filtration is 30 - 40 times the rate of filtration of slow sand filter. This filter requires the provision of pretreatment of water by coagulation and sedimentation. They are made of concrete or masonry.

Rapid sand filters are classified into two types :

(1) Gravity filter

(2) Pressure filter.

7.7.1 Components of Gravity Type Rapid Sand Filter

(1) Enclosure tank, (2) Under-drainage system,

(3) Base material,   (4) Filter media,

(5) Appurtenances.

Fig. 7.2 shows the section of a typical rapid sand filter.

1. Enclosure tank : The tank is of rectangular shape in plan and is made of concrete or masonry duly protected with waterproof material. The depth of the tank may be 2.5 to 3.5 m. The tank may have the surface area of 20 to 50 m^2, with length to breadth ratio between 1.25 to 1.35. Depending upon the quantity of water to be treated, number of such tanks are required. All of them are provided in a building called 'Filter House'.

2. Under-drainage system : It performs two functions : (a) It collects filtered water. (b) It provides passage for backwash water for washing filter media.

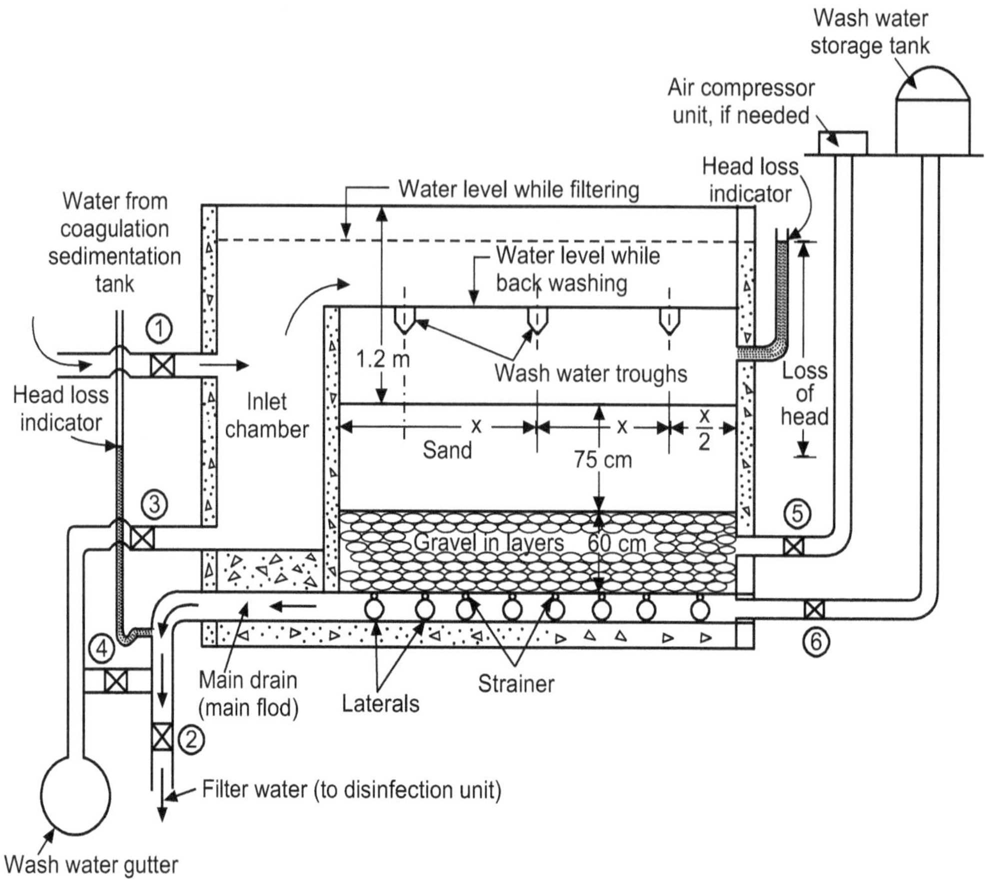

[Figure: Typical section of a rapid gravity filter — see Fig. 7.2]

Fig. 7.2 : Typical section of a rapid gravity filter

There are many under-drainage systems. Only two systems are described below :

(i) Perforated pipe system : The system consists of a central collecting pipe called 'manifold' and lateral drain pipes having 6 to 12 mm diameter holes on lower side. The holes are spaced at 7.5 to 20 cm centre to centres. Sometimes the holes are staggered. The lateral drains are supported on concrete blocks and placed on the floor of the filter. (See Fig. 7.3).

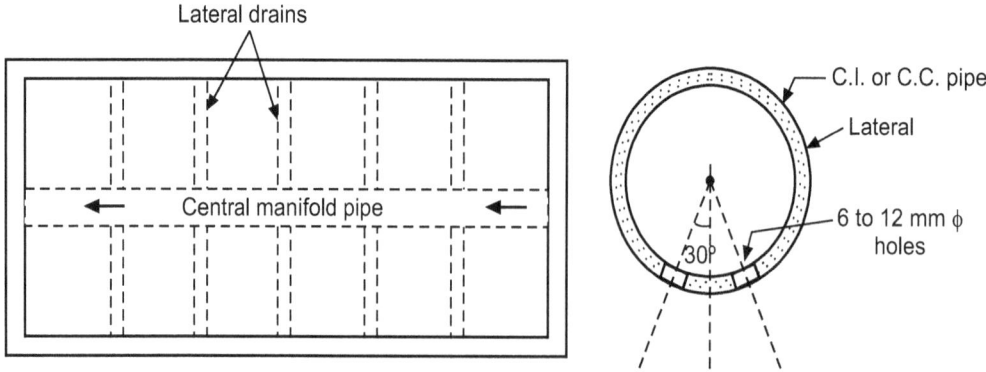

Fig. 7.3 : Perforations in lateral drain

(ii) Pipe and strainer system : In this system, laterals are provided with strainers, instead of holes in perforated system. The strainers have the holes which admit water into strainer and then to lateral. A strainer is a small brass pipe closed at top by a perforated cap. (See Fig. 7.4).

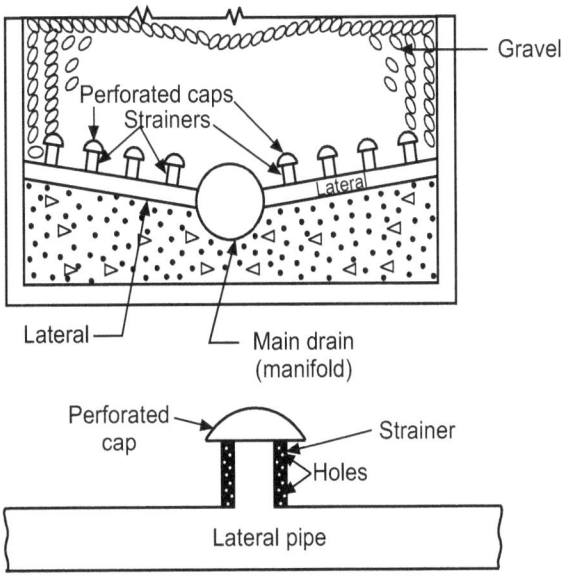

Fig. 7.4 : Strainer system

3. Base material : Gravel is the base material which supports the upper sand media. The depth of gravel may be 45 to 60 cm. The gravel free from impurities like clay, and organic matter is laid in layers of 15 cm each as follows :

Layout	Gravel size
1. Bottom most	20 to 50 mm
2. Next layer	12 to 20 mm
3. Next layer	6 to 12 mm
4. Top most	2 to 6 mm

In addition to above, a layer of 6 to 8 cm thickness of garnet sand (specific gravity 4.2) is placed on the top of filter media to avoid displacement of gravel during back wash.

4. Filter media : It consists of sand layers 60 to 90 cm thick and placed over gravel support. The effective size of sand varies from 0.45 to 0.7 mm and uniformity coefficient of 1.3 to 1.8. The finest grade is placed at top and coarse grade is placed at bottom.

5. Appurtenances : The important appurtenances are : (i) Wash water troughs, (ii) Air compressor, (iii) Rate controller, (iv) Miscellaneous accessories.

(i) Wash water troughs : These are provided at the top of the filter to collect dirty wash water coming out of filter during its cleaning. They are made of Cast Iron fibre glass R.C.C. or reinforced plastics and span across the width or length of the tanks. The position of trough is kept such that it does not carry sand during backwashing and also does not allow dirty water to be left in the filter after washing. The size of the trough is kept large enough to carry all water. The bottom of trough is 5 cm above the level of filter sand. Spacing of wash water troughs may be 1.5 to 2 m. For fixing size of trough, the following expression is used $Q = 1.376\, by^{1.5}$, where, Q is the discharge received by trough in m³/sec., b = width of trough (in m) and y = depth of water (in m) at the upper end of trough.

Typical layouts and cross-sections of wash water troughs are shown in Fig. 7.5.

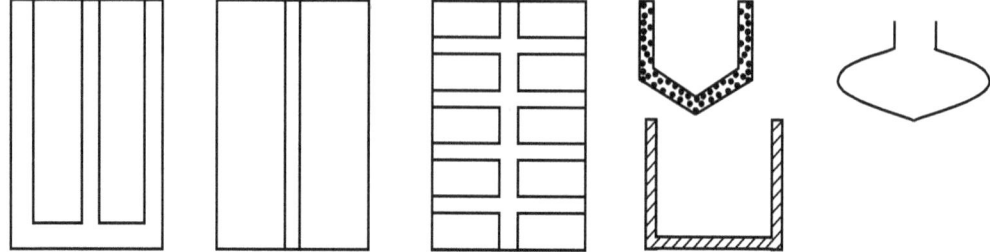

Fig. 7.5 : Typical layouts and cross-sections of wash water trough

(ii) **Air compressors :** They are used to supply air for agitating grains of sand media during cleaning of filter. For filters using air washing, strainer system is used to admit air. Alternatively, separate air distribution system through pipe is required to be installed. Air compressor and compressed air storage tank of sufficient capacity must be provided. Its air supply capacity should be 0.6 to 0.8 m³/minute per square metre of filter area, for a period of 5 minutes. The compressor should generate the air pressure sufficient to overcome frictional resistance in air pipe and also the depth of water above air supply system.

(iii) **Rate controllers :** They are fitted at the outlet end of each filter unit. It ensures uniform rate of filtration irrespective of head loss through the filter. Commonly used rate controller is Venturi Rate Controller. It works on the principle of Venturimeter. A typical controller called 'Simplex-rate of flow controller' is shown in the Fig. 7.6.

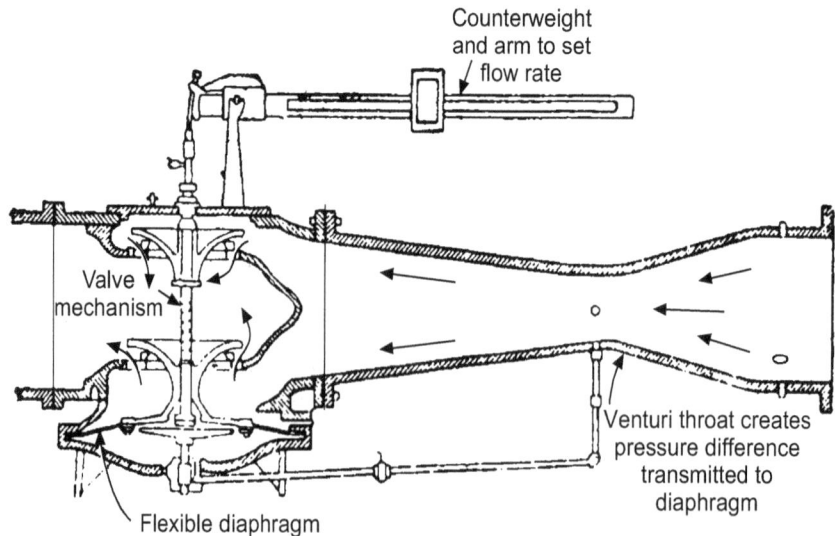

Fig. 7.6 : Simplex-rate of flow controller

(iv) Miscellaneous accessories : Instruments like meters for flow measurement, head loss indicators etc. are also required. Head loss indicator is a differential type of a mercury gauge. One arm of this gauge is connected to the water standing on filter sand bed and other end is connected to effluents coming from the filter.

Meters are installed for measuring flows at inlets and outlets. Meter is also installed to measure flow of water used for back wash of the filter.

7.7.2 Working or Operation of Filter

The working filter is managed by operating inlet valve (No. 1) to admit the effluent coming from coagulation - settling basin, to inlet chamber of filter. This water passes through filter sand bed. This filtered water is allowed to go to disinfection unit or filtered water storage tank by opening filtered water outlet valve (No. 2). These valves are shown in the Fig. 7.2 by numbers. Following valves are needed for working and cleaning of the filters.

Name of the valve	Valve number in the sketch
Inlet valve	1
Filtered water outlet valve	2
Waste water valve to drain water from inlet chamber	3
Waste water valve to drain water from main drain	4
Compressed air valve	5
Wash water supply valve	6

Hence, when the filter is in operation, only valve No. 1 and 2 will be kept open and all other valves will remain closed.

7.7.3 Cleaning of Filter by Back Washing

A separate overhead tank is constructed near the filter house to store the water required for back washing of filter. A pump is installed to lift the sufficient quantity of filtered water to be stored in wash water tank.

It is necessary to wash the filter bed when

(i) A specified period of filter run is over (say 24 to 72 hrs.)

(ii) Terminal head loss is equal to permissible value (between 2.5 to 3.5 m)

(iii) The filtered water quality is deteriorating (if effluent turbidity is > 5 mg/lit).

Procedure : Inlet valve (No. 1) admitting raw water to filter and filtered water outlet valve (No. 2) are closed. Valve (No. 5) inleting compressed air and valve (No. 6) supplying wash water are opened. Thus, air and wash water are forced upwards from under-drainage through gravel and sand bed. Air inlet valve (No. 5) is closed after required amount of air is applied. The dirty water resulting from washing, overflows into the wash water troughs, is removed by opening waste wash water drain valve (No. 4). The process of washing takes 3 to 5 minutes. After washing respective valves are closed except drain valve (No. 4). Inlet valve (No. 1) admitting raw water is opened and filter is allowed to run, but filtered water is not collected for some time and it is wasted for few minutes through drain, in order to drive out balanced amount of wash water with dirt, if any. Finally, when clear water is seen coming through drain, drain valve (No. 4) is closed. Filtered water outlet valve is opened and normal working of filter will commence.

Water required for washing is generally 2 to 3% of total water filtered.

7.7.4 Operational Troubles

(1) Air binding, (2) Mud ball formation, (3) Cracking of filter bed, (4) Sand incrustation, (5) Jetting and sand boils, (6) Sand leakage.

1. Air binding : When water passes through filter, it loses some of its head due to frictional resistance of sand. This can be measured by using two piezometer tubes. When the filter is put into operation, initially the loss of head is less (15 to 25 cm). As the filtration process continues, the head loss increases due to trapping of more and more impurities. A stage is finally reached when the frictional resistance offered by the filter bed exceeds the water head above the top of the filter bed. A negative pressure thus developes. It reduces the rate of filtration and finally sucks the water upwards due to vacuum generated, instead of getting filtered through it. The negative pressure releases the dissolved air and other gases present in water. These bubbles stick to sand grains, affecting working of filter and filtration stops. This is known as air binding as the air binds the filter and stops its working.

2. Mud ball formation : Coagulated turbid particles present in water along with floc, other binders and sand particles get accumulated and stick to one another and form mud balls. These balls are like pea and have 2 to 5 cm diameter size. These are formed due to insufficient wash of filter sand. Sometimes a dense mat is formed on the sand surface. These balls may sink down into gravel, interferring with the movement of wash water. When the formation of mud ball increases, the entire space in filter box gets filled up, seriously affecting the filter process.

Remedy :

    (i) Breaking these balls with racks and then washing off these particles.

    (ii) Washing the filter media by using chemicals like caustic soda.

    (iii) In extreme case, remove damaged sand and replace it by clean sand.

    (iv) By applying surface wash technique.

3. Cracking of filter bed : Surface clogging and cracking take place in the top layer due to entrapping of earthy particles. These earthy particles shrink and cause shrinkage cracks in the sand bed. These are usually seen near wall junctions. These cracks allow further dirty matter to go down right upto gravel layer. This seriously affects the working and washing of filter. The problem is solved by adopting remedies mentioned under mud ball formation.

4. Sand incrustation : It may take place due to accumulation of sticky gelatinous materials from the influent water. This is further enhanced by crystallization of calcium carbonate where heavy lime treatment is used during coagulation process. This causes enlargement of sand particles, thereby changing effective size of sand. These crystals of calcium carbonate deposited on sand grains are dissolved by carbonating influent. In order to keep calcium carbonate in dissolved condition, sodium hexa-meta-phosphate may be used in case of small water plants.

5. **Jetting and sand boils :** These result during back washing. The back wash water follows a path of least resistance and break through the scattered points due to small differences in porosity of sand and gravel. As jetting becomes severe, gravel as well as sand are lifted upwards, causing sand boiling. Jetting can be reduced by surface wash or air scour. It can also be reduced by interposing a layer of garnet between gravel and fine sand media.

6. **Sand leakage :** Sand leakage or downward movement of fine sand results when top layer of gravel is displaced during back wash. It can be reduced by proper proportioning gravel and sand layers. Also a coarse garnet layer can be interposed between gravel and fine sand media, as is done in sand boils.

7.7.5 Efficiency or Performance of Rapid Sand Filter

1. **Colour :** Rapid sand filter is efficient in removal of colour. The intensity of colour is reduced below three on cobalt scale. Colourless waters can be produced if polyelectrolytes are added to water before filtration.

2. **Taste and odours :** Taste and odours are not removed in rapid sand filters.

3. **Turbidity :** Filters can reduce the turbidity to the extent of 1 N.T.U. if the turbidity of applied raw water is less than 35 to 40 mg/l which is possible due to chemically assisted sedimentation.

4. **Iron and manganese :** Oxidised or oxidising iron is removed but it is less efficient in removing manganese.

5. **Bacteria removal efficiency :** In cases of low bacterial loadings, it removes bacteria to the extent of 90 - 99%. In comparison to slow sand filters, rapid filters are less efficient. Chlorination is recommended after filtration.

6. **Wash water consumption :** The filter is said to be efficient if wash water consumption does not exceed 2% of the filtered quantity.

Table 7.2 : Comparison between slow and rapid sand filters

Sr. No.	Item	Slow sand filter	Rapid sand filter
1.	Rate of filtration	100 to 200 litres per hour / m^2	3000 to 6000 litres per hour / m^2
2.	Loss of head	15 cm initial to 100 cm final	30 cm initial to 3 m final
3.	Size of bed	Requires large area	Requires small area
4.	Coagulation	Not required	Essential
5.	Filter media of sand	Effective size : 0.2 to 0.35 mm Cu : 2 to 3 Depth : 105 cm, reduced to not less than 30 cm by scrapping	Effective size : 0.35 to 0.6 mm Cu : 1.2 to 1.7 Depth : 75 cm, not reduced by washing
6.	Base material of gravel	Size : 3 to 65 mm Depth : 30 to 75 cm	Size : 3 to 40 mm Depth : 60 to 90 cm

... Contd.

7.	Under-drainage system	Split tile laterals discharging into tile or concrete main drain; or perforated pipe laterals	Perforated laterals with mains or wheeler system, or Leopald system or Wagner system for under-drainage
8.	Method of cleaning	Scrapping of top layer to 15 mm to 25 mm	Agitation and back washing with or without compressed air
9.	Amount of wash water	0.2 to 0.6% of water filtered	2 to 4% water filtered
10.	Period of cleaning	1 to 2 months	2 to 3 days
11.	Penetration of suspended matter	Superficial	Deep
12.	Supplementary treatment of water	Chlorination	Chlorination
13.	Efficiency	Very efficient in the removal of bacteria but less efficient in the removal of colour and turbidity	Less efficient in removal of bacteria, more efficient in the removal of colour and turbidity
14.	Economy	High initial cost	Cheap and economical
15.	Flexibility	Not flexible in meeting variations in demand	Quite flexible for reasonable fluctuations in demand
16.	Skilled supervision	Not essential	Essential
17.	Depreciation cost	Relatively low	Relatively high.

7.7.6 Design Criteria for Rapid Sand Filter

1. Rate of filtration : 75 – (100 – 150) – 200 litres per square metre per minute.
2. Number of filter units = $N = \sqrt{Q}/4.69$, where Q is in m³/hour
3. Filter bed size :   (a) Surface area should be between $8 - (10 - 20) - 40$ m²
   (b) Length to breadth ratio = 1.25 to 1.33
4. Depth of filter sand media = 60 to 90 cm. It depends on rate of filtration, quantity of water to be filtered, break through index for the given size of filter sand. Hudson formula gives the minimum depth of filter sand.

   Minimum depth of sand in m = $L = \dfrac{Q\,d^3 h}{29323\,B}$ in metres, where, Q = m³/hr/m² i.e. filtration rate in m³ per hour per square metre area (of filter), d = sand size in mm; h = terminal head loss in metres, B = break through index. Value of B ranges from 0.4×10^{-3} to 6×10^{-3} depending on degree of pretreatment received by the water before filtration.

5. Depth of base material (gravel) = 30 to 60 cm (well graded)
6. Sand specifications :   Maximum size = 1 mm
   Minimum size = 0.45 mm
   Effective size = 0.45 to 0.70 mm
   Uniformity coefficient = $1.3 - (1.5) - 1.7$
7. Depth of water over sand : 1 to 2 m

Design criteria for under drain system :

(i) Ratio of length of lateral to its diameter = 60

(ii) Diameter of perforations (openings) in the laterals = 5 to 12 mm

(iii) Spacing of perforations along the lateral = 8 cm for 5 mm holes
= 20 cm for 12 mm holes

(iv) Ratio of total area of perforations to the total cross-sectional area of laterals } 0.5 for 12 mm size holes
0.25 for 5 mm size holes

(v) Spacing of laterals = 30 cm for satisfactory diffusion but limited to total available head.

(vi) The ratio of total area of perforations in the under-drainage system to the entire filter area may be between 0.002 to 0.003.

(vii) Cross-sectional area of manifold = 1.5 to 2 times the total cross-sectional area of laterals.

Design of wash water troughs (gutter) :

Horizontal travel of dirty water over the surface of filter shall not be more than 0.5 to 1.0 m before reaching trough (gutter).

Bottom of trough should clear the top of expanded sand by 50 mm or more.

Upper edge of trough should be placed as far as above the surface of the undisturbed sand surface as the wash water rises in 1 minute.

For working out the size of trough with horizontal bottom, the following expression is used.

$$Q = 1.376 \, b \, y^{3/2}$$

where, Q = Total water received by the trough in m^3/sec.

b = Width of the trough in metres

y = Depth of water at the upper end of the trough in metres

Example 7.1 : Design six units of slow sand filter for the following data :

1. Population to be served = 50,000 persons
2. Per capita water demand = 150 lit/hr/day
3. Rate of filtration = 180 lit/hr/m^2
4. L/B = 2
5. Maximum demand = 1.8 × Average daily demand
6. Out of six units, one unit will act as stand by. Draw its layout.

Solution :

1. Average daily demand = Population × Rate of water supply
   = 50,000 × 150 = 75 × 10^5 lit/day

2. Maximum demand = 1.8 × Average daily demand
= 1.8 × 75 × 10⁵ = 13.5 × 10⁶ lit/day

3. Discharge per hour = $\frac{13.5 \times 10^6}{24}$ = 562500 lit/hour

4. Rate of filtration = 180 lit/hr/m²

5. Area (surface) required for filtration
= $\frac{562500}{180}$ = 3125 m²

6. Six units of filter are to be provided, including 1 unit as stand by

7. Area per unit of filter = $\frac{3125}{5}$ = 625 m²

8. L/B = 2 ∴ L = 2B and Area A = 625 = L × B = 2B × B = 2B²
Solving, B = 17.7 m, L = 2B = 2 × 17.7 = 35.5 m
∴ Provide 6 units of size 35.5 m long × 17.7 m wide.

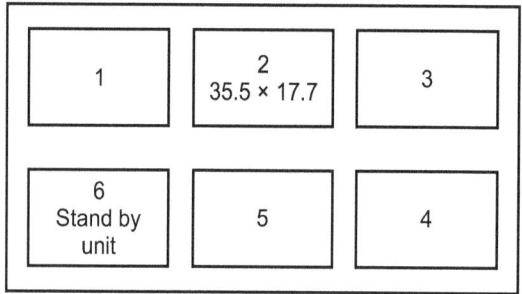

Fig. 7.7 : Layout of slow sand filter

Example 7.2 : Design a set of rapid sand filters for treating water required for a population of 80,000. Rate of water supply = 200 lit/hr/day. The filters are rated to work at 5000 lit/hr/m². Show the arrangement of filter units.

Solution : 1. Daily demand = 80,000 × 200 = 16 × 10⁶ lit/day

2. Assume 3% of filtered water is used for washing filter everyday.
Also assume that 30 minutes are required for filter washing.

3. ∴ Quantity of filtered water per hour
= $\frac{1.03 \times 16 \times 10^6}{(24 - 0.5)}$ = 0.7012766 × 10⁶ lit/hr.

4. ∴ Filter area required = A = $\frac{0.7012766 \times 10^6}{5000}$ = 140.25 ≈ 140 m²

5. Let the size of each filter unit be 9 m × 5.5 m

   No. of units required $= \dfrac{140}{49.5} = 2.82 \approx 3$

   Provide one unit as stand by. Hence, provide 4 units each of size 9 m × 5.5 m.

Design of under-drainage system :
1. Assuming total area of perforations is 0.3% of entire filter area.

   Total area of perforations $= 0.003 \times 9 \times 5.5 = 0.1485$ m²

2. Assuming 12 mm diameter perforations.

   Total cross section of laterals $= 2 \times$ Area of perforation
   $= 2 \times 0.1485$ m²
   $= 0.297$ m²

3. Keeping cross sectional area of mainfold $= 1.5 \times$ Total cross section of laterals
   $= 1.5 \times 0.297 = 0.4455$ m²

   ∴ Diameter of manifold $= \sqrt{\dfrac{0.4455 \times 4}{\pi}} = 0.75$ m

   Provide 75 cm diameter manifold laid along the length of filter unit.

   Assuming spacing of lateral of 20 cm, number of laterals $= \dfrac{9 \times 100}{20} = 45$.

4. Hence, provide 45 laterals on either side of manifold, total laterals = 90

   Length of each lateral $= \dfrac{(5.5 - 0.75)}{2} = 2.375$ m

5. Number and area of perforations :

   Let, n be the total number of perforations, each of 12 mm diameter in all the 90 laterals.

   $$h \times \dfrac{\pi}{4}(12)^2 = 0.1485 \times (1000)^2, \text{ solving } h = 1313$$

   ∴ Number of perforations on each lateral $= \dfrac{1313}{90} = 14.58 \approx 15$

   (a) Hence provide 15 perforations per lateral

   (b) Area of perforations per lateral $= 15 \times \dfrac{\pi}{4}(12)^2 = 1696.5$ mm²

   (c) Area of each lateral $= 2 \times$ Area of perforations on each lateral
   $= 2 \times 1696.5 = 3393$ mm²

   ∴ Diameter of each lateral $= \sqrt{\dfrac{3393 \times 4}{\pi}} = 65$ mm

   Hence, provide 65 mm diameter laterals at 20 cm c/c, each lateral having 15 perforations of 12 mm diameter.

Check : (i) As per design criteria, $\dfrac{\text{Length of lateral}}{\text{Diameter of lateral}}$ should not be greater than 60.

$$\therefore \quad \dfrac{2.375 \times 1000}{65} = 36 < 60 \quad \quad \ldots \text{(OK)}$$

(ii) Spacing of perforation $= \dfrac{\text{Length of lateral in cm}}{\text{No. of perforations per lateral}}$

$$= \dfrac{2.375 \times 100}{15} = 16 \text{ cm} < 20 \quad \quad \ldots \text{(OK)}$$

6. Minimum depth of filter sand, assuming mean diameter of sand = 1 mm
   and B = 2×10^{-3}
   Head loss = 2.5 m

$$L = \dfrac{Q\, d^3 h}{29323 \times B} = \dfrac{5 \times (1)^3 \times 2.5}{29323 \times 2 \times 10^{-3}}$$

$$= 0.213 \text{ m} = 21.3 \text{ cm}$$

∴ Provide 60 cm depth of sand.

7. Depth of filter tank = Depth of under-drains + Depth of gravel + Depth of sand + Depth of water + Free board

    = 60 + 45 + 60 + 100 + 30 = 295 ≈ 300 cm = 3 m

∴ Provide 4 units of size 9 m × 5.5 m × 3 m, one-unit being stand by.

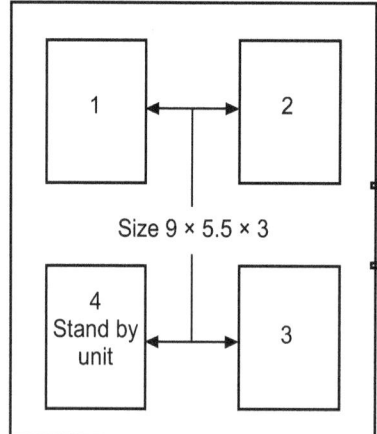

Fig. 7.8 : Layout or arrangement of rapid sand filter units

Example 7.3 : Calculate the dimensions of rapid sand filter for 1 lakh population with 150 lit/capita/day. Assume the filtration rate and mean size of sand 1.5 mm. Find the depth of sand bed for head loss of 2 m if break through index B = 0.002. Assume rate of filtration as 100 lit/min/m². **(Dec. 98)**

Solution :

1. Population = 1 lakh = 10^5
2. Water demand = 150 lit/capita/day
3. Daily demand = $10^5 \times 150 = 15 \times 10^6$ lit/day.

4. Hourly demand $= \dfrac{15 \times 10^6}{24} = 0.625 \times 10^6$ lit/hr

5. Filter area, $A = \dfrac{0.625 \times 10^6}{100 \times 60} = 104.16 \approx 105 \text{ m}^2$

6. Let the size of each filter is 7 m × 5 m, No. of units $= \dfrac{105}{35} = 3$

   Assuming one stand by provide 4 units, each of size 7 m × 5 m.

7. Minimum depth of filter sand in metre is given by Hudson formula.
$$L = \dfrac{Q d^3 h}{29323 \times B}$$
   where, Q = Filtration rate in m³/hr/m²

   $Q = \dfrac{100}{1000} \times 60 = 6$ m³/hr/m²

   $d = 1.5$ mm, h = Head loss = 2 m

   $B = 0.002 = 2 \times 10^{-3}$

   $\therefore L = \dfrac{Q d^3 h}{29323 \times B} = \dfrac{6 \times (1.5)^3 \times 2}{29323 \times 2 \times 10^{-3}}$

   $= 0.69$ m $= 69$ cm

   Hence, provide 70 cm depth of filter sand.

8. Assume gravel depth = 45 cm, depth of under-drains = 60 cm

   Water depth = 100 cm and free board = 30 cm.

   $\therefore$ Total depth of filter basin = Depth of under drains + Depth of gravel + Depth of sand + Depth of water + Free board

   $\therefore$ Total depth = 60 + 45 + 70 + 100 + 30 = 305 cm = 3.05 m ≈ 3.1 m

9. Hence, provide 4 units of filters, each of size 7 m × 5 m × 3.1 m.

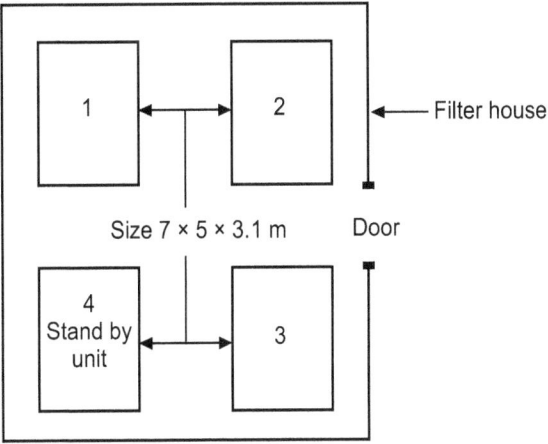

Fig. 7.9 : Layout of filter units

Example 7.4 : For 1 lakh population with 200 litres per capita per day water supply, find out the dimensions of rapid sand filter. Assume the rate of filtration. If break through index $B = 10^{-3}$ and mean size of sand = 1 mm, find the depth of sand for the terminal head loss of 2.5 m. How much water is used for back wash ?

Solution :

1. Population = 1 lakh = 10^5
2. Rate of water supply = 200 lit/hr/day
3. Daily demand = Population × Rate of water supply = $10^5 \times 200 = 20 \times 10^6$ lit/day
4. Hourly demand = $\dfrac{20 \times 10^6}{24} = 0.833 \times 10^6$ lit/hr
5. Assuming 6000 lit/hr/m² as filtration rate,
   $$\text{Area of filter} = \dfrac{0.833 \times 10^6}{6000} = 138.88 \approx 140 \text{ m}^2$$
6. Assuming size of filter as 7 m × 5 m, No. of units = $\dfrac{140}{35} = 4$
7. Minimum depth of sand = L = $\dfrac{Q\, d^3 h}{29323 \times B}$

   $= \dfrac{6 \times (1)^3 \times 2.5}{29323 \times 10^{-3}} = 0.512 \text{ m}^2 = 51.2 \text{ cm}$

   ∴ Provide 60 cm depth of sand.

   Total depth of filter basin = Depth of under-drain + Gravel depth + Sand depth
   + Water depth + Free board
   = 60 + 45 + 60 + 100 + 35 = 300 cm = 3 m

   ∴ Provide 4 units of filter, each of size 7 m × 5 m × 3 m.

   Quantity of wash water = 2% filtered quantity = 2% daily demand
   $= \dfrac{2}{100} \times 20 \times 10^6 = 4 \times 10^5$ lit/day

(Assuming filters are washed once in 24 hours)

Example 7.5 : A filter unit is of size 5.5 m × 4 m. After filtering 5500 m³ of water in 24 hours, the filter is back-washed at the rate of 10 lit/m²/sec. for 10 minutes. Calculate (i) the average filtration rate, (ii) quantity and percentage of treated water used in washing and (iii) the rate of wash water flow in each trough, if 4 troughs collect wash water.

Solution :

1. Area of filter = 5.5 × 4 = 22 m²

2. Rate of filtration = $\dfrac{5500 \times 1000}{22} = 25 \times 10^4$ lit/m²/day

3. Assuming washing time = 30 min. for washing once in 24 hours

   Average rate of filtration = $\dfrac{25 \times 10^4}{(24 - 0.5)}$ = 10638 lit/hr/m²

4. Quantity of back wash water = $10 \times 22 \times 10 \times 60$ = 132000 litres = 132 m³

   Percentage with filtered water = $\dfrac{132}{5500} \times 100$ = 2.4%

5. Wash water discharge = 10×22 = 220 lit/sec.

   ∴ Rate of wash water flow in each trough = $\dfrac{220}{4}$ = 55 lit/sec. = 0.055 m³/sec.

7.8 PRESSURE FILTERS

These are closed vessels. The coagulated raw water is admitted in the vessel under pressure greater than atmospheric pressure. Naturally these vessels must be air tight. Water is admitted by means of pumps and the pressure developed may be 3 to 7 kg/cm². They may be horizontal or vertical type. Steel cylinders, either rivetted or welded, are used as pressure vessels. Their diameters vary from 1.5 to 3 m and their lengths or heights may vary from 3.5 to 8 m. Inspection windows are provided near top for inspection. Various valves are provided for operation and cleaning. These filters contain gravel as base material and sand as filter media and working of these filters is similar to rapid sand filters. Thickness of sand bed may be 45 to 60 cm with effective size = 0.5 and uniformity coefficient of sand = 1.5.

Filtration rate is 6000 to 15,000 lit./hour/square metre of filter media. Pressure filters require more frequent cleaning.

Suitability : These are not suitable for public water supply schemes. However, they can be used for colonies, swimming pools, industrial plants and railway stations etc. The pressure filters are less efficient in removing bacteria and turbidity in comparison with rapid gravity filters.

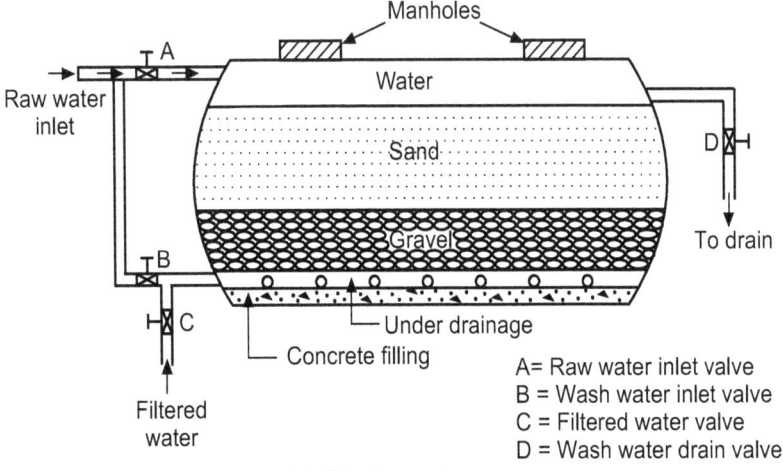

(a) **Horizontal type**

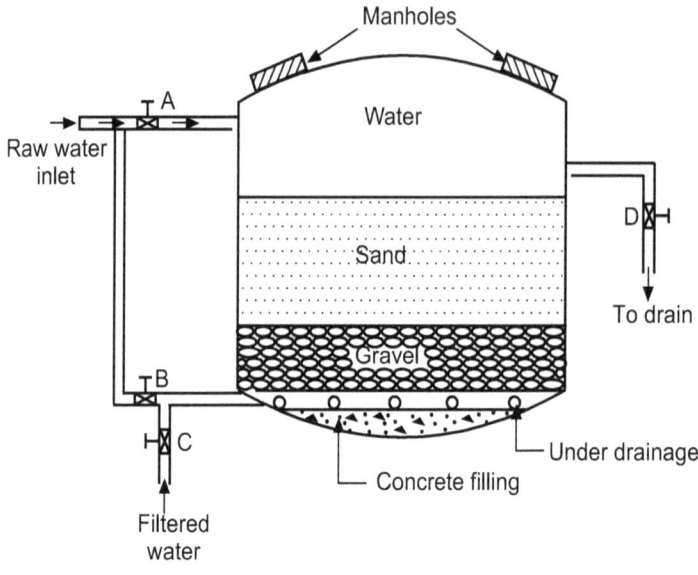

(b) **Vertical type**

Fig. 7.10 : Cross-sections of pressure filters

7.9 ROUGHENING FILTER AND DOUBLE FILTRATION

Slow sand filters yield small rate of filtration of only 100 – 200 lit/hr/m² due to entrapping of bulk of suspended impurities. The filtration of slow sand filters can be increased by providing a rapid sand filter prior to slow sand filter unit. Such a filter, which is provided earlier (i.e. before) to regular slow sand filter, is called as 'Roughening filter'.

The raw water without coagulation can also be applied to roughening filter which will reduce the suspended impurities thereby reducing the load on slow sand filters. Roughening filter has coarser grains of sand used in the filter media thereby achieving a filtration rate of 7000 - 8000 lit/hr/m².

Since, the water is passed first through roughening filter and then through the next slow sand filter, it is called as double filtration.

Sometimes other combination of filters is also practiced. Water can be passed through two consecutive rapid sand filters or water may be passed through slow sand filter first and then to rapid sand filter. Such double filtered water is of a very good quality, free from colour, turbidity and bacteria.

It is very costly and hence uneconomical for large water supply plants.

7.10 MULTIMEDIA AND DUAL MEDIA FILTERS

Now-a-days three different types of filter media are used viz. monomedia, multimedia and dual media. Following is the description of Multimedia and Dual media filters.

7.10.1 Multimedia Filter

The efficiency of multimedia filters to remove suspended particles from water is more than dual filters. Due the addition of the larger anthracite particle to the sand in a dual media filter improves head loss characteristics as well as filter run times, it also reduces the overall surface area. Adding a third layer to the dual media filter improves its efficiency. This third layer is finer than regular sand in order to increase the surface area while it is heavy enough to remain below the sand. For third layer garnet as filter media is used. The specific gravity, effective size and uniformity coefficient is 3.8-4.2, 0.25-0.3 mm and < 1.6 respectively. Table 7.3 shows configuration of multimedia filter.

Table 7.3 : Configuration of multimedia filter

Sr. No.	Type of media	Depth of media (m)
1.	Anthracite	0.40
2.	Sand	0.25
3.	Garnet	0.15

As water flows downward through the bed, it encounters layers of filtration media with decreasing porosity. The larger solids are trapped in the anthracite. The sand removes solids that penetrate that layer. The garnet layer provides the final polishing. Multimedia filters are also sometimes referred to as dual media, anthracite, granular media, multi-layer or pressure filters.

7.10.2 Dual Media Filter

A dual media filter is primarily used for the removal of turbidity and suspended solids as low as 10-20 microns. Dual media filters provide very efficient particle removal under the conditions of high filtration rate. Inside a dual media filter is a layered bed of filter media. The use of anthracite over sand retains the removal efficiency of the sand while providing greater solids storage. The anthracite is placed on the top where it can remove the heavy solids and protect the sand from plugging. Table 7.4 shows configuration of dual media filter.

Table 7.4 : Configuration of dual media and dual media filter

Sr. No.	Type of media	Size of media (mm)	Depth of media (m)
1.	Anthracite	0.90 to 1.20	0.25 to 0.30
2.	Sand	0.45 to 0.55	0.45 to 0.60

EXERCISE

1. Define filtration. What are the objects of filtration ? **(May 2007, Dec. 2010)**
2. Give the classification of filters on various basis.
3. Give the mechanisms of filtration.
4. What actions take place during filtration ?

5. Describe various filter materials. Which is the popular filter media ? Why ?
6. Enlist the various components of slow sand filter. Explain any two components.
7. Write a note on working and cleaning of slow sand filter.
8. State important guidelines for design of slow sand filter.
9. Enlist the various components of rapid sand filter and explain any two components.
10. Draw a neat sketch of under-drainage system for rapid sand filter.
11. State the design parameter for under-drainage system for RSF.
12. What is break through index ? What is its range ? On what factors it depends ?
13. What are wash water troughs ? Give various layouts and cross-sections of troughs.

(6 Marks, Nov. 2000, Dec. 2007)

14. What are strainers ? Explain their working with the help of sketch.
15. What are operational troubles in filter ? **(3 Marks, Nov. 2000)**
16. State the Hudson formula for minimum depth of filter and state the units of various components of the formula.
17. Write notes on :
    (a) Air binding (b) Mud ball formation.
18. Write about the performance of rapid sand filter.
19. Compare slow sand and rapid sand filter with reference to
    (i) Rate of filtration,
    (ii) Filter media - Effective size and uniformity coefficient of sand,
    (iii) Period and method of cleaning,
    (iv) Loss of head,
    (v) Quantity of wash water,
    (vi) Depth of gravel and sand bed. **(1 × 6 = 6 Marks, May 2000)**
20. Draw a neat sketch of a rapid sand gravity filter showing various components.

(6 Marks, May 2006, 2009, Dec. 2004)

21. Why rapid gravity filters are preferrred to slow sand filter ?
22. Describe with a neat sketch the working of pressure filter.

(4 Marks, Nov. 2002, May 2004, 2005)

23. Design rapid sand filter units for a population of one lakh to be scored by a water supply of 200 lit/hr/day. Assume the following :

    (i) Rate of filtration = 3×10^5 m³/hr/day,

    (ii) Amount of wash water required is 5% of filtered water,

    (iii) Filter dimensions of each unit are 17.5 m × 10 m,

    (iv) Filter is washed once in 24 hours,

    (v) B = 10^{-3},

    (vi) Mean diameter of sand particle = 1 mm. Assume any other data not given.

24. Find the area of a slow sand filter for a town having population of 40,000 with an average water supply of 130 lit/hr/day.

25. Explain the working of rapid sand filter. Enlist the quantities of sand required for rapid sand filter. **(Nov. 97)**

26. What are the properties of sand suitable for rapid sand filter ? **(Dec. 98)**

27. Explain the theory of filtration. Why is back wash necessary in RSF ? Give the quantity of water used for back wash and time taken for back washing. **(Nov. 94)**

28. What is the principle of filtration of water through sand beds ? Explain negative head. **(May 94)**

29. A rapid gravity filter is to be supplied with water demand of 2×10^6 per day. Filtration rate is 8400 lit./hr./m². The filter is back washed once in a day for 10 minutes, when head loss reaches 2.6 m. Design (1) The size of filter, (2) Minimum depth of filter sand bed if maximum size of sand is one mm and break through index is 1×10^{-3}. **(May 93)**

30. Write a note on roughening filter and double filtration.

31. What do you understand by loss of head and negative head in rapid sand filter ? What are their permissible values ? What will happen if negative head is excessive ? **(6 Marks, May 2000, 2002)**

32. Give reasons for following :

    (a) The negative head seriously affects the working of filter. **(2 Marks, May 2000)**

    (b) Though quality of filtered water in slow sand filter is better, rapid sand gravity filters are preferred to slow sand filters. **(3 Marks, May 2005)**

33. Compare slow sand filter and rapid gravity sand filter for following parameters ?

    (i) Rate of filtration, (ii) Characteristics of sand as filter media and

    (iii) Method of cleaning. **(6 Marks, May 2006)**

34. Explain the working of rapid sand filter with neat sketch. **(Dec. 2007)**

35. Compare slow and rapid sand filters. **(Dec. 2006)**

36. Draw a neat sketch of slow sand gravity filter showing various components. **(P.U. May 2007)**

37. Compare rapid and slow sand gravity filter. Minimum ten points of comparison are expected. **(May 2008)**

38. Explain in short, five operational troubles associated with rapid sand gravity filter. **(May 2008, 2009)**

39. What do you understand by loss of head and negative head in a rapid sand filter? What are permissible values? What will happen if the negative head is excessive? **(Dec. 2009)**

◈ ◈ ◈

CHAPTER EIGHT

DISINFECTION OF WATER

8.1 INTRODUCTION

Water, after passing through aeration, coagulation, flocculation, sedimentation and filtration tanks, contains small percentage of pathogenic micro-organisms. These processes remove only few types of bacteria. Therefore, it is necessary to destroy almost all the disease causing bacteria.

Disinfection is a process of killing all pathogens.

Sterilisation is a process in which the total and complete destruction of all types of bacteria takes place.

Safe water means :   (a) water free from bacteria
　　　　　　　　　　(b) water aesthetically acceptable
　　　　　　　　　　(c) water free from excessive minerals and poisonous matter

Thus, the process of killing pathogenic bacteria from water and make it safe for use is called disinfection. The chemicals or substances used for disinfection is called disinfectant.

8.2 DISINFECTING AGENTS

The various agents of disinfection of water are as follows :

Physical agents :

  (i) Heat
  (ii) Light (natural sun radiation, artificial)

Chemical agents :

  (i) Potassium permanganate (used in hospitals)
  (ii) Ozone, $O_3 \xrightarrow{\text{heat}} O_2 + O$ Nascent oxygen
  (iii) Chlorine and its compounds
  (iv) Bromine (used in swimming pools)
  (v) Iodine (used in tablet form)
  (vi) Phenol and phenolic compounds
  (vii) Acids and alkalies

(viii) Heavy metals and related compounds

(ix) Dyes

(x) Soaps and synthetic detergents

(xi) Hydrogen peroxide

(xii) Quaternary ammonium compounds.

Historically, the disinfectant widely used is chlorine. Chlorine may be applied as a gas (Cl_2) or as the salts of hypochlorite [$Ca(OCl)_2$, $NaOCl$]. Bromine and Iodine are occasionally used for swimming pool water.

Ozone is produced on site by passing pure oxygen, or dry, clean air in a high strength electric field. Ozone is highly effective disinfectant. Its use now-a-days is increasing.

Highly acidic and alkaline water can also be used to kill pathogenic bacteria.

Irradiation with ultraviolet light (UV) has also been used for disinfection. Although it provides no residual disinfectant, UV is effective in inactivating bacteria and viruses.

The use of electron beam as a method of disinfection is now under active research in the United States. Gamma-ray irradiation is used in Germany and along with the electron beam, is in active research in Japan.

8.3 REQUIREMENT OF AN IDEAL DISINFECTANT

Three categories of human enteric pathogens are normally of consequence : bacteria, viruses and amebic cysts. The disinfection process must be capable of killing all three.

To be of practical service, such water disinfectants must possess the following properties :

1. They should kill all types and numbers of pathogens present in water upto acceptable level.

2. They must meet possible fluctuations in composition, concentration and condition of water and waste water.

3. They must be available at reasonable cost and safe and easy to store, transport, handle and apply.

4. Residual concentrations must be determined easily, quickly.

5. They should act rapidly and should not change subsequent quality of water.

6. They must be neither toxic to humans nor domestic animals.

7. They should be able to leave some residual concentration, against its possible recontamination, after the disinfection is over.

8.4 MECHANISM OF DISINFECTION

There are four mechanisms proposed to explain the destruction or inactivation of micro-organisms :

(i) Damage to cell wall, (ii) Alteration of cell permeability, (iii) Changing the colloidal nature of cell protoplasm, (iv) Inactivation of critical enzyme system responsible for metabolic activities.

8.5 FACTORS AFFECTING THE EFFICIENCY OF DISINFECTION

1. **Nature and concentration of organisms :**

   More the concentration of organisms, the longer the time required for killing the given organisms. A relationship to explain the effect of concentration of organisms is given by

   $$C^q N_R = \text{Constant}$$

   where, C = Concentration of disinfectant
   N_R = Time required to kill a constant percentage of organisms
   q = Constant related to the strength of disinfectant

2. **Nature and concentration of disinfectant :**

   Depending upon the nature of disinfectant, it has been observed that, the effectiveness of the disinfection is related to concentration. The disinfection efficiency is generally estimated as

   $$C^n t = \text{Constant}$$

   where, C = Concentration of disinfectant
   n = Constant
   t = Time required to effect a constant percentage killing

3. **Temperature of water :**

   The effect of temperature on the rate of killing follows the Vant Hoff - Arrhenius relationship. With the increase in temperature the death rate increases. The relationship is as follows :

   $$\log\left(\frac{t_1}{t_2}\right) = \frac{E(T_2 - T_1)}{2.303 \, RT_1 T_2} = \frac{E(T_2 - T_1)}{4.56 \, T_1 T_2}$$

   where, t_1, t_2 = Times to kill given percentage at temperatures T_1 and T_2 respectively
   E = Activation energy (cal/mole)
   R = Gas constant (8.314 J/mole·K)

4. **Time of contact :**

   It has been observed that for a given concentration of disinfectant, the longer the contact time, the greater the disinfection efficiency.

   Under ideal conditions the time rate of kill follows Chick's law of disinfection.

Chick's law : The number of organisms destroyed in unit time, N_R is proportional to the number of organisms remaining N_t at the time t, the initial number being N_1.

The differential form of this equation is given by

$$\frac{dN}{dt} = -KN_t$$

where,
N_t = Number of organisms at time 't'
t = Time
K = Constant (Time^{-1})

If N_0 is the number of organisms at time t = 0, then we have,

$$\frac{dN_0}{dt} = -KN_t$$

$$\frac{dN_0}{N_t} = -K\,dt$$

On integrating, we get,

$$\frac{N_t}{N_0} = e^{-Kt}$$

Or

$$\ln\left(\frac{N_t}{N_0}\right) = -Kt$$

5. Nature of physical agent :

Heat and light are the physical agents that have been used for disinfection. The intensity of these agents affects the disinfection efficiency.

6. Nature of water to be disinfected :

The nature of suspending liquid is an important factor and must be evaluated carefully. The substances like NH_3, iron, manganese and organic matter may interfere the disinfection process. The organic matter will react with the most oxidising disinfectants and that will reduce the effectiveness of disinfection. Turbidity will also reduce the effectiveness of disinfectants by adsorption and by protecting entrapped bacteria.

7. pH of water :

The effectiveness of chlorine gets reduced with increase in pH values. The strong and effective hypochlorus acid is formed in greater quantities at low pH than at high pH values. The following table shows the formation of HOCl.

pH value	Amount of HOCl
upto 6.7	95% of total free chlorine
At 7	80% of total free chlorine
At 8	30% of total free chlorine
At 9	5% of total free chlorine

8.6 CHLORINATION

Chlorine is an element, having the symbol Cl with an atomic weight of 35.45. Gaseous chlorine is greenish yellow in colour and is approximately 2.5 times heavier than air. Under pressure, it is a liquid with an amber colour and oily nature approximately 15 times as heavy as water. Liquefaction of chlorine gas is accomplished by drying, cleaning and compressing the gas to 35 kg/cm².

When chlorine is dissolved in water at temperature between 49°F and 212°F, it reacts with water to form hypochlorus acid (HOCl) and hydrochloric acid (HCl) within few seconds according to the equation

$$Cl_2 + H_2O \rightleftharpoons HOCl + HCl \text{ (Hydrolysis)}$$

This hydrolysis reaction is reversible. The HOCl ionizes or dissociates into hydrogen ion (H^+) and hypochlorite ions (OCl^-) according to the equation,

$$HOCl \rightleftharpoons H^+ + OCl^- \text{ (Ionization)}$$

This reaction is also reversible. It is the hypochlorus acid and hypochlorite ions which accomplish disinfection.

The chlorine is available in water in the three forms :

(i) Elemental chlorine

(ii) HOCl

(iii) OCl^-.

The individual concentration will depend on pH of water.

The undissociated HOCl is about 80 to 100 times more effective or potent disinfectant than OCl^-.

At pH < 5, only elemental or molecular chlorine is present.

At pH between 5 to 10, both HOCl and OCl^- are present.

At pH > 10, only hypochlorite ions are present.

It can be seen that below pH = 7, the concentration of HOCl will be more.

Hence, pH of water to be disinfected should be maintained at less than 7 to prevent great ionisation of HOCl.

Free chlorine can also be added to water in the form of hypochlorite salts. The reactions can be represented as :

$$Ca(OCl)_2 + 2 H_2O \longrightarrow 2 HOCl + Ca(OH)_2$$

$$NaOCl + H_2O \longrightarrow HOCl + NaOH$$

8.7 REACTIONS WITH AMMONIA

When chlorine is added to water, it reacts with organic matters and forms some common compounds. The free chlorine reacts with ammonia, proteins, amino acids and phenol that may be present in water to form three types of chloroamines in the successive reactions.

$$Cl_2 + H_2O \rightleftharpoons HOCl + HCl$$
$$NH_3 + HOCl \rightleftharpoons NH_2Cl \text{ (monochloramine)} + H_2O$$
$$NH_2Cl + HOCl \rightleftharpoons NHCl_2 \text{ (dichloramine)} + H_2O$$
$$NHCl_2 + HOCl \rightleftharpoons NCl_3 \text{ (trichloramine)} + H_2O$$

These reactions are very dependent on temperature and contact time and on the initial ratio of chlorine to ammonia.

In most cases, the two species predominate, i.e. monochloramine (NH_2Cl) and dichloramine ($NHCl_2$). The chlorine in these compounds is called 'combined available chlorine.' These chloramines also will serve as disinfectants. The efficiency of disinfection is 25 times less than that of free chlorine. The trichloramine has no disinfectant properties at all.

Availability of these chloramines in water with pH is as follows :

pH < 4.4 – Trichloramine only
pH = 4.4 to 5.5 – Only dichloramine
pH = 5.5 to 8.4 – Both mono and dichloramine
    pH = 7 – Equal quantities of mono and di compounds
pH > 8.4 – Only monochloramine

8.8 CHLORINE DEMAND

Chlorine and chlorine compounds first react with organic and inorganic compounds present in water before any disinfection is achieved. Further chlorine addition will give rise to unreacted chlorine as residual either in the form of free or combined chlorine adequate for killing the pathogenic organisms.

The difference between the amount of residual chlorine after a specified contact period is defined as the chlorine demand. It varies with amount of chlorine applied, the time of contact, pH, temperature and type and quantity of residual desired.

8.9 COMBINED AVAILABLE CHLORINE

The free chlorine can react with compounds such as ammonia, proteins, amino acids and phenols that may be present in water to form chloramines and chlorine derivatives which constitute the combined chlorine. This combined available chlorine possesses some disinfecting property which is less than free available chlorine. Mono, di and tri chloramines are the forms of combined available chlorine.

8.10 FREE AVAILABLE CHLORINE

This may be defined as the chlorine existing in water as hypochlorus acid and hypochlorite ions. The undissociated HOCl is about 80 to 100 times more potent as a disinfectant than the OCl ion. Free available chlorine is more stronger than combined available chlorine.

8.11 RESIDUAL CHLORINE

Chlorine residuals are used universally in disinfection practice to control addition of chlorine so as to ensure effective disinfection without wastage of chlorine. After the completion of the chlorination at treatment works, the treated water may get contaminated due to faulty pipes in distribution system. To take care of this, it is ensured that the residual chlorine of 0.2 mg/l is present at consumers end. Also during chlorination, the organisms like Cysts of *E. hystolytica* are not destroyed but are inactivated. It takes about one hour to inactivate certain viruses. Hence, residual chlorine should be present in water.

8.12 CHLORINATION PRACTICES

(a) **Plain or simple chlorination :** The application of chlorine to raw water before releasing for drinking is called as plain chlorination. This is used when,

(i) Turbidity and colour of water is low.

(ii) Raw water is less polluted.

(iii) Iron and manganese concentration is less than 0.3 mg/lit.

(b) **Super chlorination :** This is adopted during outbreaks of epidemics and in heavily polluted waters. This is done when :

(i) The water is coloured.

(ii) Plain chlorination produces taste and odour.

(iii) Fe and Mn have to be oxidised.

(c) **Dechlorination :** Whenever higher dose of chlorine is applied during super chlorination, the water contains excess of free available chlorine which should be removed before it reaches to consumers. The partial or complete reduction of undesirable excess chlorine in water by chemical treatment is known as dechlorination. Excess chlorine can be removed by :

(i) Using SO_2, sodium thiosulphate and sodium bisulphite.

(ii) Prolonged storage and absorption on charcoal.

(d) Break point chlorination : Fig. 8.1 shows the status of the residual as a function of the dosage of chlorine. From zero chlorine applied at the beginning of the abscissa to point 'A', the applied chlorine is immediately consumed by reducing such species as Fe^{2+}, Mn^{2+}, H_2S and nitrites. As shown, no residual chlorine is produced. From A to B, chlorine reacts with organic compounds, ammonia, and amines to produce chloro-organic species and chloramines. Free chlorine is not formed. At this range of applied dosage following reactions control the production of mono and dichloramines.

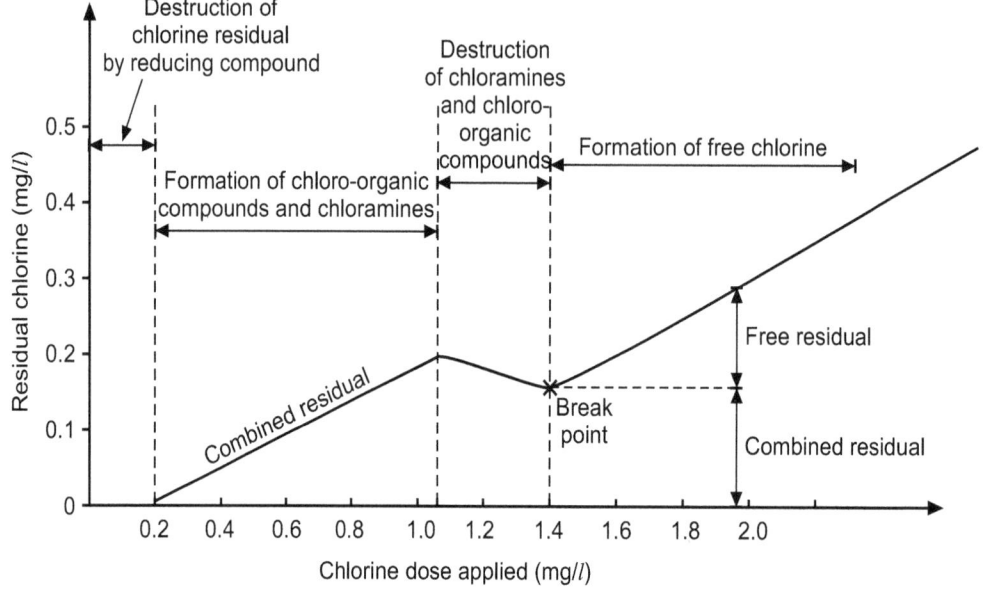

Fig. 8.1 : Break point chlorination

$$NH_3 + HOCl \longrightarrow NH_2Cl \text{ (monochloramine)} + H_2O$$

$$NH_2Cl + HOCl \longrightarrow NHCl_2 \text{ (dichloramine)} + H_2O$$

The distribution of these two forms depends on the pH and temperature. From B to the minimum, designated as the break point, dichloramine is decomposed to nitrogen trichloride as shown below :

$$NHCl_2 + HOCl \longrightarrow NCl_3 \text{ (nitrogen trichloride)} + H_2O$$

In this range of chlorine dosage, the chloramines may also decompose to N_2 and N_2O. Possible reactions for these decompositions are

$$NH_2Cl + NHCl_2 + HOCl \longrightarrow N_2O + 4\,HCl$$

$$2\,NH_2Cl + HOCl \longrightarrow N_2 + H_2O + 3\,HCl$$

The point in the chlorine dose residual curve, at which all destructible chloramines and chloro-organic compounds are decomposed and in which free residual chlorine begins to appear, is called the *break point*. Beyond the break point, the residual chlorine is composed of free and combined residual. *The break point in the chlorination of water may be defined as the point on applied residual chlorine curve at which all, or nearly all, the residual chlorine is free chlorine.*

Free residual chlorine is that part of the total residual remaining in water that will react biologically or chemically as HOCl or OCl⁻ ions.

Following are the advantages of break point chlorination :

(i) It will remove taste and odour of water.

(ii) The desired residual chlorine will remain in water.

(iii) It will remove organic matter and Mn.

(iv) It will complete the oxidation of ammonia and other compounds.

Generally the break point lies between 3 to 7 ppm of chlorine dose, though this is greatly affected by free ammonia from water.

8.13 POINTS OF CHLORINATION

1. Pre-chlorination : Application of chlorine prior to any unit treatment process. This helps in controlling biological growth in raw water pipes, and increasing the efficiency of further treatment processes.

2. Post-chlorination : Application of chlorine to treated water before it enters into distribution system. This helps to maintain the residual chlorine in treated water.

3. Re-chlorination : When the distribution system is long and complex, the residual chlorine of 0.2 mg/lit may not be available at consumers end. To achieve this, stage-wise application of chlorine in distribution system is carried out and is called re-chlorination.

8.14 APPLICATION OF CHLORINE

Chlorine is applied to water by :

(i) The addition of weak solution prepared from bleaching powder, HTH (High Test Hypo) for disinfecting small quantities of water. The chlorine compounds used for this are bleaching powder. Bleaching powder is available under different commercial brands with an available chlorine of 20 to 30%. Sodium hypochlorite and calcium hypochlorite are the chemicals used.

(ii) The addition of liquefied gas under pressure. The liquefied chlorine gas is supplied in cylinders. Chlorine dioxide gas is used for this. It is formed by reacting a strong solution of chlorine (7500 mg/lit of Cl_2 at pH 3.5) with sodium chlorite.

8.15 AVAILABLE CHLORINE

Available chlorine of a disinfectant is defined as the ratio of the mass of the chlorine to the mass of the disinfectant that has the same unit of oxidising power as chlorine.

The available chlorine in NaOCl is 95%. In other words, NaOCl is 95% effective compared to chlorine. The bleaching powder contains about 25 to 30% of available chlorine.

Example 8.1 : Calculate the quantity of disinfectant required to disinfect the 10 million litres/day of water. The dose of chlorine is 0.7 mg/lit to maintain the residual of 0.2 mg/lit. The disinfectants used may be bleaching powder or sodium hypochlorite which contains 30% and 95% available chlorine.

Solution : Chlorine required @ 0.7 mg/lit

$$= \frac{0.7 \times 10 \times 10^6}{10^6} = 7 \text{ kg}$$

Quantity of bleaching powder required :

Since, bleaching powder contains 30% of chlorine.

Amount of bleaching powder $= \dfrac{7 \times 100}{30} = 23.31$ kg

Quantity of sodium hypochlorite (NaOCl) required :

Since, NaOCl contains 95% of chlorine.

Amount of NaOCl required $= \dfrac{7 \times 100}{95} = 7.368$ kg

Example 8.2 : For the disinfection of 30,000 m³/day water, the chlorine used is 12 kg. The residual chlorine after the 10 minutes contact is 0.2 mg/lit. Calculate the dose in milligram per litre and the chlorine demand of water.

Solution : Water treated per day = 30,000 m³/day = 30×10^6 litres/day.

Chlorine consumed per day = 12 kg = 12×10^6 mg/day

∴ Chlorine used per litre of water

$$= \frac{12 \times 10^6}{30 \times 10^6} = 0.4 \text{ mg/lit.}$$

Also residual chlorine = 0.2 mg/lit.

∴ Chlorine demand = 0.4 − 0.2 = 0.2 mg/lit.

EXERCISE

1. Define : Disinfection, Sterilization.

2. What are the different disinfecting agents ? Explain.

3. What are the requirements of good disinfecting agent ?

4. What are the different mechanisms of disinfection ? Explain the factors affecting disinfection process.

5. Explain the theory of chlorination. What are the different forms of application of chlorine ? **(5 Marks, Nov. 2000)**

6. Explain chlorine - ammonia treatment. What are its advantages ?

7. What do you understand by break point chlorination ? What are its advantages ?

8. Explain :
   (a) Chlorine demand
   (b) Combined available chlorine **(May 2007)**
   (c) Free available chlorine **(May 2007, Dec. 2009)**
   (d) Residual chlorine. **(May 2007, Dec. 2009)**

9. Calculate the quantity of bleaching powder required to treat 15000 m^3/day of water with a dose of 0.6 mg/lit. Bleaching powder contains 30% of available chlorine.

10. Write short notes :
    (a) Chloramines
    (b) Effect of pH on chlorination
    (c) Pre, super and dechlorination.

11. Explain what is break point chlorination with figure. **(6 Marks, May 2000, 2009, 2010; Dec. 2008)**

12. Explain following terms : **(6 Marks, Nov. 2002, May 2006)**
    (a) Plain chlorination,
    (b) Post chlorination,
    (c) Super chlorination, and
    (d) Break point chlorination.

13. What do you mean by disinfection ? Discuss the factors affecting efficiency of disinfection. Enlist at least four disinfectants used in water treatment plant and discuss anyone in detail. **(Dec. 2006)**

14. Explain : (i) Simple chlorination, (ii) Pre-chlorination, (iii) Super chlorination, (iv) Dechlorination.

15. Comment on chlorination as the best method of disinfection for public water supplies. **(May 2009, Dec. 2010)**

16. Explain theory of chlorination. State the factors affecting chlorine demand. **(Dec. 2009, 2010)**

CHAPTER NINE

MISCELLANEOUS TREATMENT METHODS

9.1 UNIT OPERATIONS IN WATER TREATMENT

Unit operation is nothing but the procedure in which the changes produced are physical, chemical or biological.

Following are unit operations employed in Environmental Engineering :

1. Gas transfer : The gases are either released/desorbed from water or are dissolved/absorbed in water. In water treatment, this is done for removal of odourus gases and to increase oxygen content in water. Mechanical aerators, diffusers or gravity aerators can be used for this purpose.

2. Ion transfer : This takes place by means of chemical coagulation, precipitation, adsorption or ion exchange processes. Chemical coagulation is used for removal of colloidal particles which impart turbidity to the water.

For removal of Fe, Mn, carbonate and non-carbonate hardness from water, chemical precipitation process is used. Ion exchange method is used for hardness removal, demineralisation and dealkalisation of water. Adsorption process is used for the removal of odour and taste producing ions and molecules from water.

3. Solute stabilization : In this process, water is stabilized such that objectionable solutes are converted into unobjectionable forms without removal. In water treatment, chlorination, liming, recarbonation and superchlorination are the examples of solute stabilization.

4. Solids separation : In this process, suspended solids of various sizes are removed. Straining, sedimentation, floatation and filtration are the operations employed for solids separation. Straining, screening is adopted for the removal of floating objects from surface water. The purpose of sedimentation is to remove suspended solids either by plain sedimentation or sedimentation with coagulation. Filtration removes very fine suspended impurities and colloidal impurities that may not be removed in earlier treatment impurities.

9.2 DESALINATION OF WATER

Water is as vital as air for human life, animals and plants. With the increase in population, urbanisation, sophistication in human life, modernisation of agriculture and rapid industrial development, the demand for water is growing at a tremendous rate. Water is a crucial resource to be developed to cope up with the demand. India, with long coast line of over 6100 km has vital scope of developing single and multipurpose plants for the desalination of sea water to meet the shortage of fresh water. Oil rich gulf countries extract fresh water from the ocean. Kuwait alone has 50 desalination plants. Potable water for use on ship board is obtained from sea water by desalination.

9.3 DESALINATION

This is the process of reclaiming sea water by removing the dissolved salts from it to produce fresh water of potable quality. The processes of desalination of sea water envisage either removal of good water from the solution or removal of salt from the solution leaving good water behind.

9.4 METHODS OF DESALINATION

Following are the different methods of removal of salts from water. The range of applicability of one process over the other is determined primarily by the degree of salinity, composition of feed water and the economic considerations :

(i) Solvent extraction

(ii) Reverse osmosis

(iii) Electrodialysis

(iv) Solar distillation

(v) Freezing method

(vi) Distillation :   (a) Multistage flash evaporator

(b) Multieffect evaporator

(c) Vapour compression distillation.

(i) Solvent extraction : This method is adopted to remove salts from low saline waters in the range of 3000 to 10000 mg/lit of total salts. The organic solvents like secondary and tertiary amines are mixed with sea water to get more concentrated raffinate and then an extract containing the low salinity water separates on heating. The solvent is recycled and the product and raffinate are stripped of the residual solvent content.

(ii) Reverse osmosis : When the salt solution and the water are kept on the either side of the semipermeable membrane, the natural tendency of water is to diffuse through semipermeable membrane to the solute (salt water). The process is **osmosis,** the pressure is **osmotic pressure** (Fig. 9.1).

When the pressure applied to solute (sea water) is greater than osmotic pressure, then water from solute diffuses from solution through the membrane to fresh water side. This is **reverse osmosis**.

Thus, reverse osmosis the forced passage of water through a membrane against the natural osmotic pressure to accomplish separation of water from a solution of dissolved salts. The pressure applied varies between 300 to 1500 psi, with a typical range of 600-800 psi.

The quantity of product water is 70-90% for a feed of brackish ground water and about 30% for a feed of sea water.

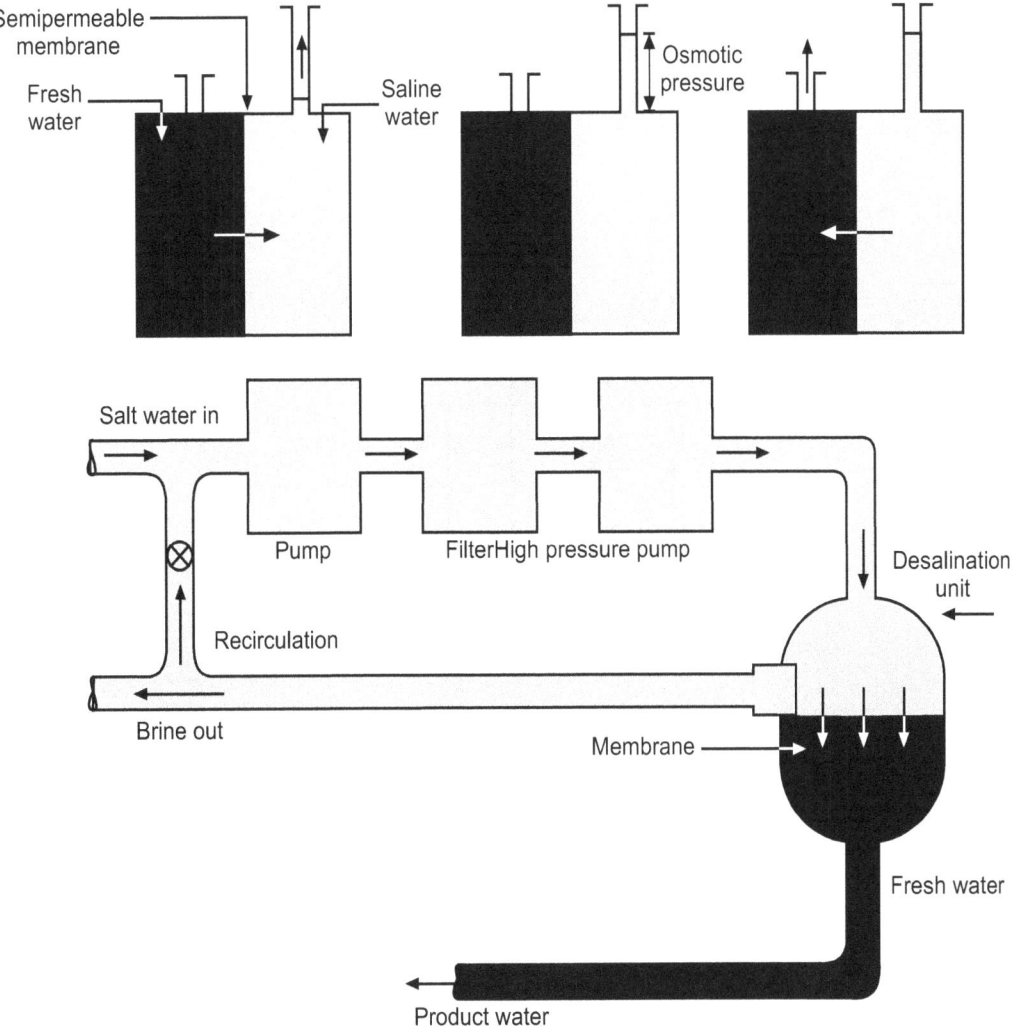

Fig. 9.1 : Reverse osmosis

The two common membrane materials are cellulose acetate and aromatic polyamide. Cellulose acetate membranes have a high flow rate per unit area and are commonly used to form tubes of spiral wound flat sheets. In contrast, polyamide membranes have a lower specific flow rate. These membranes are assembled in modular units that compact a large membrane surface in a cylindrical container fitted with inlet and outlet arrangements. A spiral wound module or a hollow fiber module can be used for this process. The water to be desalinated should be pretreated to prevent fouling of the membranes. Pretreatment may consist of coagulation and filtration to remove turbidity, suspended matter, iron, manganese, softening to remove hardness, reducing the potential of calcium carbonate and calcium sulphate precipitates and possibly filtration through granular activated carbon to remove dissolved organic chemicals. Acid is commonly used to lower the pH and prevent chemical scaling.

(iii) Electrodialysis : Electrodialysis refers to the transport of ions from a salt solution through ion exchange membranes as a result of an applied electric field. As shown in Fig. 9.2, the electrodialysis stack consists of a number of cation and anion exchange membranes arranged alternately. The saline feed is fed through the manifold in alternate compartments. The cations and anions migrate towards the cathode and anode through cation and anion exchange membranes respectively leaving the feed depleted in salt while the neighbouring compartments become concentrated.

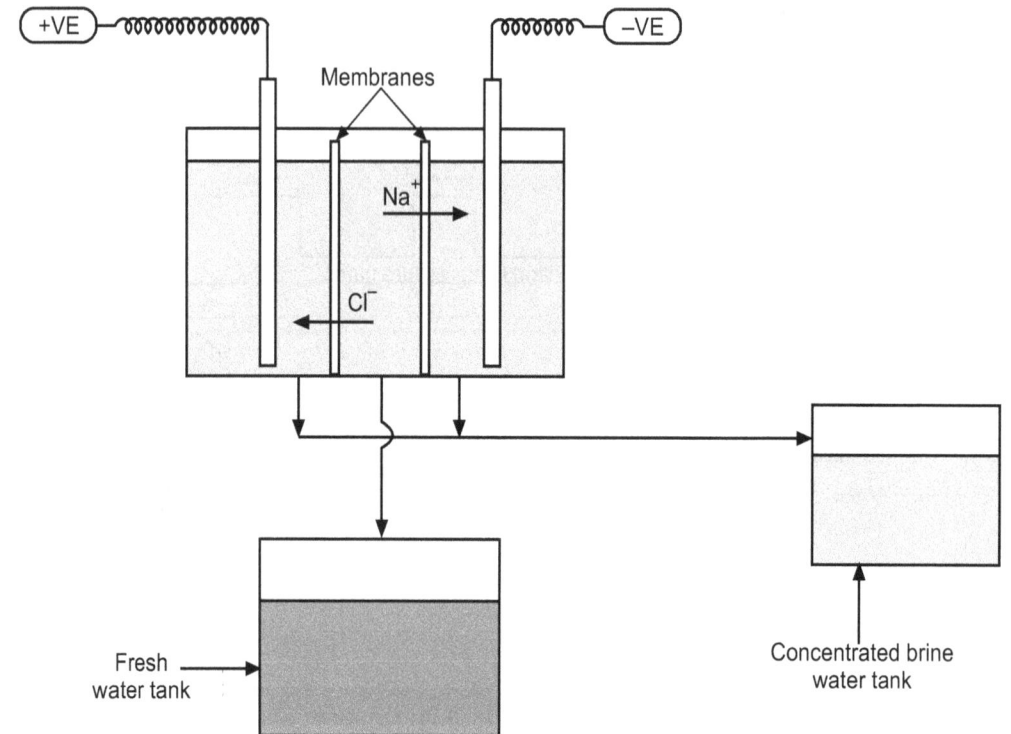

Fig. 9.2 : Electrodialysis

In electrodialysis, the power requirement increases linearly with feed salinity from about 2 kWh/m^3 (for 3000 ppm) to about 20 kWh/m^3 (for sea water). Pretreatment of the feed is required for removal of multivalent ions and foulants. Recent advances such as polarity reversal electrodialysis, use of superconducting spacers and high temperature have reduced the operational cost.

Since power requirements rise sharply with higher initial values in this method compared to distillation and freezing, this process is adopted only for waters containing less than 10,000 mg/lit of dissolved solids.

(iv) Solar stills : Solar energy can be harnessed by the use of a system of mirrors following the path of the sun to focus the sunlight on sheets of water.

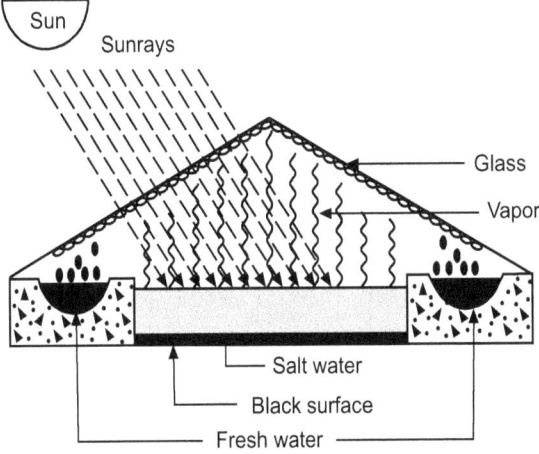

Fig. 9.3 : Solar still

In one of the popular methods, the salt water trickles down to trays mounted on an inclined compartment provided with glass sides and a heat insulated back which screens the condensing chamber from the sun. Since, the focussing mirrors form an important element in the cost of the stills, the development of cheaper non-focussing types of mirrors and use of inexpensive materials of construction have been resorted to. In basin solar stills, a commonly used design, salt water tanks, filled either by gravity or by stainless steel impeller pumps, feed the solar still whose cover is at a shallow angle of $10°$ to $18°$ with the glass pans tightly sealed to the holding frame and the joints between the still cover and the vertical walls perfectly tight. The rate of feed to the still should be such that for each 7.6 litres of salt water, 3.7 litres of fresh water is obtained and 3.7 litres of brine is discarded. The collecting troughs at the foot of the still cover must be constructed so that water will drain freely to the pipe which carries the distillate to the fresh water tank but preventing the entry of any contaminated water either from the roof or the ground in which it is constructed. In addition to the fresh water tank, it is good practice to construct additional distilled water storage so as to balance out the fluctuations between production and demand.

In general, wherever skies are generally clear, solar distillation is feasible upto $40°$ latitude, where 1000 kW/m² of energy from the sun in each year can be available, the solar radiation being more important than the mean ambient temperatures and the wind factors being negligible except as they relate to stresses upon solar distillation structures. The production of water by stills varies from month to month and even day to day depending upon the solar radiation available. The size of still is often to be designed on the basis of the least productive month. Yields of about 1000 litres/m²/year have been adopted for some of the bigger stills constructed and used successfully. The still area needed is given by the expression :

$$Q = 6.008 \times 10^{-3} \times S$$

where, Q = Output per square metre of still area in lit/day

and S = Insolation or solar radiation in calories/cm²/day

The best situations for the use of solar distillation are the isolated areas and certain arid regions where fresh water is unobtainable, solar intensities are high, fuel resources are meagre and industrial development is poor.

Table 9.1 : Technical characteristics of commercial desalination processes

Characteristics	MSF	RO	ED
Feed water	Sea water	Sea water / brackish water	Brackish water
Feed temperature (°C)	120	40	40
Feed Pretreatment	Moderate	Significant	Significant
Product quality	10 ppm	500 ppm	500 ppm
Recovery (%)	50	40/75	80
Power consumption, (kWh/m^3)	16	11 (7)*/4	2-3
Start up time	High (about 12 hrs.)	1 hr.	1 hr.
Suitability for intermittant operation	No	Yes	Yes
Maintenance/corrosion problems	Significant	Moderate	Less
Scale up advantage	Significant	Marginal	Marginal
Commercially viable capacities (m^3/day)	100 m^3/hr. or more	Any capacity	Any capacity

- With energy recovery system.

(v) Freezing method : The method is based on the principle that on lowering the temperature of sea water, it freezes and ice crystals formed are theoretically free from the saline constituents of the water. The crystals can be separated and melted to yield good water. Out of the various processes suggested for the processing of sea water by this technique the principle process envisages use of n-butane as a refrigerant. The process is prohibitive in cost because of mechanical energy and on account of the considerable quantity of pure water required to wash the salts from the ice crystals.

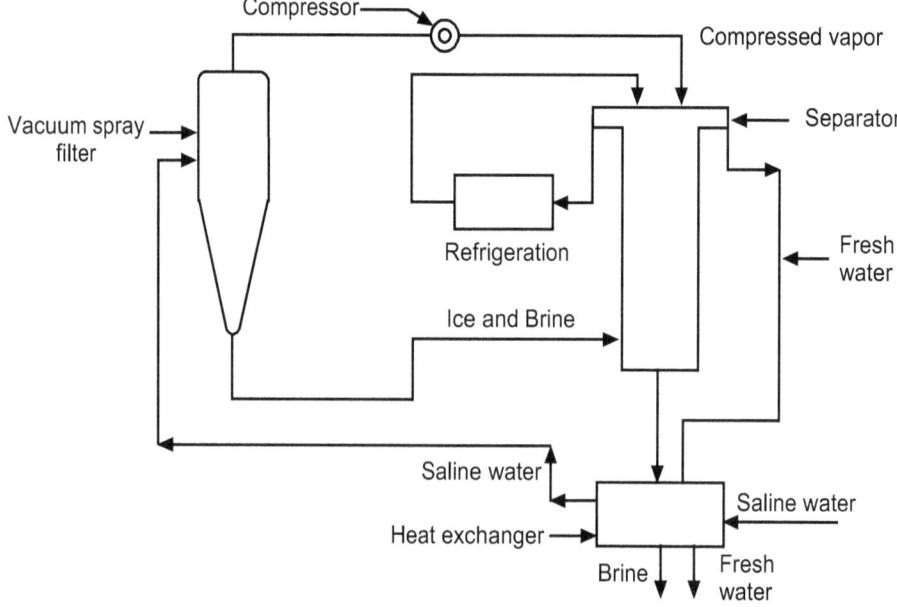

Fig. 9.4

(vi) Distillation : Distillation involves heating feed water to the boiling point and then into steam to form water vapour, which is then condensed to yield a salt free water. The principal commercial processes are :

(a) Multistage flash distillation.

(b) Multieffect distillation. (Fig. 9.5)

(c) Vapour compression distillation.

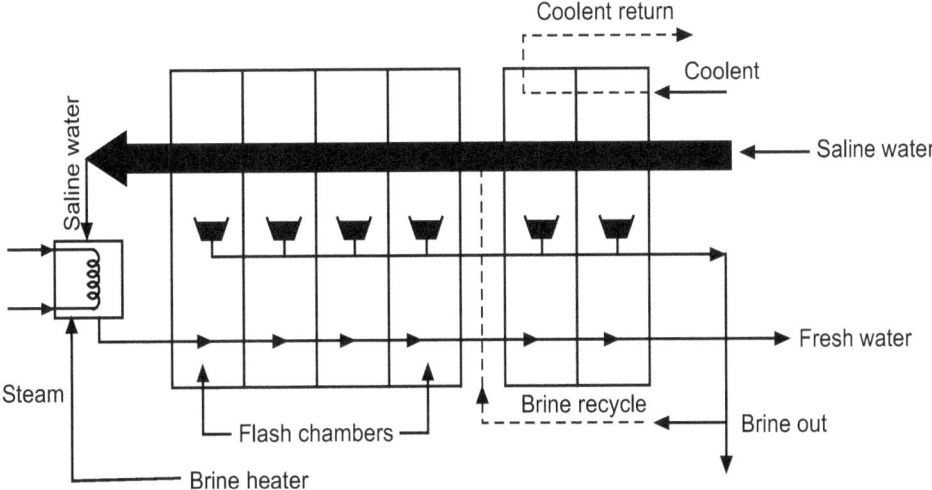

Fig. 9.5 : Multieffect distillation

(a) The raw water feed is chemically conditioned either by acid dosing or chemical addition to suppress alkaline scales inside heat transfer tubes. Oxygen and carbon dioxide are then removed to reduce their levels to 10 ppb and 1 ppm respectively to minimise corrosion and heat transfer problems. The feed water is then passed through the condenser tubes of heat recovery stages and later through brine heater to raise its temperature to 120°C. It is then flashed in stages maintained at successively lower pressures. The flashing vapour condenses on the surface of the heat exchanger tubes and the condensate is collected as product water.

(b) The steam generated in one effect condenses on the outside of long vertical tubes in the next effect, evaporating more water from a film of brine that run down the inside of the tube. The vapour leaving the first effect condenses on the tubing of the second effect, causing further evaporation of water from the brine. This process continues from effect to effect until the lowest pressure vapour is condensed in a final condenser by giving up its latent heat to circulating cooling water. The combined condensate from all affects constitute the product water.

(c) In a distillation plant, steam is used to heat and evaporate saline water. The vapour that is generated is again steam, which can be used repeatedly to evaporate more saline water. This is done in multiple effect evaporator. However, this cannot be done infinitely, because at each step or each effect the temperature of steam gets reduced and after a few steps the temperature would be too low to evaporate more saline water. However, if the lower temperature steam is compressed, its saturation temperature will increase and it can be recycled as heating steam to the first effect. This is the principle of vapour compression evaporation. Here the vapours from the boiling brine are compressed with mechanical compressor and recycled as heating steam. Though this is a distillation process, the net energy input is in the form of mechanical energy to operate the compressor and not as heat. The mechanical compressors are very expensive and also give many operation and maintenance problems. That is why this method is not popular.

In this method, steam at 100°C is compressed so that its temperature is raised to about 105°C and this compressed steam is used to raise the temperature of the feed water to boiling point. This method improves the efficiency of the reuse of the latent heat of steam.

9.5 WATER SOFTENING

This is defined as the process of removing the hardness ions of water. The hardness in water is due to the presence of Ca and Mg.

There are two types of hardness :

(a) Carbonate hardness or Temporary hardness.

– $Ca(HCO_3)_2$, $Mg(HCO_3)_2$, $MgCO_3$.

(b) Non-carbonate hardness or Permanent hardness.

– Cations (Ca and Mg), anions (SO_4, Cl_2 and NO_3)

i.e. $CaCl_2$, $CaSO_4$ or $MgCl_2$, $MgSO_4$ etc.

These are removed by adding lime and soda.

Removal of hardness :

Firstly, the calcium carbonate hardness is in the form of calcium bicarbonate. This is removed by precipitating it in the form of calcium carbonate ($CaCO_3$).

$$Ca(HCO_3)_2 + Ca(OH)_2 \longrightarrow 2\,CaCO_3 \downarrow + 2\,H_2O$$

$$Ca(HCO_3)_2 + Na_2CO_3 \longrightarrow CaCO_3 \downarrow + 2\,NaHCO_3$$

Secondly, the calcium non-carbonate hardness is because of Cl^-, SO_4^{2-} and NO_3^-. This is removed by adding soda ash. The reaction with $CaSO_4$ is

$$CaSO_4 + Na_2CO_3 \longrightarrow CaCO_3 \downarrow + 2\,NaCl.$$

Thirdly, carbonate hardness of magnesium is in the form of $Mg(HCO_3)_2$. This is precipitated in the form of $Mg(OH)_2$.

$$Mg(HCO_3)_2 + 2\,Ca(OH)_2 \longrightarrow Mg(OH)_2 \downarrow + CaCO_3 \downarrow + 2\,H_2O$$

And lastly, the magnesium ion is paired with Cl_2^-, SO_4^{2-} and NO_3^-. This can be removed by adding soda ash or a combination of lime and soda ash. Here lime will precipitate Mg^{2+} as the $Mg(OH)_2$ but will, in addition, also produce calcium non-carbonate hardness ($CaSO_4$ or $CaCl_2$). This is the reason for the addition of soda ash to precipitate the calcium ions.

Reactions :
$$MgSO_4 + Ca(OH)_2 \longrightarrow Mg(OH)_2 \downarrow + CaSO_4$$
$$CaSO_4 + Na_2CO_3 \longrightarrow CaCO_3 \downarrow + Na_2SO_4$$
$$MgCl_2 + Ca(OH)_2 \longrightarrow Mg(OH)_2 \downarrow + CaCl_2$$
$$CaCl_2 + Na_2CO_3 \longrightarrow CaCO_3 \downarrow + 2\,NaCl.$$

Note : The water to be softened contains CO_2. Therefore, when lime is added to water, it will also react with CO_2, consuming more lime.

$$CO_2 + Ca(OH)_2 \longrightarrow CaCO_3 \downarrow + H_2O$$

Water softening by ion exchange :

Ion exchange is displacement of one ion by another. In the process of softening the Ca and Mg from solution (water) are removed on the ion exchange material used. The ion exchange material may be zeolites or synthetic resins (sodium based). These are cation exchange materials. The solution from this enters into the water and Ca and Mg from water enters into these materials.

After the exhaustion of the capacity of these materials, these can be regenerated by addition of sodium chloride solution. Thus, the resins or zeolites again will be put in operation.

9.6 DEMINERALISATION / DEIONIZATION

- **Source of water :**
  1. Precipitation
  2. Sea water
  3. Storage reservoir
  4. Underground storage e.g. tube wells, open wells etc.

- **Mineralisation of water :**
  1. When water from above source, flow on ground, it comes in contact with minerals like felspar, gypsum etc., and mineral salts, sulphates, chlorides of calcium and magnesium get dissolved and this water gets mineralised.
  2. When industrial and domestic waste water finds access in any of the above water source, minerals get added to the water and water gets mineralised.

- **Need of Demineralisation :**
    1. Higher the mineral content in water, higher is the electrical conductivity, more freely electrical current flows through water, and thus corrosive power of water increases.
    2. Also mineral salts like calcium sulphate, magnesium sulphate impart hardness to water and following troubles are caused.
    (a) The water is not potable.
    (b) It makes food tasteless, tough and rubbery.
    (c) Leads more consumption of soap in laundry work.
    (d) Formation of scales on the boilers and other hot water heating systems.
    (e) Causes serious difficulties in the manufacturing processes such as paper making, canning, ice manufacturing, rayon industry etc.

    So demineralisation is needed.
- **Demineralisation is defined as removal of both cation and anion from water.**
- Demineralisation process has two steps :
    I. Cation exchange.
    II. Anion exchange.

    Cation exchange is with the help of zeolite exchanger whose patented name is zeo-karbs, catex and organolite. This zeolite is made from materials as coal and lignite. They are also called hydrogen exchangers and expressed as H_2Z, where, H represents hydrogen ions, Z represents organic part of the substance.

    They are regenerated by the use of sulphuric acid or hydrochloric acid.

    Anion exchange is with the help of a zeolite-like proprietary substance and regenerated by caustic soda solution.
- **Advantages :**
    1. Simple in operation and control.
    2. Plant is compact and requires less skilled supervision.
    3. Desired hardness water or zero hardness water obtained.
    4. No sludge problem.
    5. Economic, especially for industries manufacturing soft drinks.
- **Disadvantages :**
    1. Corrosiveness is not reduced as pH is not reduced.
    2. Water having turbidity more than 5 units injures zeolite bed.
    3. When the total hardness of raw water exceeds 850 mg/lit, this process is not economical.

Cation Exchange :

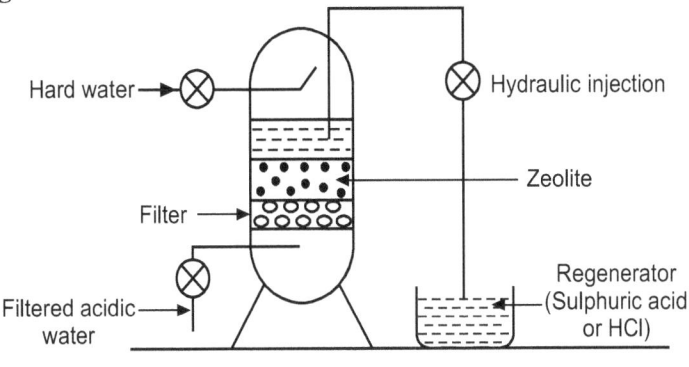

Fig. 9.6

Reactions :

$$H_2Z + CaSO_4 \longrightarrow CaZ + H_2SO_4$$
$$H_2Z + Na_2SO_4 \longrightarrow Na_2Z + H_2SO_4$$
$$H_2Z + CaCl_2 \longrightarrow CaZ + 2\,HCl$$

Now the zeolite gets exhausted of hydrogen ions and hence is regenerated by HCl or H_2SO_4.

$$CaZ + H_2SO_4 \longrightarrow H_2Z + CaSO_4$$
$$CaZ + 2\,HCl \longrightarrow H_2Z + CaCl_2$$

Anion Exchange :

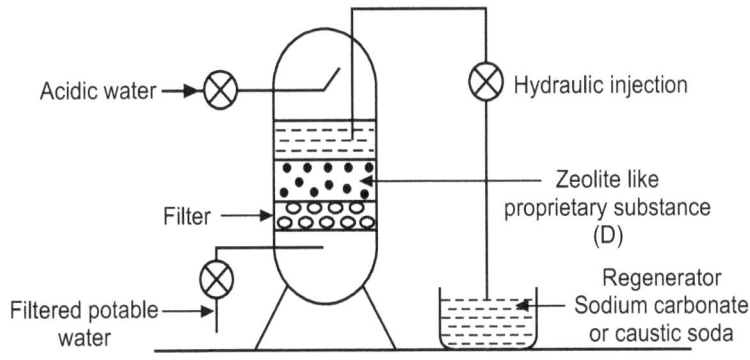

Fig. 9.7

Reactions :

$$D + (H_2SO_4 \text{ or } 2\,HCl) \longrightarrow D\,(H_2SO_4 \text{ or } 2\,HCl)$$

and $\quad D\,(H_2SO_4 \text{ or } 2\,HCl) + Na_2CO_3 \longrightarrow D + Na_2\,(SO_4 \text{ or } Cl_2) + H_2O + CO_2$

Now this zeolite-like proprietary substance (D) gets exhausted of OH^- ions and is regenerated by caustic soda.

9.7 WATER TREATMENT OF SWIMMING POOLS

For swimming pool water should be treated to remain clear and clean, free from harmful substances, bacteria, viruses, algae and other pathogens.

The following are the steps of the treatment of swimming pool water.

1. The water is discharged from swimming pools to a water treatment plant.
2. First water will flow through screens which remove solid particles, hairs, plasters and leaves from water. The screens are in different shapes and sizes. The size of particles to be removed decides the shape of the screen.
3. Then a flocculant is added to reduce the turbidity which may cause by colloidal particles. Due to a flocculant colloidal particles bind together. Colloidal particles are visible floating particles of organic matter, such as skin tissue and textile fibres. This group of pollutants also concerns colloidal pollutants, such as soap remains, cosmetic products and skin fats.
4. Floating particles are removed from water in a sandfilter. Filter is made of different layers of sand that varies in size. However, often many particles escape filtration in this method. In that case secondary filtration is required. The sandfilter is backwashed periodically.

   There is another method of filtration that uses semipermeable membrane for filtering salts and some dissolved matters. Membrane filtration can be done by using following methods :

   (a) **Microfiltration :** Microfiltration is used for filtering solids of very small size that range from 0.1 to 1.5 microns. All the suspended particles of that size and some microorganisms can be removed by it easily.

   (b) **Ultra filtration :** The particles that escape from micro filtration are effectively removed by ultra filtration process. By this method, particles whose size range from 0.005 to 0.1 microns can be removed. Apart from suspended solids, salts and proteins are also can be easily removed by ultra filtration.

   (c) **Nanofiltration :** Particles of size 0.0001 to 0.005 microns are removed by this method. This method is also effective for removal of viruses, herbicides and pesticides from the water.

   (d) **Reverse Osmosis :** This is most effective means of filtration that uses semipermeable membrane. Metal ions and dissolved salts can be effectively removed by this method.

5. To remove organic suspended matter, microorganisms such as bacteria are used for decomposition of organic suspended matter. Anaerobic or Aerobic bacteria are used for treating pool water.

After treatment water is disinfected. Disinfection is an important process in treating the water. They are used for killing microorganisms. Water can disinfect by using chemicals like chlorine, ozone or through ultra violet (U.V.) radiation.

9.8 ADSORPTION – ODOUR AND COLOUR REMOVAL

The presence of colour in water may be due to organic and inorganic matter (iron and manganese). Natural organic matter comes largely from decaying vegetation and can be completely soluble or suspended. Colour is not a health concern and as such is not regulated for health reasons. Colour is considered a contaminant for aesthetic reasons and secondary standards exist to maintain the aesthetic quality of treated water supplies.

Odour in drinking water is caused by sediment and by chemical impurities which can contribute to the formation of lime scale. In ground water, the most common odorous compounds are sulfides, oligosulfides and polysulfides emitted by aquatic microorganisms like actinomycetes, cyanobacteria and other aerobic and anaerobic bacteria.

Odour, tastes and refractory organics can be removed from the water by adsorption processes. Adsorption can be defined as the accumulation of substances at the interface between two phases. In water treatment plant, the interface is between liquid and solid surface that are artificially provided. The material removed from the liquid phase is called the adsorbate and the material providing the solid surface is called the adsorbent.

Activated carbon is most commonly used as adsorbent in water treatment plant. Activated carbon in manufactured from carbonaceous material such as wood, coal, petroleum residues, bamboo, coconut shell etc. The activated carbon is having very large surface-area-per mass ratio, ranging from 500 to 1500 m^2/g. Activation removes hydrocarbons from coal and creates an active adsorptive surface having the power to adhere the impurities on the surface. Activated carbon is crushed into granules ranging from 0.1 to 2 mm in diameter or pulverized to a very fine powder. Dissolved organic material adsorbs both exterior and interior surfaces of the carbon. When the surfaces become covered, the carbon must be regenerated.

Granular activated carbon (GAC) consists of cylindrical tank which contain a bed of material as shown in Fig. 9.8. The water is passed through the bed with sufficient residence time allowed for completion of the adsorption process. The system may be operated in either a fixed bed or moving bed system. Fixed bed systems are batch operations and moving bed system are continuous process. In fixed bed system, GAC is regenerated by removing adsorbed organics through burning (800°C) in the absence of oxygen and oxidizing agent (usually steam) is applied at slightly higher temperatures to remove the residue and reactivate the carbon.

The major problem associated with GAC system is plugging of the bed by suspended solids in water. Back washing provisions may be made in design, similar to filter back wash process in water treatment plant. Design of GAC system is based on flow rates (0.08 to 0.4 m^3/m^2 min.) and contact time (10 to 50 min.) Carbon column can be arranged in parallel to increase the capacity and in series to increase the contact time.

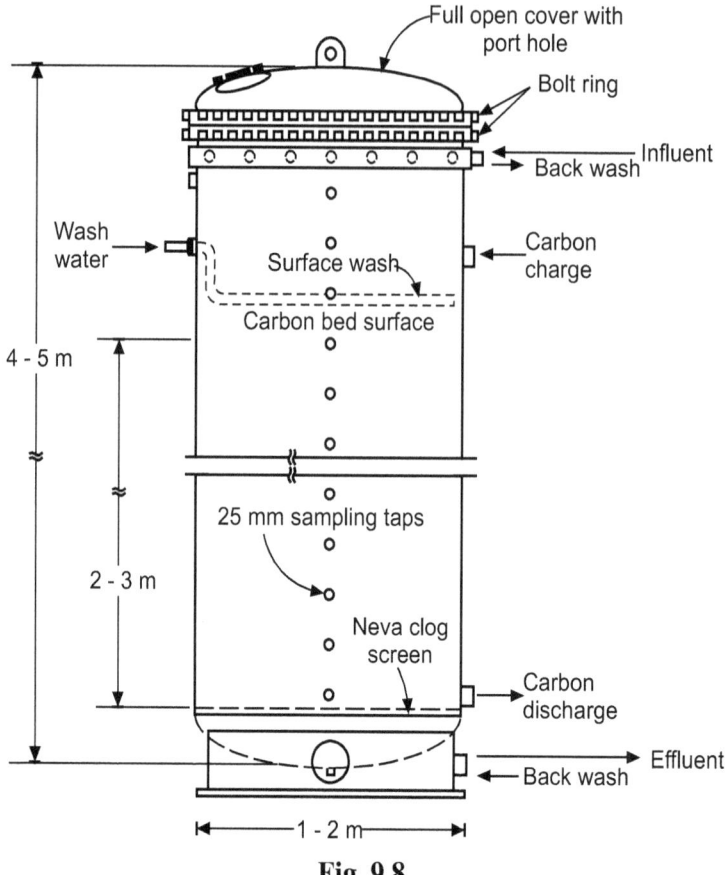

Fig. 9.8

Fig. 9.9 : Activated adsorption column

9.9 FLUORIDATION AND DEFLUORIDATION

The content of fluoride at excessive levels in drinking water in developing countries is a serious problem. Similarly, the control of fluorosis in drinking water is a difficult task.

For defluoridation of water following three processes are used :

(i) Bone charcoal, activated alumina and clay resemble sorption media, generally packed in columns to be used for a period of operation.

(ii) Aluminium sulfate and lime in the Nalgonda technique, polyaluminium chloride and lime act as co-precipitation chemicals to be added daily and in batches. Precipitation techniques produce a certain amount of sludge every day.

(iii) Calcium and phosphate compounds are the so-called contact precipitation chemicals to be added to the water upstream of a catalytic filter bed. In contact precipitation, there is no sludge and no saturation of the bed, only the accumulation of the precipitate in the bed.

(a) Bone charcoal :

Bone charcoal is a blackish, porous, granular material. The major components of bone charcoal are calcium phosphate 57–80%, calcium carbonate 6–10% and activated carbon 7–10%. In contact with water, the bone charcoal is able, to a limited extent, to absorb a wide range of pollutants such as colour, taste and odour components. Moreover, bone charcoal has the good ability to adsorb fluoride from water. This is believed to be due to its chemical composition, mainly as hydroxyapatite, $Ca_{10}(PO_4)_6(OH)_2$, where one or both the hydroxyl groups can be replaced with fluoride.

The principal reaction is as follows :

$$Ca_{10}(PO_4)_6(OH)_2 + 2F \longrightarrow Ca_{10}(PO_4)_6 F_2 + 2(OH)_2$$

(b) Contact precipitation :

In this process fluoride is removed from the water through addition of calcium and phosphate compounds and then bringing the water in contact with an already saturated bone charcoal medium. In solutions containing calcium, phosphate and fluoride, the precipitation of calcium fluoride is theoretically feasible, but practically impossible due to slow reaction kinetics. The calcium chloride and sodium dihydrogen phosphate are used for the removal of fluoride, the reaction of the same is as follows.

Dissolution of calcium fluoride

$$CaCl_2 \, 2H_2O \rightleftharpoons Ca^{2+} + 2Cl^- + 2H_2O$$

Dissolution of sodium dihydrogenphosphate:

$$NaH_2PO_4 \, H_2O \rightleftharpoons PO_4^{3-} + Na^+ + 2H^+ + H_2O$$

Precipitation of calcium fluoride :

$$Ca^{2+} + 2F^- \rightleftharpoons CaF_2$$

Precipitation of fluorapatite :

$$10\,Ca^{2+} + 6PO_4^- + 2F^- \rightleftharpoons Ca_{10}(PO_4)_6\,F_2$$

(c) Nalgonda :

This process was developed in India by the National Environmental Engineering Research Institute (NEERI). In this process, aluminium sulfate is used for coagulation-flocculation sedimentation, where the dosage is designed to ensure fluoride removal from the water. Aluminium sulfate, $Al_2(SO_4)_3 \cdot 18H_2O$, is added to the water and efficient stirring in order to ensure initial complete mixing. Aluminium hydroxide micro-flocs are produced rapidly and gathered into larger easily settling flocs. Due to that specific gravity of particles increased. Thereafter the mixture is allowed to settle. During this flocculation process many kinds of micro-particles and negatively charged ions including fluoride are partially removed by electrostatic attachment to the flocs.

Following are the reactions during the process :

Alum dissolution :

$$Al_2(SO_4)_3 \cdot 18H_2O \rightleftharpoons 2Al_3^+ + 3SO_4^{2-} + 18H_2O$$

Aluminium precipitation (Acidic) :

$$2Al_3^+ + 6H_2O \rightleftharpoons 2Al(OH)_3 + 6H^+$$

A much larger dosage of aluminium sulfate is normally required in the defluoridation process than normal drinking water flocculation. The aluminium sulfate solution is acidic, therefore simultaneous addition of lime is often required to maintain neutral pH in the treated water and complete precipitation of aluminium. Surplus lime is used as a weighting agent, i.e. to facilitate more complete settling. The treated water can be decanted. Filtration is, however, removal of excessive Fluoride.

(d) Activated alumina (Al_2O_3) :

Activated alumina is manufactured from aluminium hydroxide by dehydroxylating it in a way that produces a highly porous material; this material can have a surface area significantly over 200 square metres/g.

The efficiency of the activated alumina for adsorbing fluoride is generally poor on the first adsorption cycle unless the alumina is pretreated. A pretreatment which involves allowing a dilute aluminum sulfate solution to remain in contrast with the alumina for 1 hour is found to be particularly satisfactory. This pretreatment is very important if the alumina is being used on a once through basis or where good performance is necessary on the first cycle.

Activated alumina is aluminium oxide grains prepared to have a sorptive surface. When the water passes through a packed column of activated alumina, pollutants and other components in the water are adsorbed onto the surface.

(e) Clay :

Clay is an earthy sedimentary material composed mainly of fine particles of hydrous aluminium silicates and other minerals and impurities. Clay is fine-textured, plastic when moist, retains its shape when dried and sinters hard when fired. These properties are utilized in manufacture of pottery, brick and tile. Both clay powder and fired clay are capable of sorption of fluoride as well as other pollutants from water. The clay is also good for removal of turbidity of water.

EXERCISE

1. What is desalination ? What are the different methods ?
2. Explain – Reverse osmosis, Electrodialysis. **(Dec. 2008, May 2009)**
3. Write a detailed note on solar stills.
4. Compare MSF, RO and ED.
5. Explain the different methods of distillation used for desalination.
6. Explain the process of demineralization. **(Dec. 2007)**
7. Why softening of water is necessary ? Explain the process of water softening.
8. Explain advantages and disadvantages of lime-soda process of water softening. **(May 2006, 2008; Dec. 2009)**
9. Explain any one method of declination. **(May 2006, Dec. 2009)**
10. State the methods of water softening. Explain zeolite process in details with sketch. **(Dec. 2006)**

11. Write short notes on : **(Dec. 2007)**
    (i) Water softening by lime-soda process.
    (ii) Electrodialysis.

12. Explain ion exchange method of water softening. **(Dec. 2008)**

13. Explain in short zeolite process to remove hardness. **(May 2010)**

14. Explain electrodialysis. **(Dec. 2010)**

15. Explain zeolite process to remove hardness. Give the approximate chemical equations. **(Dec. 2010)**

CHAPTER TEN

WATER DISTRIBUTION SYSTEM

10.1 INTRODUCTION

Distribution of water is the last phase of any water supply scheme. The function of distribution system is to furnish treated water in required quantity maintaining its quality under required pressure wherever it is needed in the city or town. The consumption of water may be for residential, industrial, commercial or public purpose etc.

The distribution system consists of the following :

1. Network of pipes comprising of –

    (a) Mains of large diameter

    (b) Submains

    (c) Branches

    (d) Feeders or laterals.

2. Valves for controlling the flow in the pipes

3. Fire hydrants

4. Service connection

5. Water meters

6. Distribution reservoir (Service reservoir)

7. Pumps.

10.2 FACTORS OR REQUIREMENTS CONSIDERED IN THE DESIGN OF DISTRIBUTION SYSTEM

The following factors or requirements should be considered in the design of distribution system :

1. It should satisfy all the types of demands including fire demand of the town.

2. It should be capable to meet the maximum hourly flow.

    The manual of government of India has given the following peak factors according to population :

Population	Peak factor
(a) Upto 50,000	3.0
(b) Between 50,000 to 2 lakhs	2.5
(c) More than 2 lakhs	2.0

3. It should provide water at consumer's tap with adequate pressure head.

4. It should maintain the degree of purity while conveying the treated water from water works to consumer.

5. Pipes in the distribution network should be completely water-tight to avoid contamination of water.

6. The cost of construction and maintenance of the distribution system should be minimum. The cost of distribution system is about 65 to 70% of the total cost of the water supply scheme.

7. During repairs, there should not be any obstruction to traffic. Also there should be alternate path of flow of water to be served to the people in the area during repairs.

8. The shell of pipes used should be sufficiently thick to avoid bursting of pipe due to pressure flow.

10.3 ZONEING OF AREAS

The nature of topography of the area occupied by town or city cannot be expected to be flat. It will have natural undulations. To know the nature of ground, contour map is prepared by carrying out contour survey. The map will enable the design engineer to divide the city or town into high level, low level to medium level portions, with reference to treatment works. Such portions or areas are called as *zones*. Each zone may be further subdivided into small areas called *'districts'*. The population of each district may vary from 10 to 20 thousand or more. Water can be distributed independently to each zone by a separate service reservoir.

Water can be supplied by gravity flow to low lying zone. For medium and high level zones, suitable site is selected for errecting service reservoirs. Water can be pumped in such reservoirs and then distributed under gravity in that zone.

Water in all the zones should be available to tail end consumer with a minimum pressure of 8 to 10 metres of water.

10.4 CLASSIFICATION OF DISTRIBUTION SYSTEM

Depending upon the topography of the town, the water may be distributed by

1. Pumping
2. Gravity or
3. Combination of pumping and gravity (Dual System).

10.4.1 Pumping System

The treated water is directly pumped into distribution mains, without storing in high level reservoirs. High lift pumps are provided for forcing water into mains.

Since, the demand of water is fluctuating, the pumps have to operate at various rates during the whole day. A continuous attendance is required at the pumping station to regulate the flow by running only the required number of pumps out of the total number of pumps installed.

During failure of pumps or electric supply, the water supply to the town may be interrupted. To avoid this, it is desirable to have some units of pumps running on diesel.

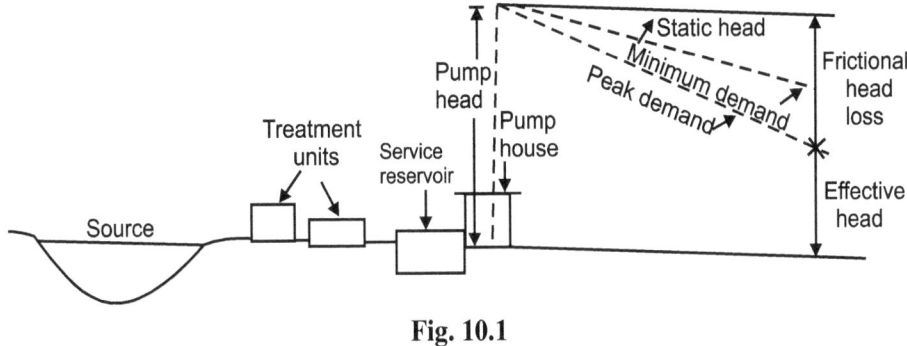

Fig. 10.1

Pumping system can supply the required quantity of water for fire fighting by running all the pumps including standby. The system is costly and its use should be discouraged as far as possible.

10.4.2 Gravity System

In this system, the gravity force is used in distributing water from high level source to the low level zone consumers.

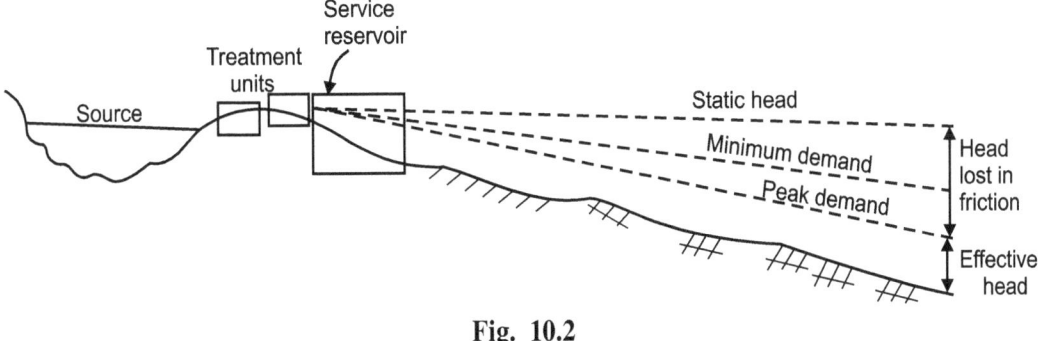

Fig. 10.2

This eliminates pumping altogether. The method is economical, reliable and requires less maintenance. For proper working of the system, the difference of head available between service reservoir and low level zone should be sufficient to develop enough pressure at the consumer's tap. The method also minimises wastages and leakages.

10.4.3 Combination of Pumping and Gravity (Dual System)

In this system, the water after treatment is pumped and stored in the Elevated Service Reservoir (ESR). According to the supply hours, the stored water is supplied to the public by gravity. The Fig. 10.3 shows pump house, ESR and hydraulic grades for minimum and peak demands. The system enables the pumps to operate at constant speeds, at designed optimum efficiency, reducing wear and tear and overall cost.

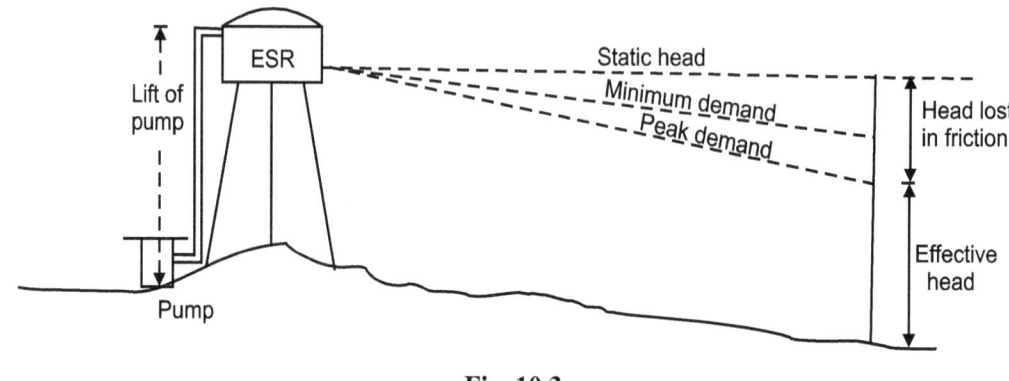

Fig. 10.3

Advantages :

1. The system is economical, efficient and reliable and adopted practically everywhere.
2. Pumping at constant rate increases efficiency.
3. Special supervision is not required.
4. Fire demands can be efficiently met with.
5. Water is available even during failure of pump or power.

10.4.4 Layouts of Distribution Pipe Network

Distribution pipes are always laid below the roads prevailing in the town. Also they are laid on one side of the road, keeping the other side of the road for laying of sewers in future. The layout of pipe-lines naturally follows the patterns of roads. Following are the four types of systems. They can be used singularly or in combination as required by local conditions.

1. Tree or Dead end System
2. Ring or Circular System
3. Grid or Interlaced System
4. Radial System.

(a) Tree or Dead end system :

The layout of pipe-lines resembles the nature of the 'tree' and hence the name. There is one main pipe-line from which number of submains are taken out according to number of roads. From each submain, number of branch lines are taken out. From each branch lateral feeder is taken out, from where service connections are given to the consumers. Branch lines are sometimes used for giving service connections. Water flows from main line to submain and then to branches. The water thus flows only in one direction through all pipes till it comes to dead ends. Hence, the system is popularly known as *dead end system*. The system is suitable for old towns having unplanned roads and localities having uncontrolled growth. Such layout is shown in Fig. 10.4.

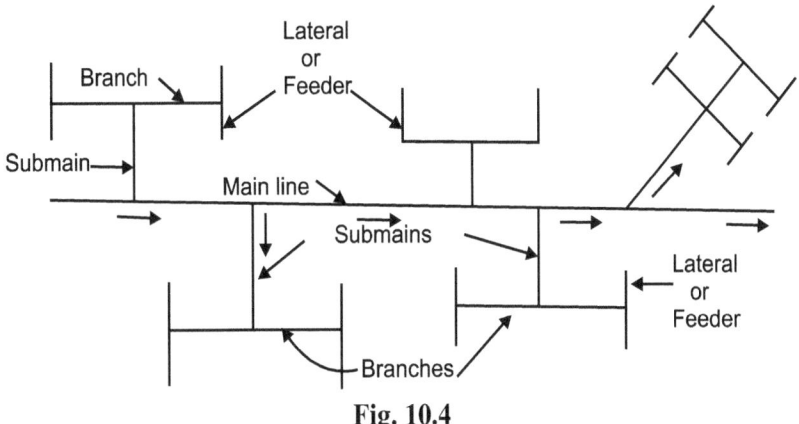

Fig. 10.4

Merits :
1. The system is simple, economical and can be extended according to the growth.
2. For controlling flow of water, the number of sluice valves (also called as cut-off valves) required are less.
3. The discharge and pressure head at various points in the system can be worked out easily.
4. The diameter and length of feeder pipe required is small as it serves a restricted population.

Demerits :
1. For fire fighting, sufficient water may not be available as only one pipe is supplying water.
2. Due to numerous dead ends, water does not have free circulation which may lead to contamination.
3. In case of repairs of damaged pipe-line, the water supply fed by that pipe will be completely stopped till the repairs are completed.

(b) Ring or Circular system :

In this system, main pipes are laid around the area of the zone to be served. Depending upon the pattern of roads, the closed ring may be circular or rectangular. The discharge is divided into two parts each going along the boundary enclosing the area in the zone, and meet again at other end. Cross pipes connecting two mains form submains. The system is suitable for towns having well planned roads crossing one another at right angles. The layout is shown in Fig. 10.5.

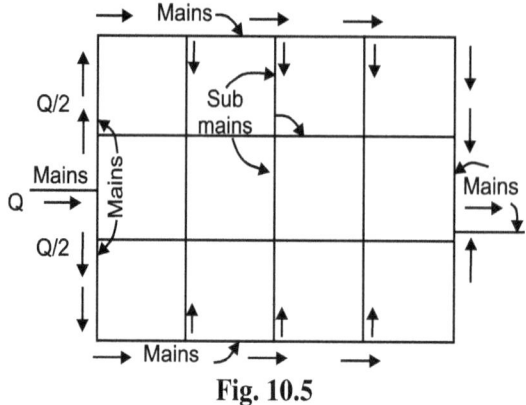

Fig. 10.5

Merits :
1. The water reaches at a particular point from two routes or directions.
2. Water is available from all directions for extinguishing fire.
3. During repairs, water supply can be made from other submains.
4. Designing of pipe is simple and easy.

Demerits :
1. The system is costly to construct.
2. It requires more length of pipes and more number of sluice valves.

(c) Grid or Interlaced system :

It is also known as *reticulation system*. In this system mains, submains and branches are all inter-connected. In well planned city, growth of town is allowed to take place in a predetermined manner. The roads are planned in a grid iron form. The pipe-lines laid under such roads naturally form grid iron shape. This system is provided in Chandigarh in Punjab. The system is therefore recommended for well planned towns. The layout is shown in the Fig. 10.6.

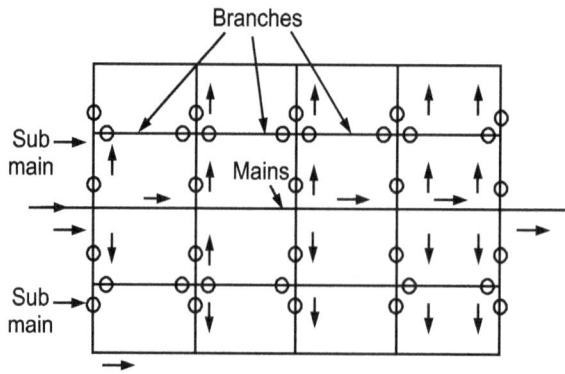

Fig. 10.6

Merits :
1. Since there are no dead ends, there is a free circulation of water.
2. Head loss is minimum in the system.
3. For fire fighting, water is available from all directions.
4. During breakdowns, water supply can be made from other submains.

Demerits :
1. The system requires more valves and longer pipes making the system costly.
2. Calculation of diameter of pipe and pressure at point is not easy.

(d) Radial System :

The system consists of laying pipe-lines radially, ending at the periphery of the area of the zone. In each zone, elevated service reservoir is placed at its centre, from where water is admitted to these radially laid pipes known as branches, as shown in Fig. 10.7. Water is pumped into these service reservoirs through mains and water is withdrawn through radially laid branches for consumers during supply hours.

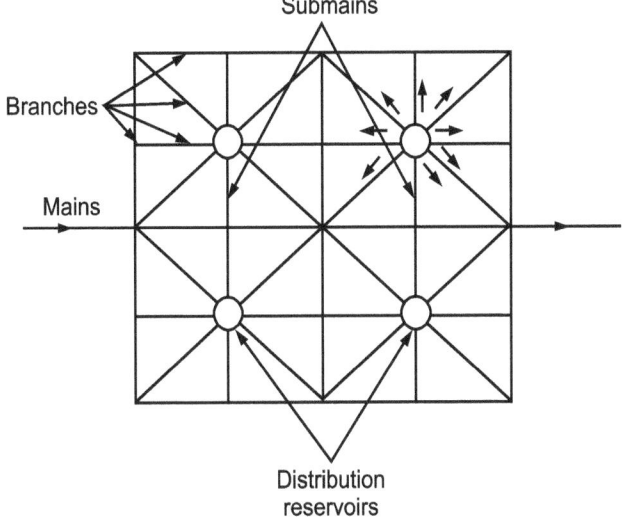

Fig. 10.7

Merits :
1. Water is supplied to the consumers with high pressure.
2. Designing of pipe sizes is simple.
3. There is quick and efficient supply of water.

Demerits :

As every zone requires a separate service reservoir, number of reservoirs required are more, and hence the system becomes costly.

10.5 SYSTEMS OF WATER SUPPLY

There are two systems of water supply to the public :

1. Continuous system
2. Intermittent system

(i) Continuous System :

In this system, water is supplied throughout the day i.e. for 24 hours without any break. When the water available for distribution is in abundance, this system is used. The system is ideal, since the water is not remaining stagnant at any time in the pipe-line and fresh water is always available to the public.

(ii) Intermittent System :

In this system, water is supplied to the public during some fixed hours of the day. Hence, the supply is said to be *intermittent*. Generally, the water supply is 3-4 hours in the morning as well as in the evening. The system is required to be adopted when sufficient quantity of water is not available or when sufficient pressure cannot be maintained in the system. Under such circumstances, various zones in the town are supplied with water by rotation. This system is most widely used in India.

Comparison between Continuous and Intermittent System :

Continuous System	Intermittent System
1. Consumers are not required to store the water and no danger of water pollution.	1. Consumers are forced to store the water for non-supply hours, which may get polluted.
2. Water is available for fire-fighting in case of fire break.	2. In case of fire during non-supply hours, water may not be available causing damage to property.
3. Smaller sizes of pipes are needed for distribution of water throughout the day in the pipe.	3. Large sizes of pipes are required as the daily demand is to be supplied in a small period.
4. Water is under constant circulation and hence remains fresh.	4. During non-supply hours, pipes get emptied and outside water may finally enter in the pipe through cracks and leaky joints leading to contamination of water during supply hours.
5. Less number of valves and fittings are required as the water flows.	5. Large number of valves and fittings are required.

... Contd.

6. Water will be kept closed by the consumers and no wastage of water.	6. Water taps may be left open by consumers during non-supply hours leading to wastage. Also people have a tendency to throw stored water to get fresh water.
7. This system is very much convenient to all consumers as the water is available at any time.	7. This system is unsuitable to all consumers as they are to wait till the supply starts when the stored water gets exhausted.
8. For carrying out repairs, the supply is required to be stopped causing great inconvenience to consumers.	8. Repairs can be conveniently done during non-supply hours.
9. Operational staff like valve man, etc. required is less.	9. Extra staff is required to operate and maintain various valves in the system.

10.6 PRESSURE IN THE DISTRIBUTION SYSTEM

When the water enters the distribution system, progressively it loses head as it flows through pipes, bend valves and other fittings due to friction. The effective head available at the service connection of the consumer should be sufficient so that the water will rise to the top floor of the building. The pressure required at a particular point in the system depends upon :

1. The height of the tallest building in that zone.
2. The distance of the point from the service reservoir.
3. The pressure to be maintained near fire hydrant.
4. The provision of water meters, since there is a high loss of head when water flows through meter.
5. Funds available for the water supply scheme. Higher pressure at consumer's end means higher elevation of distribution reservoir, increasing the cost of the scheme.

The following pressures are considered satisfactory in residential and commercial areas.

(a) Residential areas :

Upto 3 storeys	– 2 kg/cm^2
3 to 6 storeys	– 2 to 4 kg/cm^2
6 to 10 storeys	– 4 to 5.5 kg/cm^2
Above 10 storeys	– 5.5 to 7 kg/cm^2

(b) Commercial areas : (5 kg/cm^2)

In the areas with single storeyed structures, the residual pressure of 1 kg/cm^2 should be maintained.

For fire fighting, Board of Fire Underwriters recommends a pressure of 5 kg/cm^2 at the fire nozzle, where there are more than ten buildings having more than three storeys, in that locality. In the areas with less risk, the pressure at the nozzle may be upto 4 kg/cm². In the thinly populated areas, fire pressure upto 3.5 kg/cm² is sufficient.

When fire engines are used for fire fighting, a minimum pressure of 1.5 kg/cm² must be available under normal conditions.

In the distribution system, a minimum velocity of 0.6 m/sec. should be maintained. Also maximum velocity should not be more than 3 m/sec. The velocities in the various pipes should be as follows :

Pipe diameter in mm	Velocity in m/sec.
100	0.9
150	1.2
250	1.5
400	1.8

10.6.1 Methods for Maintaining the Adequate Pressure in the Distribution System

1. Balancing reservoir : Balancing reservoir is constructed, which stores the water when demand is less than the rate of supply. When demand exceeds the rate of supply, water flows from the balancing reservoir to supply line, such reservoirs are needed in case of direct pumping of water into the distribution system.

2. Central location of reservoir : A reservoir is constructed in a central place of that zone. This will reduce the lengths of supply pipe-lines causing reduction in frictional losses and increasing residual pressure at consumer's end.

3. Booster Pumps : For tail end distant localities, provision of booster pumps can maintain the adequate pressure in the system.

10.6.2 Distribution or Service Reservoirs

These are the tanks, either constructed or fabricated, to store the treated water to be supplied to various consumers of the town or city, as and when required with minimum interruption. They serve the following functions :

1. They provide and maintain the desired constant pressure in the distribution system, including remote areas.
2. They reduce pressure fluctuations.
3. They provide emergency storage for fire, failure of pump or power and bursting of mains.
4. They absorb hourly variations in demand.
5. They enable the pumps to run at uniform rate during designed pumping hours (8 to 16 hours pumping).
6. They help in reducing the sizes of pipes and capacities of the pumps thereby making the distribution system economical.
7. In case of small installations, they avoid 24 hours pumping.

Classification of Service Reservoirs :

1. **Based on materials of construction :**
   (a) Masonry
   (b) Steel
   (c) R.C.C.

2. **Based on elevation with respect to ground :**
   (a) Surface reservoirs or ground reservoirs
   (b) Stand pipes
   (c) Elevated reservoirs

3. **Based on shape :**
   (a) Rectangular tanks
   (b) Circular tanks
   (c) Intze type tanks.

10.6.2.1 Surface Reservoirs

These reservoirs are constructed either at ground level or below ground level and hence are known as *ground reservoirs*. They are rectangular or circular in shape and are made of masonry or concrete. To control leakage of water from the reservoir, inside surfaces are lined with granite, concrete, asphalt or asphaltic membrane.

Sometimes these reservoirs are built underground when they are large and garden is developed on their top. One such hanging garden is existing in Mumbai city.

A typical section of surface reservoir is shown in Fig. 10.8. It is generally constructed into two or three compartments. During the repairs and cleaning, one compartment will be completely emptied and other compartment will remain in operation. There is interconnection between two compartments controlled by shut off valve. A drain pipe with scour valve is provided at the bottom of reservoir for cleaning.

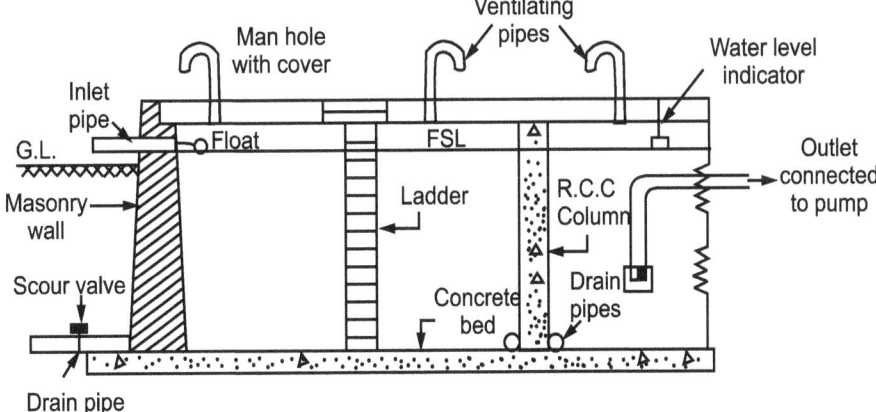

Fig. 10.8 : Surface reservoir

Manholes with access ladders are provided in each compartment for cleaning and inspection purposes. Ventilating pipes, covered with wire mesh are provided in adequate number on the roofs of the reservoir. The inlet pipe is placed slightly above the designed full supply level with automatic float valve to close inlet to stop flow when water reaches F.S.L. A water level indicator is also installed to indicate existing level of water in the tank.

These are elevated tanks supported on the ground only, without any R.C.C. or steel form work tower like support. They are generally made of steel shell containing 0.2% copper to reduce corrosion and are cylindrical in shape. These tanks may be 10 to 12 m in diameter and 15 to 20 m high. These are provided with different arrangements like inlet and outlet pipes to operate them, water level indicator, manholes and ladders etc. for proper functioning of the tank.

The total storage capacity of the tank consists of two portions :

1. Useful storage and
2. Supporting storage.

The useful storage is that portion of water which is above the elevation of highest point in the distribution area to be served by the stand post.

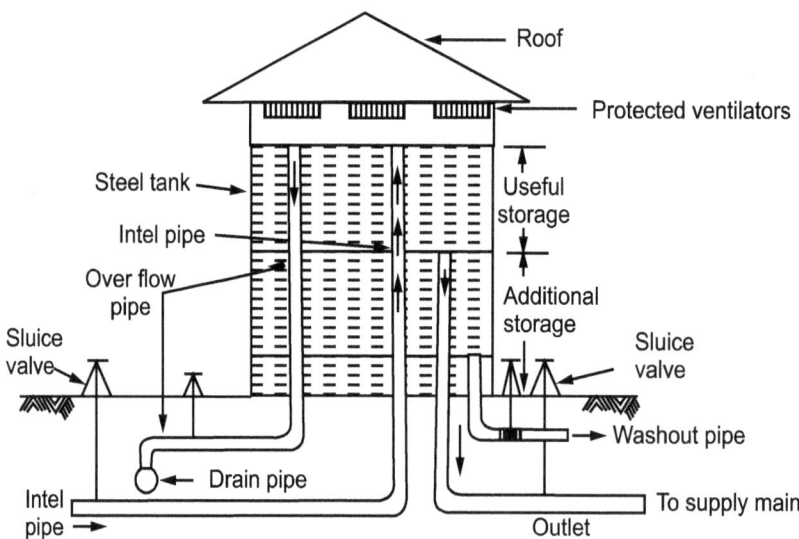

Fig. 10.9 : Stand pipe

Water below this level in the tank acts as an additional storage and also supports the upper useful storage. The supporting storage may be used for distribution in low level areas or for fire fighting purpose using booster pumps. The Fig. 10.9 above shows the sketch of a typical stand pipe.

10.6.2.2 Elevated Reservoirs

When the water is to be supplied with high pressure, the provision of stand pipe becomes impracticable as well as costly. Elevated reservoirs, made of R.C.C. or steel, are supported by structured frame work.

All elevated reservoirs are popularly called as Elevated Service Reservoirs (E.S.R.). Sometimes they are also called as overhead tanks. Formerly, steel tanks were constructed on large scale. But it is seen that their life is short due to corrosion and they require constant maintenance. Hence, now-a-days R.C.C. reservoirs of various shapes as shown in Fig. 10.10 are constructed for water supply schemes.

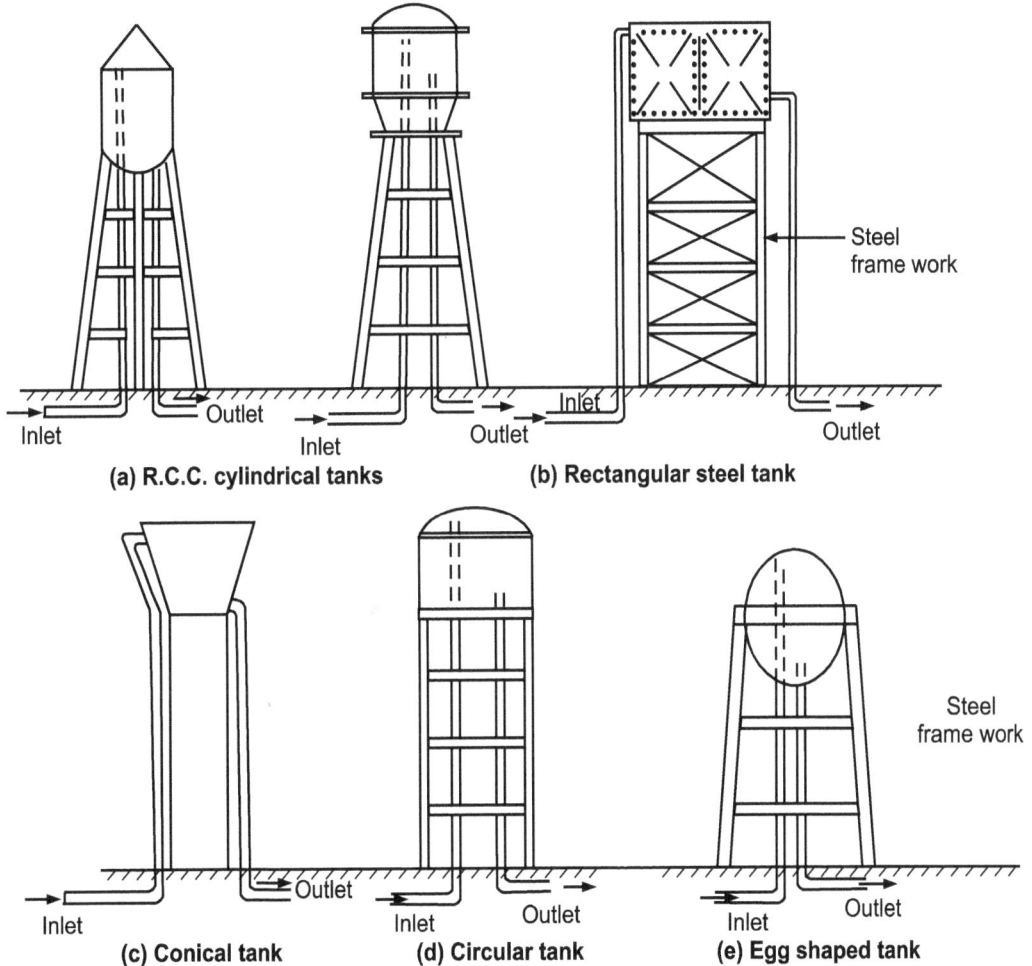

Fig. 10.10 : R.C.C. reservoirs of various shapes

R.C.C. reservoirs are supported by frame work of beams and columns. Prestressed cement concrete tanks are also constructed in many cities and towns. For all types of reservoirs, the following accessories are provided.
1. Rellux valve in the inlet pipe and gate valve in the outflow pipe.
2. Ventilating pipes or air vents in the roof.
3. Float valve for automatic controlling of inflow.
4. Water level indicator.
5. A ladder.
6. Drain pipe and overflow pipe.
7. Manhole for inspection and cleaning.

10.6.2.3 Intze Type Tank

It is an R.C.C. elevated tank of cylindrical shape. The tank is having dome shaped roof and as well as dome shaped bottom. The tank is provided with all required accessories as shown in the Fig. 10.11.

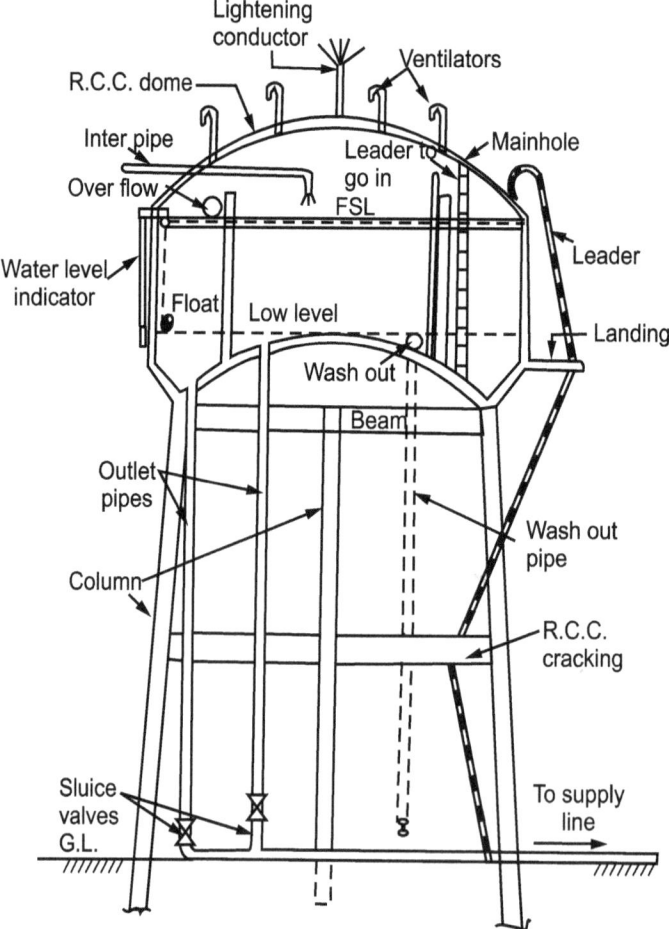

Fig. 10.11 : Intze type tank

10.7 CAPACITY OF DISTRIBUTION OR SERVICE RESERVOIR

The total capacity of the reservoir is the sum of the following storages :
1. Balancing storage
2. Fire storage
3. Breakdown storage.

Above storages are many times called as *reserve*.

1. Balancing storage or reserve : The demand of water of the town is always fluctuating. The function of this balancing storage is to cope up with the variable demand with a constant rate of water supply from the treatment units.

The quantity of water that must be stored in the reservoir for equalising (or balancing) this fluctuating demand against constant supply is called as *balancing storage* or *reserve*. This also reduces heavy pumping at peak demand periods.

This quantity is calculated by using hydrographs of inflow and outflow by Mass Curve Method. It can also be worked out by analytical method. The procedure for calculating this amount is discussed separately.

2. Fire storage : The quantity of water required to be stored for extinguishing fires is called as *Fire storage*. The National Board of Fire Underwriters recommends that the reservoirs should be capable to supply water for extinguishing a serious fire for 10 hours having population 6000 and more. For smaller population, the rate of supply of water remains same, but for reduced duration as given below.

Population	Duration in hours
4000	8
2000	6
1000	4

These requirements are very high and are not practicable in India.

In general, water at the rate of 1 to 4 lit/head may be stored as a fire reserve depending upon the importance of that zone.

In the elevated reservoirs, the quantity to be stored for fire reserve is calculated from the equation

$$R = (F - P) T \qquad \ldots (10.1)$$

where,
R = Fire reserve in litres
F = Fire demand in lit/min.
T = Duration of fire in minutes
P = Reserve fire pumping in lit/min.

Many times for economy, fire reserve is stored in a separate tank at ground level and then pumped directly into distribution system. When fire takes place, ofcourse, such pump should be maintained in working order and should be checked intermittently.

3. Breakdown storage reserve : This is also known as emergency storage. It is required to be stored to meet the demands in case of failure of pump or failure of driving unit like electric motor or diesel engine driving the pump. It is difficult to estimate the amount of water to be stored on account of breakdown, as it is not known the nature of failure and time required to repair. Hence, it is customary to make a lump-sum provision of 20 to 25% of the total storage. This confirms the need of keeping some standby units of pump with different types of driving power.

The total storage capacity of the reservoir is thus the summation of balancing fire reserve and breakdown reserve.

Calculations of balancing storage or reservoir :

There are three methods :

1. Mass curve method.
2. Hydrograph method.
3. Analytical method.

10.7.1 Mass Curve Method

A mass curve is graph of cumulative demand (outflow) versus time or cumulative supply (inflow) versus time. The mass curve of demand and mass curve of supply are plotted on the same graph. The quantity of balancing reserve is worked out by adding maximum ordinates between the demand and supply curves as explained below. The mass curves are plotted as follows :

1. For the maximum demand day, obtain hourly demands for 24 hours.
2. Work out cumulative demand starting from a fixed time like 8.00 a.m. or 12.00 night etc.
3. Plot the graph of cumulative demand against time to get a mass curve of demand.
4. On the same graph paper, plot the cumulative supply against time. Depending upon the pumping hours, the curve will be for 24 hours or for certain period of the day as shown in the Fig. 10.12 and Fig. 10.13.

5. Find maximum ordinates between the two curves. (AB and CD are maximum ordinates in the figures.)

6. The sum of two maximum ordinates is the required balancing storage.

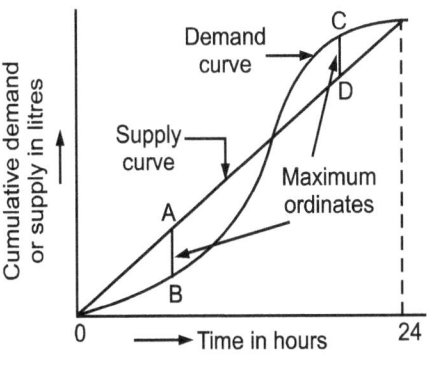
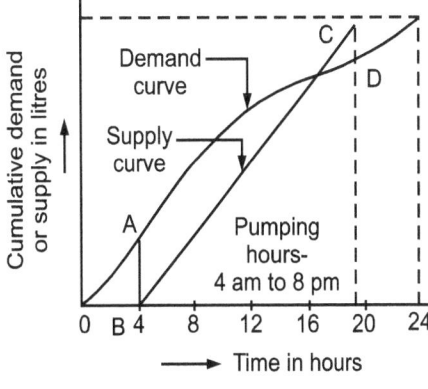

Fig. 10.12   Fig. 10.13

10.7.2 Hydrograph Method

The hourly demand of the maximum day is plotted with respect to time, as shown in the Fig. 10.14. The curve PQRSTU obtained is called hydrograph. As seen from the graph, the demand is more in the morning and evening and less during the other hours of the day. If there is a pumping for 24 hours, the rate of pumping will be equal to the average hourly demand which is shown by the dotted line QT. The area QRST enclosed by the demand line and constant pumping line AB represents the required storage.

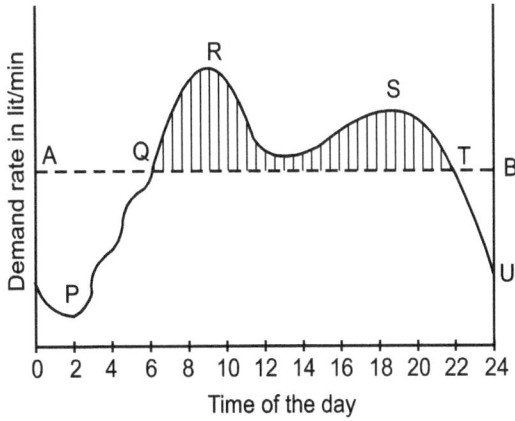

Fig. 10.14

10.7.3 Analytical Method

From the available data of hourly demand, the cumulative hourly demand and the cumulative hourly supply are worked out and tabulated for 24 hours of the day. The hourly excess or shortage of cumulative demand by comparison with cumulative supply are worked out for every hour. The sum of maximum excess of demand and maximum excess of supply gives the balancing reserve capacity of the reservoir.

Example 10.1 : The average demand of a firm having population of 1.5 million, is 260 lit/capita/day. The demand is to be satisfied by continuous pumping for 24 hours. The break up of demand is as follows :

Time	lit/capita/day
4 am to 10 am	90
10 am to 2 pm	45
2 pm to 8 pm	80
8 pm to 12 mid-night	27
12 mid-night to 4 am	18

Water is to be stored in the elevated reservoir by uniform pumping.

Determine the balancing reserve.

Solution :

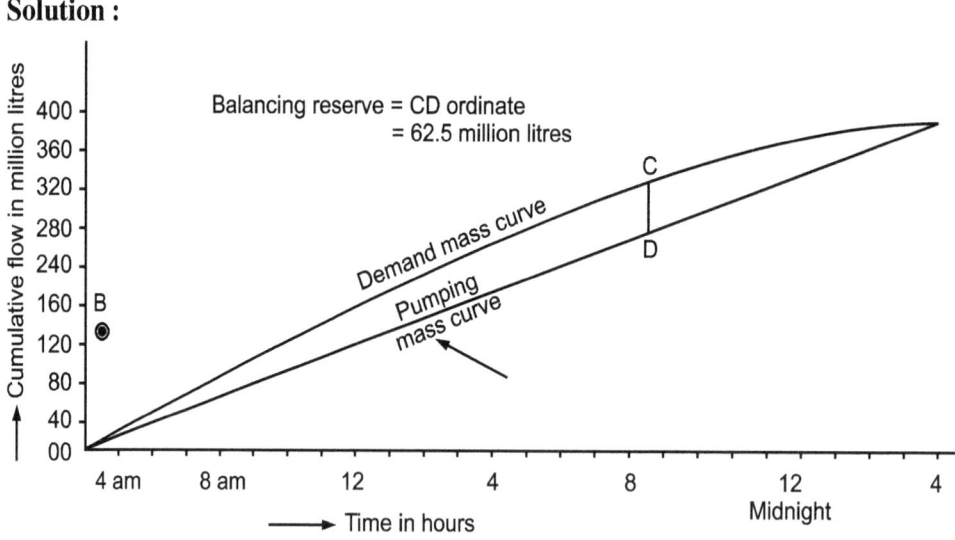

Fig. 10.15

Total daily supply = Population × Rate of water supply

= $1.5 \times 10^6 \times 260$

= 390×10^6 litres

The water supplied is converted into cumulative demand as shown below :

Time	Per capita demand lit/day	Demand of town in Ml/d	Cumulative demand in Ml/d
(1)	(2)	(3)	(4)
4 am to 10 am	90	135	135
10 am to 2 pm	45	67.5	202.5
2 pm to 8 pm	80	120	322.5
8 pm to 12 mid-night	27	40.5	363.0
12 mid-night to 4 am	18	27	390.0

The mass curve for demand is plotted from the data in columns (1) and (4) as shown in Fig. 10.15.

Now the full demand of 390 million litres is to be pumped in 24 hours. Hence, hourly rate of pumping = $\frac{390}{24}$ = 16.25 M lit/hour.

From the curves it is seen that CD is the only maximum ordinate which gives 62.5 million litres as balancing reserve.

Example 10.2 : Solve Example 10.1 by analytical method.

Solution : Work out cumulative demand as well as cumulative supply through pumping as shown in the following Table 10.1. Then work out the excess demand and also excess supply. The sum of maximum values in excess demand and excess supply gives the required quantity of balancing storage. All calculations are shown in the following table.

From the table, it is noticed that

Maximum excess demand = 62.5 million litres

Maximum excess supply = Nil

Hence total balancing storage = 62.5 million litres.

By comparing this result with the result obtained by Mass Curve in the previous example, it is seen that both results are agreeing.

Table 10.1

Time in hours	Per capita demand in lit/day	Demand of town in Ml Pop × Rate = 1.5 × col. 2	Comulative demand in Ml	Pumping rate in Ml/hour	Cumulative pumping in Ml	Excess demand in Ml (3 – 6)	Excess supply in Ml
1	2	3	4	5	6	7	8
4 am to 10 am (6 hrs.)	90	135	135	16.25	16.25 × 6 = 97.5	37.5	–
10 am to 2 pm (4 hrs.)	45	67.5	202.5	16.25	16.25 × 10 = 162.5	40.0	–
2 pm to 8 pm (6 hrs.)	80	120.0	322.5	16.25	16.25 × 16 = 260	62.5	–
8 pm to 12 night (4 hrs.)	27	40.5	363.0	16.25	16.25 × 20 = 325	38	–
12 night to 4 am (4 hrs.)	18	27.0	390.0	16.25	16.25 × 24 = 390	Nil	–

Example 10.3 : A town with a population of one million has a continuous water supply. Rate of water supply is 270 lit/hr./day. Break-up of water demand is as follows :

Time	Litres per capita
5 am to 11 am	95
11 am to 3 pm	55
3 pm to 9 pm	80
9 pm to 12 pm	25
12 pm to 5 am	15

Water is supplied from the treatment plant at a uniform rate of 11.25 million lit/hour for all 24 hours. Find the balancing capacity of the reservoir required by

1. Analytical method
2. Mass curve method.

(Dec. 2006)

Solution : 1. By analytical method : Calculations are shown directly in the Table 10.2.

Table 10.2

Time	Demand of the town in million litres	Cumulative demand in million litres	Supply in million litre in the interval	Cumulative supply in million litres	Excess in million litres	
					Demand	Supply
5 to 11 (6 hrs.)	95	95	11.25 × 6 = 67.5	67.5	27.5	–
11 to 3 (4 hrs.)	55	150	11.24 × 4 = 44.96	112.5	37.5	–
3 to 9 (6 hrs.)	80	230	11.25 × 6 = 67.5	180.0	50.0	–
9 to 12 (3 hrs.)	25	255	11.25 × 3 = 33.75	213.75	41.25	–
12 to 5 (5 hrs.)	15	270	11.25 × 5 = 56.25	270.00	Nil	–

Balancing storage = Max. value in excess demand + Max. value in excess supply
= 50 + 0 = 50 million litres

2. Mass curve method : The mass curves for cumulative demand and supply are drawn as shown in the Fig. 10.16. From the graph, it is seen that the maximum ordinate is 'CD'. Another ordinate AB = 0. Hence, 50 million litres is the required balancing storage.

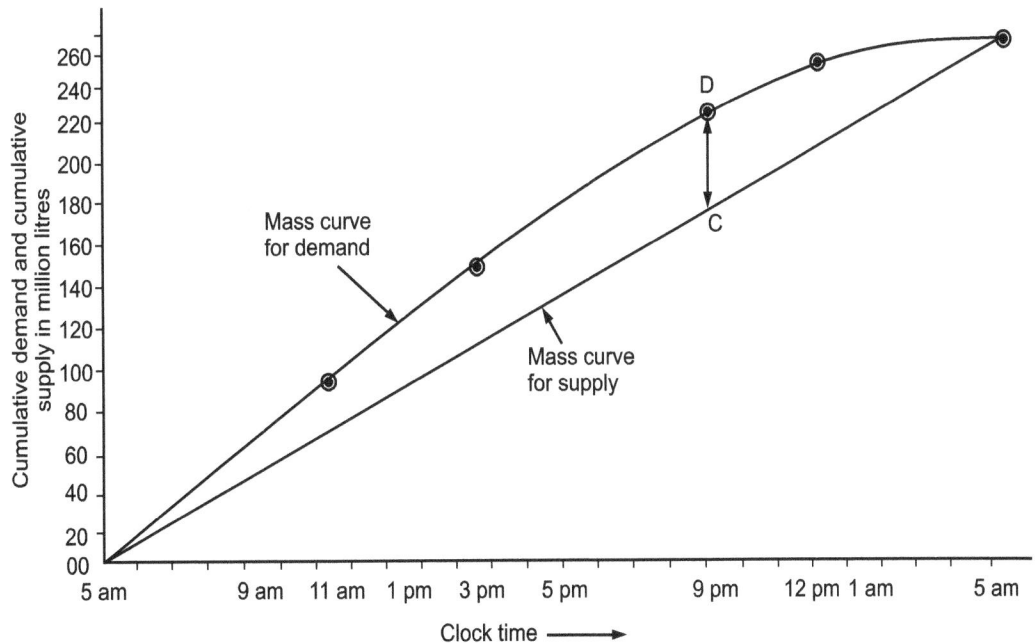

Fig. 10.16

Example 10.4 : Calculate the storage capacity of the distribution reservoir from the following data.

1. Daily demand = 2,25,000 litres
2. Pumping hours = 9 hours per day between 8 am to 5 pm.
3. Pattern of draw off is as follows :

Supply hours	Percentage of day's supply
7 am to 8 am	30%
8 am to 5 pm	35%
5 pm to 6.30 pm	30%
6.30 pm to 7 am	5%

Solution : A given demand is converted into cumulative demand as tabulated below. Similarly from pumping hours, cumulative supply in flow is worked out. From both cumulative demand and supply, excess in demand as well as supply is worked and shown in the Table 10.3.

Table 10.3

Supply hours	% Rate of demand	Demand in litres	Cumulative demand $\times 10^3$	Cumulative supply $\times 10^3$	Excess
7 am to 8 am	30	$\frac{30}{100} \times 25 \times 10^3$ = 67.5×10^3	67.5	–	– 67.50
8 am to 5 pm	35	$\frac{35}{100} \times 225 \times 10^3$ = 78.75×10^3	146.25	225	+ 78.75
5 pm to 6.30 pm	30	$\frac{30}{100} \times 225 \times 10^3$ = 67.5×10^3	213.75	225	+ 11.25
6.30 pm to 7 am	5	$\frac{6}{100} \times 225 \times 10^3$ = 11.25×10^3	225.00	225	Nil

Full demand is to be obtained by pumping in 8 hours

∴ Rate of pumping = $\frac{225 \times 10^3}{9}$ lit/hours = 25×10^3

∴ Balancing storage = Maximum excess demand value + Maximum supply value
= $(67.5 + 78.75) \times 10^3 = 146.25 \times 10^3$ litres
= 1,46,250 litres

Plot the mass curve of demand and also supply with time on x axis and cumulative demand and supply on y axis. The curves are shown in the Fig. 10.17. (Graph)

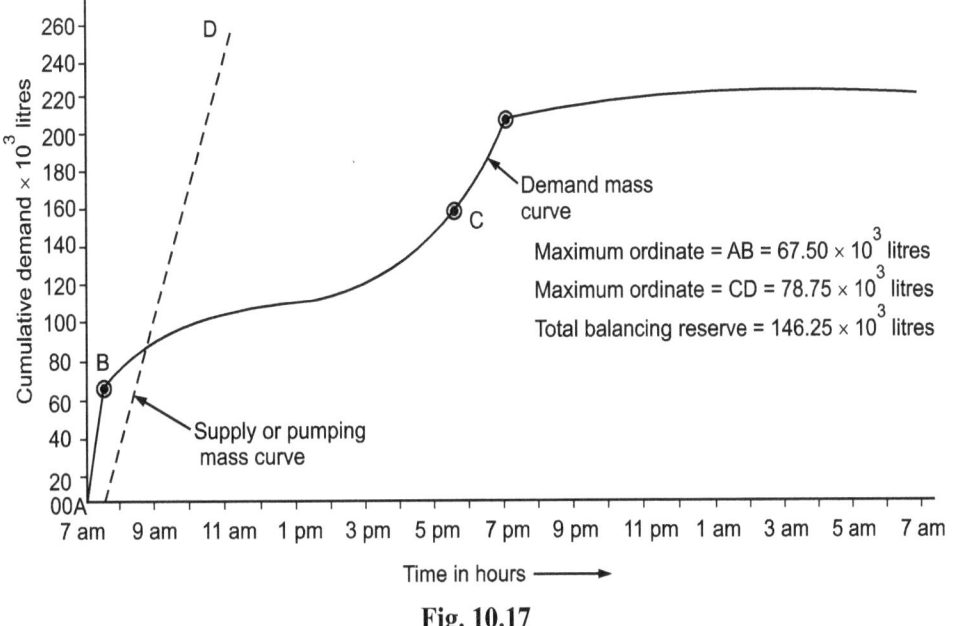

Fig. 10.17

Measure maximum ordinates AB and CD.

Total balancing storage = $67.5 \times 10^3 + 78.75 \times 10^3$
= 146.25×10^3 litres = 1,46,250 litres

Examples 10.5 : The designed demand of a community is 4 Ml/d. Water is pumped into an elevated reservoir from 5 am to 1 pm. The supply to the community is from 5 am to 10 am and 5 pm to 10 pm at a uniform rate. Design the balancing capacity of the reservoir.

(1983)

Solution :

1. Supply hours : Morning 5 am to 10 am = 5 hrs.

    Evening 5 pm to 10 pm = 5 hrs.

    Total supply hours = 10 hrs.

2. Design demand = 4 Ml/d

3. Rate of demand per hour = $\frac{4}{10}$ = 0.4 Ml/hour

4. Pumping hours 5 am to 1 pm = 8 hrs.

5. Rate of pumping = $\frac{4}{8}$ = 0.50 Ml/hour

Let us now work out cumulative demand and supply as shown in the Table 10.4.

Table 10.4

Time	Rate of demand in Ml/h	Cumulative demand in Ml	Rate of supply (Pumping Ml/hour)	Cumulative supply in Ml	Excess Cumulative demand in Ml	Excess Cumulative supply in Ml
5 am to 10 am (5 hrs.)	0.4	2.0	0.5	2.5	–	0.5
10 am to 1 pm (3 hrs.)	Nil	2.0	0.5	4.0	–	2.0
1 pm to 5 pm (4 hrs.)	Nil	2.0	Nil	4.0	–	2.0
5 pm to 10 pm (5 hrs.)	0.4	4.0	Nil	4.0	–	0.0

Maximum value under cumulative supply = 2 Ml. Hence, the balancing capacity of the reservoir = 2 Ml.

Alternatively, balancing capacity can be obtained from mass curves as shown in Fig. 10.18.

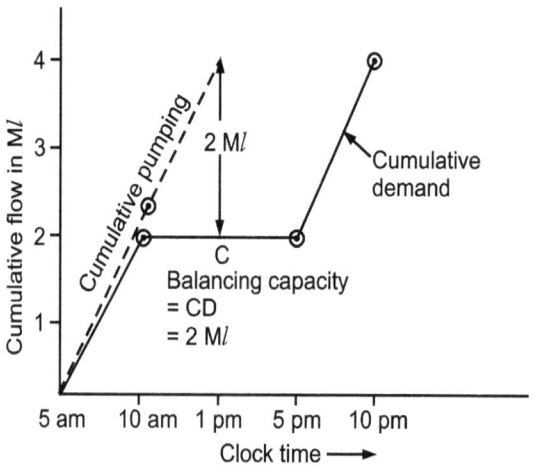

Fig. 10.18

Example 10.6 : The designed demand of a town is 5 Ml/d. It is pumped into an elevated service reservoir at a uniform rate from 5 am to 9 am and 5 pm to 9 pm. The variations in consumption of water are detailed below.

Period	5 am to 9 am	9 am to 5 pm	5 pm to 9 pm	9 pm to 12 pm	12 pm to 5 am
Consumption as a % of D.D.	40%	15%	30%	10%	05%

Design the balancing capacity of the reservoir (1981).

Solution : (A) By analytical method :

1. Pumping hours
   – Morning – 5 am to 9 am = 4 hours
   – Evening – 5 pm to 9 pm = 4 hours
   – Total pumping hours = 8 hours

2. Designed demand of town = 5 Ml/day

3. Rate of pumping = $\frac{5}{8}$ = 0.625 Ml/hour

4. Consumption during the specified period is worked out as shown in the following Table 10.5.

Table 10.5

Period	Percentage consumption	Consumption during the period in Ml	Cumulative consumption in Ml	Rate of pumping in Ml/hour	Cumulative pumping	Excess	
						Consumption in Ml	Supply in Ml
5 am to 9 am	40	5 × 40% = 2.0	2.0	0.625	2.5	–	0.5
9 am to 5 pm	15	5 × 15% = 0.75	2.75	–	2.5	0.25	–
5 pm to 9 pm	30	5 × 30% = 1.5	4.25	0.625	5.0	–	0.75
9 pm to 12 pm	10	5 × 10% = 0.5	4.75	–	5.0	–	0.25
12 pm to 5 am	05	5 × 0.5% = 0.25	5.00	–	5.0	Nil	Nil

From the Table 10.5 it is seen that the

$$\text{Maximum excess consumption} = 0.25 \text{ M}l$$

and $\quad$ Maximum excess supply $= 0.75$ Ml

$\therefore \quad$ Balancing capacity $= 1.00$ Ml

(B) By mass curve method : (See Fig. 10.19)

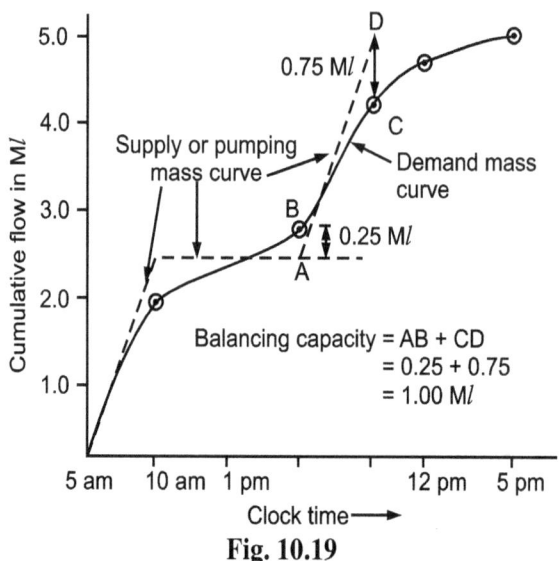

Fig. 10.19

Example 10.7 : Design the balancing reserve of an elevated service reservoir with the following data :

Time	Uniform rate of consumption as percentage of demand
5 am – 9 am	50%
9 am – 5 pm	12%
5 pm – 9 pm	35%
9 pm – 5 am	03%

The daily demand of 6 Ml/d is pumped up at a uniform rate into ESR from 5 am to 5 pm. State the time :

1. When FSL is reached.
2. When LWL is reached in the reservoir.

(Dec. 1984)

Solution : 1. By analytical method : Rate of pumping $= \dfrac{6}{12} = 0.5$ Ml/hour.

Table 10.6

Time	Percentage consumption	Actual consumption percentage × 6 Ml	Cumulative consumption	Rate of pumping in Ml/hour	Cumulative pumping in Ml	Excess Consumption in Ml	Excess Supply in Ml
5 am to 9 am (4 hrs.)	50	3.00	3.00	0.5	2	1.0	–
9 am to 5 pm (8 hrs.)	12	0.72	3.72	0.5	6	–	2.28
5 pm to 9 pm (4 hrs.)	35	2.10	5.82	–	6	–	0.18
9 pm to 5 am (6 hrs.)	03	0.18	6.00	–	6	–	00

Reservoir balancing capacity $= 1.0 + 2.28 = 3.28$ Ml
FSL will be reached at 5 pm. LWL will be reached at 9 am.

2. By mass curve method : The mass curve is plotted as shown in Fig. 10.20. From the curve, balancing capacity = 3.28 Ml.

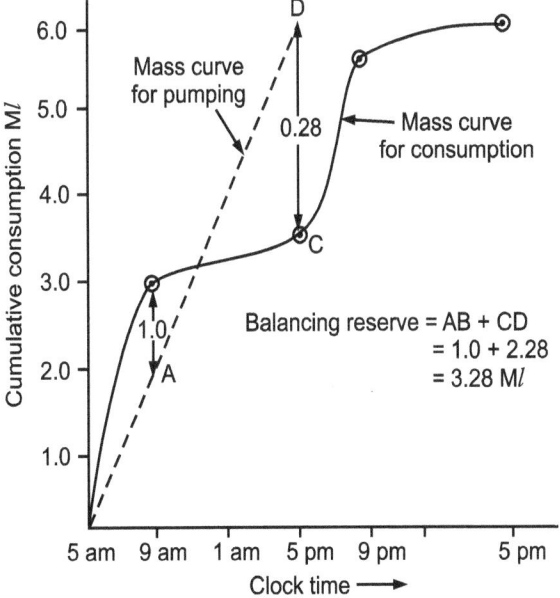

Fig. 10.20

Example 10.8 : Design balancing reserve of a service reservoir with the following data :

Time	6 am to 10 am	10 am to 6 pm	6 pm to 10 pm	10 pm to 6 am
Consumption in percentage of day's demand	45	15	38	02

Designed demand of 12 Ml/day is to be pumped at a uniform rate to the reservoir for all 24 hours. State the time :

1. When FSL is reached and
2. When LWL is reached in the reservoir.

Solution : The example is solved by analytical method. The method used is slightly different from cumulative calculation method. This method adopted gives us the condition of reservoir i.e. whether it is getting filled or getting emptied during the given intervals of the time. Tabulated calculations are self explanatory.

Rate of pumping $= \dfrac{12}{24} = 0.5$ Ml/hour.

Table 10.7

Time	Percentage consumption	Actual consumption in Ml percentage × 12	Rate of consumption in Ml/hour	Rate of pumping / filling in Ml/hour	Water in the service reservoir in ml	
					Filling	Emptying
6 am to 10 am (4 hrs.)	45	5.40	1.35	0.50	–	(1.35 – 0.5) × 4 = 3.40
10 am to 6 pm (8 hrs.)	15	1.80	0.225	0.50	(0.5 – 0.225) × 8 = 2.20	–
6 pm to 10 pm (4 hrs.)	38	4.56	1.140	0.50	–	(1.14 – 0.5) × 4 = 2.56
10 pm to 6 am (8 hrs.)	02	0.24	0.03	0.50	(0.5 – 0.03) × 8 = 3.76	–

From the columns of emptying and filling of the above table, storage levels are shown in following Fig. 10.21 with respect to clock time. This gives us FSL, LWL and also the amount of storage required.

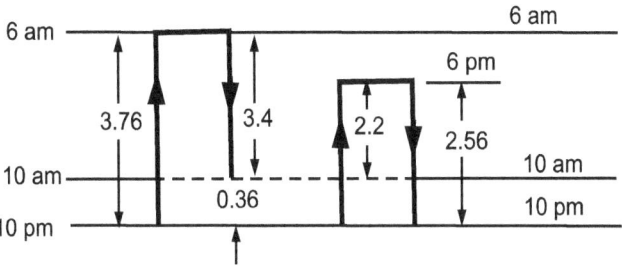

Fig. 10.21

1. Balancing reserve = 3.76 Ml
2. FSL is reached at 6 am
3. LWL is reached at 10 am.

10.8 LOCATION AND SIZE OF DISTRIBUTION RESERVOIR

Location : The topographical conditions of a zone of the town generally suggest the location of the reservoir. A central elevated location of a reservoir in the zone will be an ideal location. This will command the maximum area around it and will reduce the lengths of pipes and frictional losses. The higher natural elevation in the form of hillock will be useful to maintain an adequate pressure in the distribution system. Also availability of hillock in the centre of the zone will reduce the height of framework to support the reservoir and consequently the cost of the whole reservoir.

Size : The capacity of distribution reservoir and the shape to be adopted will generally affect dimension of the reservoir.

Masonry and concrete reservoirs constructed at ground level are generally rectangular. The depth of small reservoirs may range from 3 to 6 metres. For large capacity reservoirs, depth may be from 6 to 9 metres.

Elevated service reservoirs constructed on a fairly level ground are generally made of R.C.C. and are cylindrical in shape, with circular dome at top and duly supported on R.C.C. framework of columns and beams and adequately strengthened by number of bracers.

10.9 APPURTENANCES IN THE DISTRIBUTION SYSTEM

For proper functioning of the distribution system, the different devices fixed on it are called as *appurtenances*. The following purposes are served by these devices :

1. To control the flow of water efficiently.
2. To fulfil the demand in emergencies like fire etc.
3. To expel or admit air in pipe in the intermittent system through air valves etc.
4. To detect leakages etc.

Types of appurtenances :

1. Various valves like check valve, air valve, scour valve and sluice valve etc.
2. Fire hydrants.
3. Water meters.
4. House service connection.
5. Water taps and cocks in the consumer's property.

1. Various valves :

These are already dealt within the water transportation previously.

2. Fire hydrants :

A fire hydrant is a device in the form of outlet from which water is withdrawn during fires, from main or submains of distribution system.

Fire hydrants are provided at all road crossings and turnings and at an interval of 100 to 120 m on straight roads.

Pressures at fire hydrants :

(i) When the water is to be pumped by using motor pumps, the pressure head of 7 to 14 m of water must be available.

(ii) When water is to be withdrawn directly from fire hydrants without pumping, the pressure head of 35 to 50 m of water must be available.

Requirements of good fire hydrants :

1. It should be cheap.
2. It should supply undisturbed continuous flow of water for extinguishing fire.
3. Its arrangement should be simple so that it will be in working order for all the time.
4. Its outlet should be simple so that fire house pipe can be easily and quickly connected.

Types of fire hydrants :

There are two types of hydrants which are commonly used.

(a) Flush type fire hydrant

(b) Post type fire hydrant.

(a) Flush type fire hydrant : It is provided underground and its top is flush with the ground and hence it is called as *flush fire hydrant*. It is installed in a cast iron or brick chamber and is connected to water pipe-line under the ground. It cannot be seen easily and hence the letters 'FH' are painted on nearby structure. Sometimes FH letter plate is welded to the bar and it is embedded in the ground with 'FH' plate projecting above ground by 5 to 10 cm, to indicate the location of flush fire hydrant.

location of flush fire hydrant

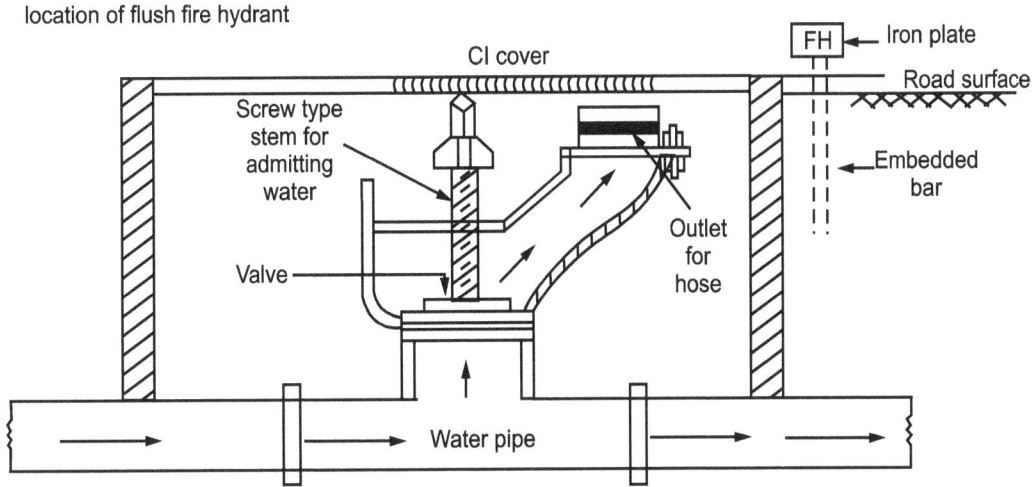

Fig. 10.22 : Flush type fire hydrant

(b) **Post type fire hydrant :** It remains projected above ground or road level in the form of post by above 80 to 100 cm. It should be made very sturdy, otherwise it is likely to be damaged by destructive mentality persons. It is in the form of barrel made of C.I. with bronze surfaces to avoid rusting. For withdrawal of water, it may have more than one outlet. Depending upon the number of outlets provided, the hydrants are classed as one, two, three or four way hydrant. The Fig. 10.23 shows the sketch of post hydrant.

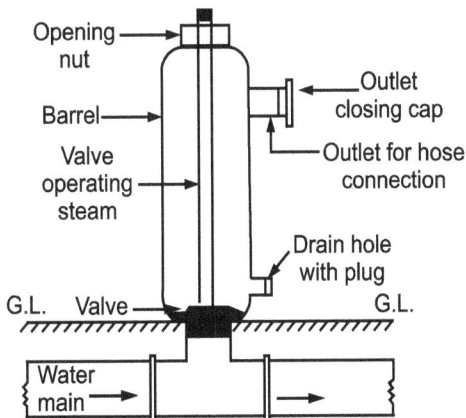

Fig. 10.23 : Post type fire hydrant

During fire, hose pipe is connected to nearby hydrant to its outlet. By loosening the opening nut, the valve is operated to supply water through the connected hose. The other end of hose pipe is then connected to fire engine mounted on the vehicle of fire brigade. The engine withdraws water and boosts its pressure and the water stream or jet (if nozzle is fitted) is available at high pressure to extinguish the fire. The nozzle diameter may be 25 to 30 mm. After the control of the fire, the hose is disconnected, the nut is operated and the flow is stopped.

The water from the hydrants may be withdrawn for other purposes like construction of municipal roads, sprinkling on roads, flushing of underground sewers or for public gardens.

3. Water meters :

These are the devices provided on pipes to measure the quantity of water flowing through it. This enables the water supply authorities to charge the consumer according to the amount of water supplied. Patented water meters are available in market. An ideal water meter should satisfy the following points.

1. It should be cheap and simple in construction.
2. It should record any amount of flow under variable pressures, within the permissible limits of error.
3. It should cause minimum loss of head.
4. Its moving parts should not get corroded due to the chemicals present in flowing water.
5. It should be easy to repair and should not clog as far as possible.

Types of meters :

Meters are classified as follows :

(a) Displacement or Positive meters

(b) Inferential or Velocity meters.

(a) Displacement or positive meters : These meters are accurate than the other type. There is filling and emptying of the meter chamber. The quantity of water passed through meter is measured by counting the number of times the process of filling and emptying is taking place. There are various types like disc, oscillating or reciprocating available in the market. Out of these, disc type meter is widely used for measuring the amount of water supplied in domestic houses. It consists of a disc placed in the chamber of meter. It has inlet and outlet for the water to flow through. This causes oscillation of disc. This is transformed in the form of reading through the train of gears. They are available in 15 to 150 mm diameter sizes. They are capable to measure the flow from 90 to 4500 lit/min. They cannot be installed on pipe-line where hammer effect is expected.

(b) Inferential or velocity meters : These meters measure the horizontal velocity of water when it is passing through them. By continuity equation, the discharge is equal to the cross-sectional area into velocity. Hence, the measured velocity when multiplied by cross-sectional area gives the discharge. The meter is provided with certain arrangement which records the amount of flow of water through it.

These meters are used in the following conditions :

1. When the pipe is carrying large amount of flow to supply to industries or trade centres.
2. When the flowing water contains suspended impurities like raw water.

They are unsuitable for domestic supplies as they are not so accurate for low discharges.

Following are the types of velocity meters :

(i) Venturi meter

(ii) Rotary meter

(iii) Turbine meter.

(i) Venturi meter : It is based on the principle of Bernoulli's theorem. It consists of a converging cone from a normal section of pipe upto a point called as throat followed by a diverging cone emerging to normal size again. Two piezometers, one at the beginning of the convergent cone and other at the throat are provided which measure heads at these points. The discharge through the pipe is directly proportional to the difference in heads (h) indicated by two piezometers.

They are very much suitable for measuring large flows through pipes with minimum loss of head. They are used on mains having diameter 7.5 cm or more.

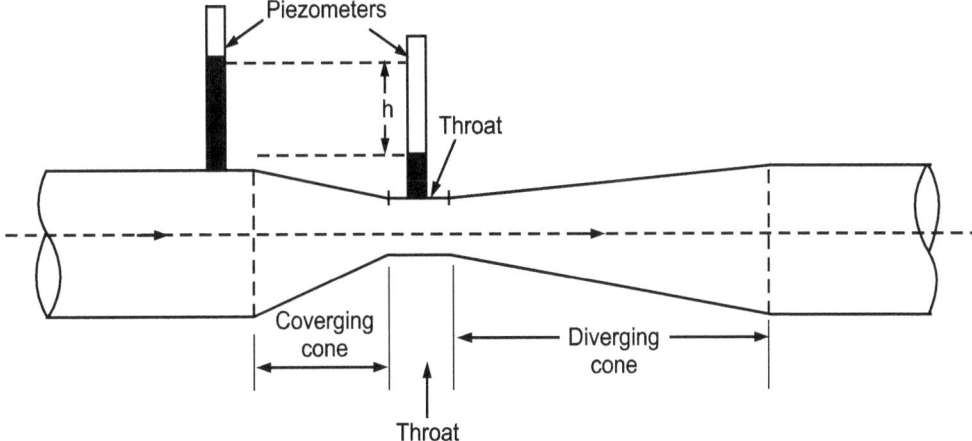

Fig. 10.24 : Venturi meter

(ii) Rotary meter : It consists of a shaft on which radial vanes are attached. The whole assembly is enclosed in a bronze casing. When the water passes through the meter, it forces the radial vanes to rotate causing the rotation of the shaft. The rotation of the shaft will be proportional to the velocity of water flowing through the meter and hence the meter is calibrated to read directly flow of water by a system of gears. The line sketch of the rotary meter is shown in the Fig. 10.25.

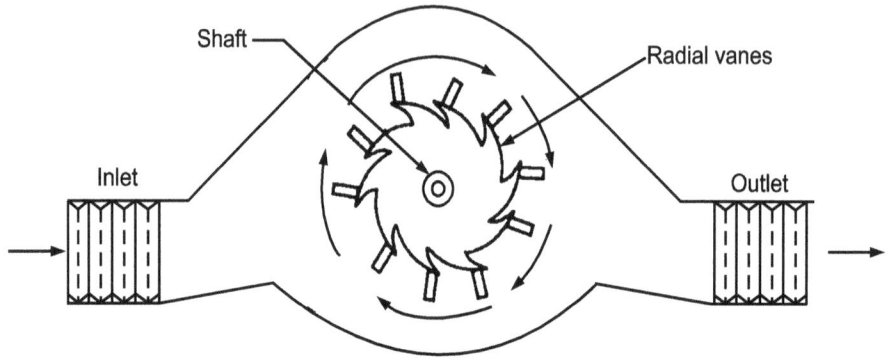

Fig. 10.25 : Rotary meter

(iii) Turbine meter : It consists of a turbine wheel which rotates due to water flowing through it. Its working is similar to rotary meter. The number of revolutions made by the turbine wheel records the discharge reading on the dial through set of gears.

Comparison between displacement meter and velocity meter

Displacement meter	Velocity meter
1. They show more accurate readings.	1. They show less accurate readings.
2. They are installed to measure small discharges in residential houses.	2. They are installed to measure large discharges in mains or submains etc.
3. The working of the meter gets seriously affected due to shock of water hammer.	3. The working of this type of meter is not seriously affected due to shock.
4. They are costly.	4. They are cheap.
5. Loss of head of water is more.	5. Loss of head of water through them is less.
6. They go out of order if water contains suspended impurities.	6. They can be safely used even for raw water containing sediments.
7. They can be installed on horizontal or vertical or inclined pipe.	7. They can be installed on horizontal pipes.

4. Service pipe connection :

To supply the water to the consumer from the feeder line of the distribution system, service pipe connection is required to be given. It consists of a service pipe of 15, 25 or 40 mm diameter made of galvanised iron connecting feeder line to the internal water supply pipe line. The residual pressure in the service should be between 0.4 to 0.7 kg/cm^2.

For giving house service connection, first the hole of required diameter is threaded in the feeder pipe. In this threaded hole, a 'ferrol' (corporation cock) is screwed. Ferrol is a kind of tap which can be closed or opened by rotating it through 90°. A bend pipe made of lead, called 'Goose Neck' is then inserted between the ferrol and the internal pipe of the consumer. Flexibility of goose neck takes care of any settlement of the pipe. To control the flow of water to the consumer, a stop cock often called as curb valve is provided in a box below footpath with a cover at top. This service pipe is then taken into the premises of the consumer where one more stop cock which is owned by the consumer is provided. This cock enables the consumer to carry out the internal pipe repairs, if any, by closing it. After this stop cock, generally a water meter is provided to enable the local W.S. authority to take regular, monthly or bilmonthly reading and charge the consumer.

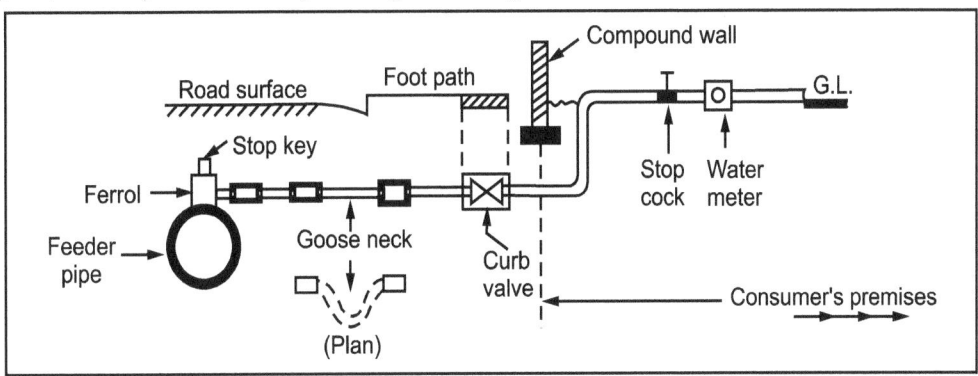

Fig. 10.26

In case of non-payment of water supply bill, the local authority, by operating the curb valve, supply of water can be shut off.

Pipe fitting and taps for internal water supply :

Various kinds of pipe fittings and taps are required for proper supply of water in the premises of the consumer either inside the building or outside of it. All these fittings and accessories which are provided beyond the water meter are known as "Internal water supply plumbing".

Following pipe fittings are required for proper distribution of water in toilets, bathrooms, wash hand basins and kitchen sinks – Bends, tees, elbows, unions, nipples crosses, wye pieces, plugs, plastic couplers, etc. They are shown in the Fig. 10.27. They are always threaded either internally or externally to fit them in proper position in the internal pipe-line.

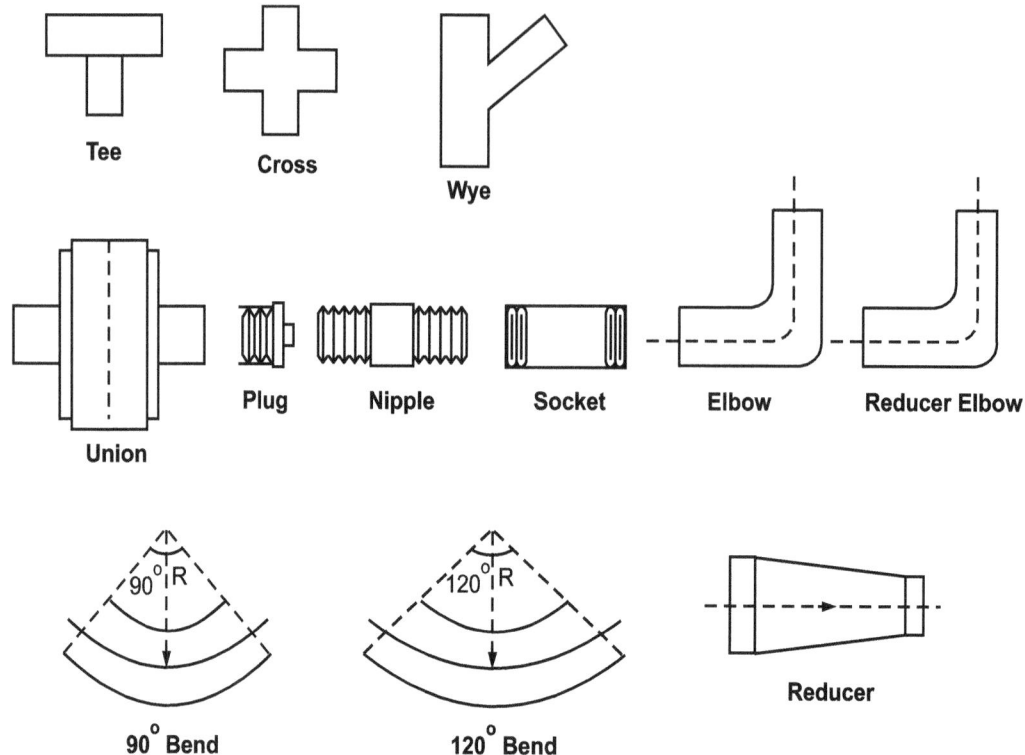

Fig. 10.27 : Various pipe fittings and specials

All the internal pipes and pipe fittings are made of galvanised iron and shortly written as G.I. pipes and fittings. Sometimes they are called as pipe special. Now-a-days PVC pipes and fittings are also popularly used for internal water supply. It should be remembered that for conveying hot water, PVC pipes cannot be used.

5. Water taps and stop cocks :

Water taps are types of accessories provided to withdraw water from the pipe-line at several places in the building. Many varieties of the taps are available in the market. A most commonly used tap is a 'Bib Cock'. It is fixed to the 'tee' piece along the pipe-line. It has a handle at top and by rotating the handle the opening to release the water can be controlled. When it is fully opened, it will supply the full discharge. It has one end threaded and the other end is suitably bend and is called as spout. It is available in sizes from 10 mm to 50 mm diameters. Rubber or leather washer is provided at the end of a threaded stem which is replaced occasionally when cock starts leaking.

Stop cock is a kind of tap having both ends threaded. It is placed along the pipe-line to control the flow of water from one side to another. It is provided at the following positions.

1. Before the location of water meter to stop the flow of water in the entire internal water supply pipe-line.

2. Along the pipe-line leading to withdrawing water from the overhead tank.

3. Before the water enters either flushing tanks in toilets or wash hand basins.

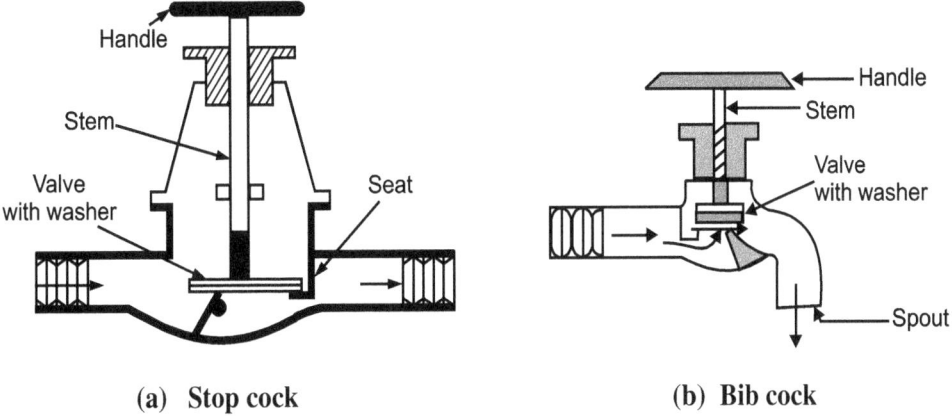

(a) Stop cock (b) Bib cock

Fig. 10.28

10.10 DESIGN OF DISTRIBUTION SYSTEM

It is already discussed that depending upon the topography of the town, it is divided into various zones. Existing and proposed layouts of the town affect the arrangement of laying of distribution pipe-lines. This pipe network may consists of circle system, grid iron system, radial system or dead end system. In a particular zone, many times combination of two or more systems may be beneficial.

The drawing of the town showing the existing and proposed road is prepared. On it the layout of distribution pipes, valves, fire hydrants etc. are shown along with the R.Ls. of various points. The population to be served by the pipe-line is also shown on the plan. The positions of highest building etc. are also marked on the plan. The minimum water pressures required at tail ends are also noted on the plan.

The next step is to determine the diameters of various pipes so that they will carry the required discharge of water at the desired pressure. This is discussed below.

Design of pipe diameters :

The hydraulic calculations of distribution system are complicated and not amenable to the usual methods. So far no suitable and accurate method is developed to determine the sizes of pipes in the distribution.

The sizes of pipes are first assumed and terminal pressure heads available after losses in friction and various accessories while carrying the designed maximum discharge, are calculated. The discharges entering at junction (input) and discharges leaving (take offs) these points are determined in advance by knowing the population and the maximum rate of demand.

While fixing diameters generally the following points are considered :

(a) In the zones having population more than 50000, the pipe should be capable to carry 2.25 times the average rate of supply. For population between 5000 to 50000, pipe should be capable to carry 2.5 times average rate of supply. For population less than 5000, pipe should be capable to carry 3 times the average rate of supply.

(b) When fire demand is also included in the system, the diameter of pipe should not be less than 150 mm.

(c) At every 300 metres, the pipes should be interconnected.

(d) For finding velocities, suitable formula from amongst the following may be used.

1. Hazen's formula $\quad V = 0.85 \, C_H \, R^{0.63} \times S^{0.54}$

2. Manning's formula $\quad V = \dfrac{1}{n} \, R^{2/3} \times S^{1/2}$

   (where, n = 0.015 for concrete pipes and n = 0.013 for C.I. pipes)

3. Crimp's and Bouge's formula $\quad V = 83.5 \, R^{2/3} \, S^{1/2}$

   where, V = Velocity of flow in pipe in m/sec, **c** and **n** are the coefficients of roughness of the surface.

   R = Hydraulic mean depth (Hydraulic Radius) in m

and   S = Hydraulic slope

It will be noticed that the velocities are dependent on hydraulic radius i.e. on the pipe diameter which itself is to be finalised. Hence, as an approximate assumption, the velocity may be assumed between 1 to 1.5 m/sec. and then by knowing the discharge of water to be supplied (Q), the diameter (d) of the pipe is calculated by the relation $d = 2\sqrt{Q/\pi \cdot V}$.

Hazen –William's formula is popularly used for this purpose. To reduce the tedious calculations, Nomograms based on Hazen formula for C.I. pipes with $C_H = 100$ are invariably used.

If the hydraulic slope $S = \dfrac{H_L}{L} = \dfrac{\text{Loss of head due to friction}}{\text{Length of pipe}}$ is substituted in Hazen's equation, friction head loss will be given by the equation

$$H_L = \dfrac{1}{0.094}\left[\dfrac{Q}{C_H}\right]^{1.85} \times \dfrac{L}{d^{4.87}}$$

The use of nomogram is already discussed earlier. Out of four unknowns, two unknowns like discharge and velocity are assumed and the other two unknowns like diameter of pipe and hydraulic gradient i.e. loss of head per 1000 m are directly read out when a straight edge is placed along the two known valves of discharge and velocity, from the nomograms. From the layout plan, the length of the pipe under calculation is known and hence the total head loss is worked out by multiplying the length of pipe by the value of head loss per 1000 m, read out from the nomogram. Similarly the head loss is calculated for other pipes. These head losses in different pipes are then used to work out the terminal pressure since the pressure at starting point like pump or ESR is known. If it is noticed that this terminal pressure is less or more than permissible values, the diameter of the pipe is assumed with a suitable new value and the whole process is then repeated till the permissible residual pressures (terminal) are obtained.

The above method or process is applicable for solving simple networks like tree or dead end layouts. The method is made more clear by solving the following example.

Example 10.9 : A big residential complex is to be provided with tree type pipe layout for supplying water from a R.C.C. elevated reservoir. The average rate of water is assumed as 180 lit/capita/day. Design the diameter of the distribution mains XY and YZ for the peak demand equal to three times the average demand with the following data.

1. R.L. of bottom of elevated reservoir = 300 m, R.L. of X = 280 m, R.L. of Y = 270 m and R.L. of Z = 261 m.

2. The minimum terminal pressure head = 15 m

3. The length of pipe XY = 600 m and YZ = 700 m.

4. The population in various buildings may be taken as shown in the Fig. 10.29.

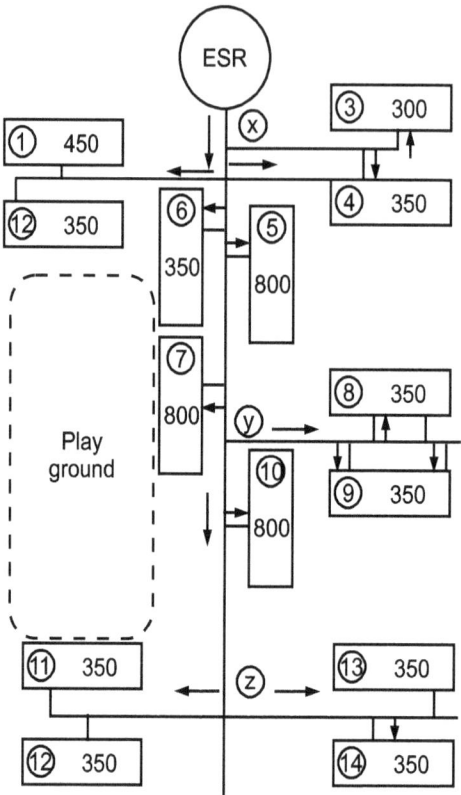

Fig. 10.29 : Layout of residential complex

Solution : The design work consists of working from the tail end towards the reservoir. The population served by the pipe lengths XY and YZ are tabulated in Table 10.8 as shown in columns 2, 3 and 4. Since, the peak demand (3 × average daily demand) per day is known, total demand for the population served by pipe YZ is first worked out. Pipe diameter of 140 mm is then assumed and from the Hazen's nomogram the head loss per 1000, read out to be 12.5 m. Since, the length of pipe is 700, the actual head loss comes to be 8.75 m as shown in column 9.

Table 10.8

| Pipe section | Population served | | | Peak demand $\frac{3 \times 180 \times P}{24 \times 3600}$ lit/sec. | Assumed pipe diameter in mm | Length of pipe in metres | Head loss | | Hydraulic level worked out from reservoir bottom in metres | G.L. in metres | Net head available in metres |
	Previous	Local	Total				Rate per 1000	Actual head loss (Rate × Length)			
1	2	3	4	5	6	7	8	9	10	11	12
YZ	700 + 700	800	2200	13.75	140	700	12.5	8.75	285 − 8.75 = 276.25	261.00 at z	15.25 OK
XY	2200 + 700 900 650	800 + 800 + 350	6400	40.00	180	600	25	15.00	Y = 300 − 15 (Actual loss of head) = 285.00 X − 300	270 at y 280 at x	15.00 OK 20 OK

Since, the net head available of 15 m is permissible, provide 180 mm diameter for pipe XY and 140 mm diameter for pipe YZ.

Similarly the actual head loss for the pipe XY comes out to be 15 m. Since R.L. of bottom of tank is 300 m at X, at Y hydraulic head available = 300 – 15 (head loss) = 285. Similarly at Z, hydraulic head available = 285 – 8.75 = 276.25. These hydraulic heads are compared with corresponding ground levels to know the net heads available at points X, Y and Z as indicated in column 12.

EXERCISE

1. State the requirements which are considered while designing the distribution system.

2. Explain with sketches the following : **(May 2007)**

    (a) Gravity

    (b) Pumping and

    (c) Pumping cum gravity system for water distribution. **(Nov. 1988)**

3. Explain the following layout systems for distribution : **(May 2007, Dec. 2008, 2010)**

    (a) Dead end system

    (b) Radial system. **(Nov. 1988)**

4. Name various systems of water distribution and discuss in detail the dual system of distribution. **(Dec. 2006, May 2009, 2010)**

5. Explain the necessity of distribution reservoir and the way in which its capacity is fixed. **(Dec. 2008, May 2009)**

6. What are the functions of Elevated Service Reservoir ? **(May 2006, Dec. 2008)**

7. Differentiate between continuous and intermittent system.
    (May 2006, 2007, 2008, 2009, 2010; Dec. 2006, 2009, 2010)

8. State the classification of reservoirs.

9. Differentiate between Fire reserve and Break down reserve.
    (May 2007, Dec. 2008)

10. How is the elevation of ESR determined ?

11. State the reasons for the following : (May 2006)

    (a) Water meters are installed for each consumer in his premises.

    (b) Water is supplied intermittently in most of the Indian towns.

    (c) Dead end system of layout is used in old cities.

    (d) Many times ESR is provided centrally in the distribution system.

12. Write short notes on :

    (a) Zoning of areas (May 2006, 2009, Dec. 2006, 2009)

    (b) Pressure in the distribution system

    (May 2006, Dec. 2006, 2007, 2008, 2009)

    (c) Appurtenances in the distribution system

    (d) Mass curve method (May 2006, 2009; Dec. 2006, 2007, 2009, 2010)

    (e) Post type fire hydrant

    (f) Stand pipes

    (g) Method of maintaining the adequate pressure in the distribution system.

    (Dec. 2006)

    (h) Stop cock and bibcock.

    (i) Flush and post type fire hydrant. (Dec. 2007)

    (j) Capacity of service reservoir. (Dec. 2007)

13. Draw a line sketch of R.C.C., ESR and give the list of accessories provided for EAR. (May 2006)

14. Draw a neat sketch of flush type fire hydrant and explain its working.

15. What are the functions of elevated service reservoir ? Draw a sketch of intze type tank. (Dec. 2006)

16. Write a short note on mass curve method. (May 2007)

17. How is the elevation of ESR determined ? **(Dec. 2007)**

18. Enlist any eight appurtenances used in the water distribution system. Explain the requirements of a good water meter. **(May 2008)**

19. What is the purpose of providing an ESR ? Explain how its capacity is calculated. **(Dec. 2009, May 2010)**

❖ ❖ ❖

CHAPTER ELEVEN

HEAVY METALS, NON-BIODEGRADABLE ORGANICS AND NON-DEGRADABLE ORGANICS

11.1 HEAVY METALS

The sources of trace metals are associated with both human activities such as mining, manufacturing, and natural processes of chemical weathering and soil leaching. Corrosion in water distribution pipes and customers plumbing can also add heavy metals in drinking water.

Arsenic, barium, cadmium, chromium, mercury, nickel, selenium, and thallium are toxic metals affecting internal organs of the human body.

1. Zinc

Zinc is essential element for humans, animal and plants. It is also an important cell component in several metalloenzymes. Infants need 3–5 mg/day, adult males 15 mg/day, pregnant and lactating females 20–25 mg Zn/day. However, heavy doses of Zn salts (165 mg) for 26 days causes vomiting, renal damage, cramps, etc.

2. Iron

It is one of the essential mineral for humans and animals. Degree of absorption depends upon solubility and stability of compound. It is a component of blood cells and liveral etalloenzymes. However, more than 10 mg per kg of body weight causes rapid respiration and pulse rates, congestion of blood vessels, hypertension and drowsiness. It increases hazard of pathogenic organisms, as many of them require Fe for their growth.

3. Cadmium

Like mercury, cadmium and its compounds enter the environment only from geological or human activities (metal mining, smelting and fossil fuel combustion). Cadmium and its compounds are black-listed materials, which by international agreement may not be discharged or dumped into the environment. Cadmium is a cumulative poison. Cd is very toxic, 50 mg may cause vomiting, diarrhoea, abdominal pains, loss of consciousness. It takes 5–10 years for chronic Cd intoxication. During first phase, discolouration of teeth, loss of sense of smell, mouth dryness occurs. Afterwards it may cause decrease of red blood cells, impairment of bone marrow, lumber pains, disturbance in calcium metabolism, softening of bones, fractures, skeletal deformations, damage of kidney, hypertension, tumor formation, heart disease, impaired reproductive function, genetic mutation, etc.

4. Chromium

Most of the more common soluble forms found in soils are mainly the result of contamination by industrial emissions. The major uses of chromium are for chrome alloys, chrome plating, oxidising agents, corrosion inhibitors, pigments for the textile glass and ceramic industries as well as in photography. Hexavalent chromium compounds (soluble) are carcinogenic.

Any chromium compound is toxic but haxavalent Cr greater than 70 mg is very toxic. It causes cancer, anuria, nephritis, gastrointestinal ulceration, perforation in partition of nose. It penetrates cell membrane and badly affects central nervous system. Causes respiratory trouble, lung tumors when inhaled. May cause complications during pregnancy. Has adverse effects on aquatic life. Trace amount of Cr III is essential for normal glucose, protein and fat metabolism and hence it is a essential trace element in diet.

5. Lead

Lead is a cumulative poison. Most of the lead produced in metallic form, in batteries, cable sheathing, sheets and pipes, etc., is recovered and recycled. But most lead used in compound form, like paints and petrol additives is lost to the environment, eventually ending up in the aquatic environment. More than 400 mg of lead in human body can cause brain damage, vomiting, loss of appetite, convulsions, uncoordinated body movements, helplessly amazed state, coma. It is retained in liver, kidney, brain, muscle, soft tissues, bones. Leads to high rate of miscarriages, affects skin, and respiratory system, damages kidney, liver and brain cells.

Disturbs endocrine system, causes anaemia, and long term exposure may cause even death.

6. Mercury

Mercury from natural sources can enter the aquatic environment via weathering, dissolution and biological processes. Although extremely useful to man, mercury is also highly toxic to the human organism, especially in the form of methyl mercury, because it cannot be excreted and therefore acts as a cumulative poison. Mercury is very toxic. Excess mercury in human body (more than 100 mg) may cause headache, abdominal pain, diarrhoea, destruction of haemoglobin, tremors, very bad effects on cerebral functions and central nervous system, paralysis, inactivates functional proteins, damage of renal tissues, hyper coagulability of blood, mimamata disease, and even death. It may cause impairment of vision and muscles and even coma. It disturbs reproductive and endocrine system. Also causes insomnia, memory loss, gum inflammation, loosening of teeth, loss of appetite, etc.

7. Nickel

Nickel is ubiquitous in the environment. Nickel is almost certainly essential for animal nutrition, and consequently it is probably essential to man. Nickel is a relatively non-toxic element; however, certain nickel compounds have been shown to be carcinogenic in animal experiments.

8. Copper

Excess of Cu in human body (more than 470 mg) is toxic, may cause hypertension, sporadic fever, coma. Copper also produces pathological changes in brain tissue. However, Cu is an important cell component in several metalloenzymes. Lack of Cu causes anaemia, growth inhibition and blood circulation problem.

9. Arsenic

Arsenic is notorious as a toxic element. When water is found to contain arsenic at levels of 0.05 ppm, an attempt should be made to ascertain the valency and chemical forms of the element. Arsenic is commonly associated as an alloying additive with lead solder, lead shot, battery grids, cable sheaths and boiler piping. Nowadays, most arsenic originates from paints or pharmaceuticals and is commonly found in sewage. The primary concerns are carcinogenicity and mutagenicity. Arsenic is oisonous to fishes, animals and humans. Greater than 25 mg of arsenic causes vomiting, diarrhoea, nausea, irritation of nose and throat, abdominal pain, skin eruptions inflammations and even death. It binds globulin of blood haemoglobin in erythrocytes. May cause cancer of skin, lungs and liver, chromosomal aberration and damage, gangrene,

loss of hearing, injury to nerve tissue, liver and kidney damage. Minor symptoms of As poisoning, weight loss, hair loss, nausea, depression, fatigue, white lines across toe nails and finger nails.

10. Asbestos

Asbestos is commonly found in domestic water supplies. The use of asbestos cement (170 g of asbestos per kg - 80% chrysotile and 20% crocidolite) for pipes in distribution systems could contribute to the asbestos content of drinking water. Background levels are reported to be in the range of less than 1 million to 10 million fibres per litre. The primary concern is carcinogenicity.

11. Barium

Barium is present in traces in many foodstuffs, such as nuts. Barium is also used in various industrial processes, such as in vacuum tubes, spark-plug alloys, Getter alloys, Fray's metal and as a lubricant for anode rotors in X-ray machines. Excess of Ba (more than 100 mg) in human body may cause excessive salivation, colic, vomiting, diarrhoea, tremors*, paralysis of muscles or nervous system, damage to heart and blood vessels.

12. Beryllium

The primary source of beryllium in the environment is the burning of fossil fuels, although contamination is normally light. Beryllium can enter the water system through weathering of rocks in ground acquifers, atmospheric fallout on rain water collection systems and industrial and municipal discharges. Beryllium

13. Selenium

Selenium has been identified as an essential nutrient in several animal species, including man. Dietary selenium levels of 5 mg/kg of food or more may cause chronic intoxication. There is a range of selenium intake by humans that is consistent with health, and outside this range deficiency or toxicity can occur. Selenium is widely used in the electronics industry, TV cameras, solar batteries, computer cores, rectifiers, xerographic plates and ceramics as a colourant for glass. It is also used as a trace element for animal feeds. Signs of Se poisoning (more than 4 mg) are fever, nervousness, vomiting, falling of blood pressure, causes damage to liver, kidney and spleen, loss of nails and hair, causes blindness to animals. Cats are most

susceptible. It affects enzyme systems and interfere with sulphur metabolism. It can cause growth inhibition, skin discolouration, bad teeth, psychological problem, gastro intestinal problems, but trace amount of Se is protective against poisoning by Hg, Cd, Ag.

11.1.1 Remedial Measures

1. The management of proper crop production methods like crop rotation, cover crop, appropriate selection of crop and seeds, proper drainage systems and equipments etc can be the good methods for controlling the water contamination.

2. The use of proper conservation buffer is also a good source for trap the chemicals like pesticides, sediments, bacteria, fertilizers etc to prevent the surface water contamination.

3. The conservation practices like the best management practices is a useful tool to measures and control the loss of soil and water quality due to nutrients, waste, toxics etc.

4. The water contamination can be controlled by the selection of appropriate chemicals, pesticides and other organic and inorganic substances, their disposal sites of wastes of industries, and the mixing procedures.

5. Waste treatment

6. Waste water reclamation

7. Reutilization, recycling, renovation, and recharge of waste
8. Reduction of waste at source
9. Removal of pollutants

11.2 NON-BIODEGRADABLE ORGANICS : PESTICIDES

Pesticides that may be of importance to water quality include chlorinated hydrocarbons and their derivatives, persistent herbicides, soil insecticides, pesticides that are easily leached out from the soil, and pesticides systematically added to water supplies to control disease vectors, such as mosquito larvae (Malaria and Dengue fever). Of these compounds, only the chlorinated hydrocarbon insecticides occur frequently and these are very persistent in the environment where they have become ubiquitous.

Pesticides may enter aquatic ecosystem either directly, indirectly or unintentionally through the following sources:

1. Rain water
2. Runoff from agricultural fields
3. Domestic sewage
4. Industrial effluents

Typical Pesticides Include:

DDT (Dichloro Diphenyl Trichloroethane), a persistent insecticide, stable under most environmental conditions and resistant to complete breakdown by enzymes present in the soil microorganisms.

Aldrin and Dieldrin, two related and very persistent pesticides which accumulate in the food chain. Currently may be used for termite control around the roots of fruit trees.

Chlordane, a broad-spectrum insecticide also used for termite control and for homes and gardens.

HCB or hexachlorobenzene, produced commercially for use as a fungicide.

Heptachlor, another broad-spectrum insecticide used to control agricultural soil insects. Heptachlor is very persistent.

Lindane, a wide-spectrum insecticide of the group called organochlorine insecticides and used in a wide range of applications, including treatment of animals, buildings, water (for mosquitoes), plants, seeds and soil.

Methoxychlor, an insecticide used for the treatment of agricultural crops and livestock.

Pesticides/Insecticides are Highly poisonous for humans and animals. Also they lower seed germination, plays a role in development of Parkinson's disease, destruction of nerve cells in certain regions of brain resulting in loss of dopamine which is used by nerve cells to communicate with brain.

Some of these are physical poisons, some are protoplasmic poisons causing liver damage, some are respiratory poisons and some are nerve poisons.

Trihalomethanes

Trihalomethanes (chloroform and bromoform) in drinking water occur principally as products of reaction of chemicals used in oxidative treatment reacting with naturally occurring materials present in the water. Their formation is particularly associated with the use of chlorine for disinfecting water supplies. Notwithstanding this, it is important to recognize the fact that chlorine is an effective water disinfectant and the hazards of disease arising from microbiological contaminants resulting from incomplete disinfection are substantial. Trihalomethanes have several adverse effects on health.

11.3 PHOTO CATALYSIS

In chemistry, photocatalysis is the acceleration of a photoreaction in the presence of a catalyst. In catalysed photolysis, light is absorbed by an adsorbed substrate. In photogenerated catalysis, the photocatalytic activity (PCA) depends on the ability of the catalyst to create electron–hole pairs, which generate free radicals (e.g. hydroxyl radicals: •OH) able to undergo secondary reactions. Its practical application was made possible by the discovery of water electrolysis by means of titanium dioxide. The commercially used process is called the advanced oxidation process (AOP). There are several ways the AOP can be carried out; these may (but do not necessarily) involve TiO2 or even the use of UV light. Generally the defining factor is the production and use of the hydroxyl radical.

11.3.1 Types of Photocatalysis:

(A) Homogeneous Photocatalysis

In homogeneous photocatalysis, the reactants and the photocatalysts exist in the same phase. The most commonly used homogeneous photocatalysts include, ozone and photo-Fenton systems (Fe+ and Fe+/H_2O_2). The reactive species is the •OH which is used for different purposes. The mechanism of hydroxyl radical production by ozone can follow two paths.

$$O_3 + hv \rightarrow O_2 + O(1D)$$

$$O(1D) + H_2O \rightarrow \bullet OH + \bullet OH$$

$$O(1D) + H_2O \rightarrow H_2O_2$$

$$H_2O_2 + h\nu \rightarrow \bullet OH + \bullet OH$$

Similarly, the photo-Fenton system produces hydroxyl radicals by the following mechanism

$$Fe_2+ + H_2O_2 \rightarrow HO\bullet + Fe_3+ + OH-$$

$$Fe_3+ + H_2O_2 \rightarrow Fe_2+ + HO\bullet_2 + H+$$

$$Fe_2+ + HO\bullet \rightarrow Fe_3+ + OH-$$

In photo-Fenton type processes, additional sources of OH radicals should be considered: through photolysis of H2O2, and through reduction of Fe^{3+} ions under UV light:

$$H_2O_2 + h\nu \rightarrow HO\bullet + HO\bullet$$

$$Fe_3+ + H_2O + h\nu \rightarrow Fe^{2+} + HO\bullet + H+$$

The efficiency of Fenton type processes is influenced by several operating parameters like concentration of hydrogen peroxide, pH and intensity of UV. The main advantage of this process is the ability of using sunlight with light sensitivity up to 450 nm, thus avoiding the high costs of UV lamps and electrical energy. These reactions have been proven more efficient than the other photocatalysis but the disadvantages of the process are the low pH values which are required, since iron precipitates at higher pH values and the fact that iron has to be removed after treatment.

(B) Heterogeneous Photocatalysis

Heterogeneous catalysis has the catalyst in a different phase from the reactants. Heterogeneous photocatalysis is a discipline which includes a large variety of reactions: mild or total oxidations, dehydrogenation, hydrogen transfer, $^{18}O_2-^{16}O_2$ and deuterium-alkane isotopic exchange, metal deposition, water detoxification, gaseous pollutant removal.

Most common heterogeneous photocatalyts are transition metal oxides and semiconductors, which have unique characteristics.

Photocatalysis over a semiconductor oxide such as TiO_2 is initiated by the absorption of a photon with energy equal to, or greater than the band gap of the semiconductor.

Oxidative reactions due to photocatalytic effect:

$$UV + MO \rightarrow MO (h + e-)$$

Here MO stands for metal oxide ---

$$h+ + H_2O \rightarrow H+ + \bullet OH$$

$$2 h+ + 2 H_2O \rightarrow 2 H+ + H_2O_2$$

$H_2O_2 \rightarrow HO\bullet + \bullet OH$

The reductive reaction due to photocatalytic effect:

$e- + O2 \rightarrow \bullet O_2-$

$\bullet O_2- + HO\bullet 2 + H+ \rightarrow H_2O_2 + O_2$

$HOOH \rightarrow HO\bullet + \bullet OH$

Ultimately, the hydroxyl radicals are generated in both the reactions. These hydroxyl radicals are very oxidative in nature and non selective with redox potential of (E0 = +3.06 V)

A wide range of semiconductors may be used for photocatalysis, such as $TiO2$ ZnO, MgO, WO_3, Fe_2O_3, CdS. The ideal photocatalyst should process the following properties (i) photoactivity, (ii) biological and chemical inertness, (iii) stability toward photocorrosion, (v) suitability towards visible or near UV light, (vi) low cost, and (vi) lack of toxicity

TiO_2 is known to have and excellent pigmentary properties, high ultraviolet absorption and high stability which allow it to be used in different applications, such as electroceramics, glass and in the photocatalytic degradation of chemicals in water and air. It has been used in the form of a suspension, or a thin film in water treatment

Applications:

Photocatalysis has large capability for the water treatment. It can be utilized for the decomposition of organic and inorganic compounds, and removal of trace metals as well as destruction of viruses and bacteria. It can be used also to decompose natural organic matter (humic substances), which has many environmental and industrial impact. The drawback of this method is that of being slow compared with traditional methods but it has the advantage not leaving toxic by product or sludge to be disposed.

Removing Trace Metals

Trace metal such as mercury (Hg), chromium (Cr), lead (Pb) and others metals are considered to be highly health hazardous. Thus, removing these toxic metals are essentially important for human health and water quality. The environmental applications of heterogeneous photocatalysis include removing heavy metals such as (Hg), chromium (Cr), lead (Pb), Cadmium (Cd), lead (Pb), Arsenic (As), nickel (Ni) cupper (Cu). The photoreducing ability of photocatalysis has been used to recover expensive metals from industrial effluent, such as gold, platinum and sliver

Destruction of Organics

Photocatalysis has been used for the destruction of organic compounds such as alcohols, carboxylic acids, phenolic derivatives, or chlorinated aromatics, into harmless products e.g, carbon dioxide, water, and simple mineral acids. Water contaminated by oil can be treated efficiently by photocatalytic reaction. Herbicides and pesticides that may contaminate water such as 2,4,5 trichlorophenoxyacetic acid, 2,4,5 trichlorophenol, s-triazine herbicides and DDT can be also mineralised.

Removing Inorganic Compounds

In addition to organic compounds, wide ranges of inorganic compounds are sensitive to photochemical transformation on the catalyst surfaces. Inorganic species such as bromate, or chlorate, azide, halide ions, nitric oxide, palladium and rhodium species, and sulfur species can be decomposed. Metal salts such as $AgNO_3$, $HgCl$ and organometalic compound (e.g CH_3HgCl) can be removed from water, as well as cyanide, thiocyanate, ammonia, nitrates and nitrites.

Water Disinfections

Photocatalysis can also be used to destroy bacteria and viruses. Streptococcus mutans, Streptococcus natuss, Streptococcus cricetus, Escherichia coli, scaccharomyces cerevisisas, Lactobacillus acidophilus, poliovirus 1 were destructed effectively using heterogeneous photocatalysis. The increasing incidence of algal blooms in fresh water supplies and the consequent possibility of cyanobacterial microcystin contamination of potable water Microcystin toxins is also degraded on immobilized titanium dioxide catalyst. Photodisinfection sensitized by TiO_2 had some effect on the degradation of Chlorella vulgaris (Green algae), which has a thick cell wall.

Degradation of Natural Organic Matter

Humic substances (HS) are ubiquitous and defined as a category of naturally occurring biogenic heterogeneous organic substances that can be generally characterised as being yellow-brown and having high molecular weights. These are also defined as the fraction of filtered water that adsorb on XAD-8 resin (non-ionic polymeric adsorbent) at pH 2. They are the main constituents of the dissolved organic carbon (DOC) pool in surface waters (freshwaters and marine waters), and ground waters, commonly imparting a yellowish-brown color to the water system. The concentration of humic substances varies from place to place; the values in seawater being normally from two to three mg l-1. Their size, molecular weight, elemental composition, structure, and the number and position of functional groups vary, depending on the origin and age of the material.

EXERCISE

1. What do you mean by heavy metals?

2. What is a non – biodegradable organics: Pesticides?

3. What are typical material includes in pesticides?

4. Explain the photocatalysis?

5. What are the types of photocatalysis and explain it?

6. Write down the applications of photocatalysis.

❖ ❖ ❖

www.ingramcontent.com/pod-product-compliance
Lightning Source LLC
Chambersburg PA
CBHW062127160426
43191CB00013B/2218